CALL
of
ANGELS

SECOND EDITION

BALDIP KAUR

CALL
of
ANGELS

CALL
of
ANGELS

BALDIP KAUR

ARPress
45 Dan Road Suite 5
Canton MA 02021

Hotline: 1(800) 220-7660
Fax: 1(855) 752-6001

Ordering Information:
Quantity sales. Special discounts are available on quantity purchases by corporations, associations, and others. For details, contact the publisher at the address above.

Printed in the United States of America.

ISBN-13:   Paperback   979-8-89330-773-3
            eBook   979-8-89330-774-0

Library of Congress Control Number: 2024903738

When the sun rises without me
It will be
because I heard an angel
call my name
she whispered
that my time in the world was short
but a place was prepared for me
In the sky far above

Prologue

Covid-19
London 2020

Almost every year, the world faces and tackles devastating typhoons, wildfires, tsunamis, and earthquakes.

Amelia adjusted her face mask over her ears for they were amidst a global pandemic and drove down a street that was dimly lit, the only light originating from a streetlamp at the corner of the road.

She was aware of the panic and fear, however justified, that the virus had created amongst the populace, and was relieved that her family, Mark, and sister-in-law Rasna, had not been affected by it. She loved her brother and admired his wife, for not only was Rasna kind and affectionate, she was an exotic and beautiful woman, with skin that was a sultry brown and soft black hair that encircled her charming face.

Both of them had been already traumatised by one disaster, the tsunami of 2004, which had separated them temporarily, however, Amelia, together, with her parents, had believed in the purity of their love, which they had thought to be like a deep seam of gold sewn in their heart, a love that had bound them during adversity and that was so strong that it had eventually re-united them.

Mark and Rasna had told her endless stories about the tsunami, and, as she steered her car down the road, the scene of the tsunami shaped and unfolded itself before her eyes —on Boxing Day of 2004, the tsunami's destruction had been caused by an underwater disturbance or earthquake - and the sheer force and power of the seawater had become a tall wave that had travelled inshore at high speed.. A wave that was so strong and fierce, that, when it receded, it had depleted the land of its people, buildings and trees and left devastation in its wake.

However, the virus that was currently floating around did not class as a natural disaster, but a health and public crisis because the virus was so highly contagious and transmissible that it had been declared a pandemic by the World Health Organisation who were not equipped to deal with a deadly virus like Covid-19.

So, whilst governments of the world blundered through their early responses to the pandemic by trying to formulate and implement effective decisions that would protect their citizens, the virus silently and rapidly rippled through the communities, infecting huge number of people and killing millions globally.

Amelia was a kind and gentle woman who loved her job as a nurse at the new Nightingale hospital and she worked hard and selflessly attending to the vast number of people suffering from Covid-19. However, neither she, nor the doctors could cure them, nor could they minimise the pain of their near and dear ones.

In the silent environment of the intensive care unit, lying on beds and attached to ventilators, were heavily sedated patients with intravenous drips inserted in their arms. The noise of the wheezing of the patients on ventilators echoed around the ICU unit, where Amelia was based. She had come to compare the virus to a monstrous and massive infection that attached itself to people, a virus that had tentacles that quickly curled and snarled around first the lungs then to other organs of their bodies.

She yawned with exhaustion, which was both mental and physical, for each day, she looked on helplessly at the rapid spread, consequences, disruption, and fear that was being caused by Covid-19.

The doctors and nurses felt powerless as they tried to save Covid-19 patients, distressed and disappointed that they could not even help some of their colleagues who had died in the process of saving others. The doctors who had had the courage and humility to tear of their layers of ego to attain new levels of exceptional selfless qualities.

Amelia felt a gentle breeze and wondered if was shedding soothing tears for the innocent souls, the souls that the angels had called for? For all the agony and grief suffered by patients and their families, she felt that there had to be cries and voices to be heard in the wind to reflect the human pain.

And if it were not so, it maybe because the universe would drown in its own tears if it remembered the grief of the innocent and untimely death of millions of people?

There were stories about the charitable deeds of people, and how they were uniting and helping those in need; unfortunately, the Coronavirus was also bringing out another darker side of some people: fear, anger, resentment, domestic abuse; and, recently, of racial discrimination, against which protests were taking place globally.

Amelia stopped at a red light and looked at the dashboard clock.

It was Thursday, 8 p.m., a time when she knew that millions of people would be standing at their front doors and gardens, open windows and on balconies, clapping and making loud noises in gratitude and thanks to the NHS staff.

The racket of hand clapping, whistles and cheering echoed along the street she was driving on. There was an uproar as children and adults banged on pots and pans, all expressing their gratitude to doctors and nurses alike. Amelia was comforted by their appreciation, for, she thought, what would happen to this world if doctors and nurses, or anyone who was caring and compassionate was ignored and rejected?

This gratitude was being expressed by people in all countries hit by the virus. From city centres to suburbs, the explosion of appreciation for NHS staff, care workers, pharmacists and supermarket staff was heartfelt and heavy with emotion, as the country struggled to protect themselves against the virus and adjust to the lockdown.

This show of appreciation boosted the NHS's staff's spirit and optimism, for they were constantly stressed and exhausted as they worked under difficult conditions, in isolation most of the time, conscious and afraid of the fact that they could, unwittingly, be carriers of a highly contagious disease that could ultimately put their families and friends at risk.

Although most people were following the Government guidelines of remaining indoors, there were others who were disregarding them by frequenting parks and beaches. These people did not realise that death was too high a price to pay for a brief period of freedom. These people were either unaware or careless of the fact that they were caught in the web of the virus, and that to ignore this reality would not only endanger their lives but that of others - which in turn would only tighten and extend the lockdown.

It was true, there were many people who were fed up with the lockdown and waited impatiently for real life to resume after the deadly virus vanished. The lockdown was a daily reminder to people that their freedom was dependant on the government, who, in turn only had their well-being at heart, However, it did raise a question; if and when the guidelines were relaxed, would the people have the strength to face the virus head on, or would they have become too compliant and caged, preferring to stay in an enclosed space rather than fly out into the vast frightening blue sky?

Amelia drove down the street towards her home, thinking that how, because of the Pandemic, her days currently only consisted of dealing with Coved-19 patients, managing and prioritising doctors' orders and messages, tending to each patient each day, and in some cases, connecting them to their relatives via zoom. But, irrespective of their efforts, and, repeatedly, following the chaos and turmoil in the ward, there would be a deathly silence as most of her patients lost their battle against the virus.

Amelia turned into a driveway, pressed the button of a remote to open the garage door, switched off the ignition, and undid her seatbelt. She opened the car door and ran into a house, then quickly into a large kitchen that had bookshelves crammed with law books.

She ran quickly towards the bathroom to change and wash, past Sanduni and Mayusha, her niece and nephew, who were watching television, and Rasna who sat in an armchair, looking nostalgically at the photos of her family that she had so lovingly positioned on the mantlepiece.

Rasna missed them all, her father, mother and sister, and each absence bought with it a gaping wound. Her sadness had become a puff of cloud on which she had become accustomed to living in, for she had learnt to shape herself around them.

They had been in the lockdown for about 4 weeks, with no end of it in sight, for each day there was news that the death toll in London and most countries was rising, there were programmes on television showing that the hospitals and mortuaries round the world were being inundated with dead bodies, so much so and that artificial graves were being dug.

They were worried about Marks's father, Caleb, who was eighty-five years of age and a diabetic, so had decided that he would be safer in a care home, unaware that the care homes would soon become a hotspot for Covid-19.

Later that night, Rasna woke from a dream that had dispersed before she could hold on to it. She could not fully comprehend the nightmare, only that it had frightened her and that it was somehow connected to water.

She got up and rubbed her eyes, confused, then recalled that the daily news report about the global pandemic and deaths of millions had, perhaps, unconsciously bought another global disaster, the tsunami of 2004, to mind?

If only she had prevented her family from going on holiday to Sri Lanka, and Mark from his vacation in Thailand on December 2004, a lot of pain and loss that she and her family had suffered could have been avoided.

As she found it difficult to get back to sleep, and Mark was peacefully asleep, she recalled the events, leading up to the tsunami, events that had commenced from the tsunami's 1st anniversary, that is – December 26th 2005

Tsunami (Anniversary)

Thailand 2005

Chapter 1

Rasna stood silently on the shore of Koa Lak beach in Thailand under a sky that shone with a hazy glow. This afterglow, she deduced, must be faintly emanating from the chain of candles that lit the beach and the stars that were clustered across the sky.

It had been a year since the paradise beach's beauty, encircled by palm trees and a calm emerald, green sea, had been hit by the tsunami, and the calmness of the sea had been replaced by a power and anger that had hurled a huge towering tidal wave towards the island. Admiration of the exotic country had changed into fear on the faces of the tourists and residents alike as a giant wave battered the shorelines and destroyed everything in its path on Boxing Day of 2004.

However, a year on, the countries that had faced the sea's wrath were having a day of remembrance, and Rasna had first come to Thailand before going on to Columbo, Sri Lanka.

The glow on the beach was softened by faint shadows that Rasna thought appeared to be angels gently floating over the shore, and wondered if they were the same angels that had called for the innocent lives that had perished in the tsunami?

Its destruction had spread as far as Sri Lanka, where Rasna had been on holiday with her family, and where she had felt like a spectator observing, in amazement two distinct kinds of world.

At first, she saw a paradise of golden beaches with palm trees and emerald, green sea, then suddenly the very same paradise had turned into a dark and dirty bowl, a bowl that was full of debris and dead bodies. The force of the high wall of water had travelled with such force and speed that it stretched and destroyed beaches and land as far as East Africa.

She thought of her sister, Kirti, and her child, who would have been a year old, had it survived, and of the children who had. She considered the trauma they had suffered, but to what extent could one measure their ordeal? The children called out for their mother at night, for she lived only in their dreams and not in their reality as she had been seized by the sea.

Some children had been injured while running away from the tsunami, others while trying to survive in wreckages. Similarly, even if they somehow managed to get to the refugee shelters for protection, the children there were kidnapped, mainly for the purposes of human-trafficking, slavery, rape or some other sinister and disturbing purpose – cruelties that were organised and carried out by corrupt people for money.

Subsequently, the few children that had managed to survive would become a generation that would grow old with their approach to life being shaped by their experiences of the tsunami, for the trauma of losing loved one and its outcome, would be far more devastating than the aftermath of any tsunami.

Being an adult, she thought of her own reaction to the tsunami. She had cut herself off for a year from people, hiding behind a wall of grief that she had built around her. She had had friends who tried to get in touch with her but, she could not bring herself to talk to anyone, so when they had not received any calls from her, nor bothered to answer theirs, they had eventually stopped contacting her.

In Koa-Lak beach, there was an atmosphere of sorrow amongst the survivors,' friends and relatives of the victims, who had gathered to remember those killed by one of Nature's deadliest disasters. For them, the past and the present had become interwoven and each had one thought – why had so many innocent people lost their lives whilst others had survived? There were those who had lost their homes and lived in tents-in affected areas whilst others still survived in the hope that somehow their missing loved ones would be found.

Rasna held hands with the people who had lived through the tsunami, thereby making a human circle, each one reminiscing and praying for their lost loved ones. Everyone held a lantern which symbolised the life of their loved one who had been a victim of the tsunami.

Rasna clasped in her hand a paper lantern for Mark, her fiancé, with an inscription that read simply 'I love you, sleep gently forever."

They then let loose the lanterns that gently glided towards the sky, and Rasna looked up at them with tears as she thought how loss ran through her life like thread entwined in tapestry.

The lamps floated upward into the horizon, glowing like fireflies to a backdrop of the beat of drums – whilst clear notes of a flute played softly into a melody that fused into soft peal of bells.

"It's the uncertainty of it all," a petite elegant woman said. "My daughter disappeared and to this day I do not know what happened to her."

Everybody in the circle blinked back their tears and nodded.

"I hate to tell you this, but even knowing with certainty that your loved one is dead, does not help that much either!"

A petite woman wiped her eyes than turned towards Rasna. "I miss my family every day! The swirling waters of the tsunami swept away my parents. My mother and young son could not fight the current but luckily my father somehow managed to fight his way back to the debris of what was left of our hotel."

"I survived for five days, but only by clinging to a palm tree and eating its fruit," another woman added. "The cries for help and screams still ring loudly in my ear. Words cannot describe the extent of the horror that I have seen. Holding on to the tree, I saw bodies floating by, some of young children."

A shudder passed through all, who, although were unhappy at the loss of their loved ones, also felt guilty at being grateful they had survived.

Rasna peeled back the layers of time, and the present went to pause like a video as her mind became a tape that replayed the terrible carnage of nature.

The wind rustled through her hair and a strand fell across her face. She habitually looped it over her ear with her delicate hand, then smiled wistfully for Mark had always teased her about it. She recalled his tender gaze and boyish grin when he called her 'my Indian princess'.

A warm feeling coursed through her body as she thought of him, the sentences and nicknames of love and endearment they had bestowed on each other as tenderly as precious gifts.

Her lips trembled and she wiped the tears flowing down her cheeks as she struggled to control the surge of emotion that had been unleashed. Were broken hearts only the result of romantic dreams that had no place in real life, she thought?

She looked down at the emerald, green ring gleaming and glowing like green fire on her finger, and she felt that it twinkled like Mark's green eyes. The ring sparkled on the delicate and long finger of her hand and she stroked it gently, for it was the only reminder she had left of Mark.

The ring blurred and shimmered through her tears and she wished she had told Mark how much she loved him, then wondered if she could salvage something from their love that had been destroyed by the Tsunami?

Her only hope to find any kind of peace was to simply accept that injustice and unfairness existed in life – still she felt that Mark's love spoke to her across time, and as the impact of her emotions was so intense, she even envisioned their love could transcend time and space! And as the sea tumbled and rolled on to the beach and the waves tossed a white thunder of foam onto the shore, she believed that his spirit was now as free as the doves that had been set lose in some countries that were commemorating the anniversary of the tsunami.

However, she wondered if she would have willingly forgone the brief period of happiness with Mark in order to escape the misery that it had brought? Forces which caused girls to abandon tradition and inhibitions had always been a mystery to her, but now she understood only too well why a woman would sacrifice everything to be with the man she loved. She realised why her aunt Lakshmi had defied her parents and society by marrying the man she loved, however tragically that had ended.

She was to fly to Colombo, Sri Lanka, the following day as there was to be the lowering of the Sri Lankan flag at half-mast in memory of the victims of the tsunami being held in Colombo's Central Independence Square, This was to be followed by a two minute silence, and Rasna was keen to attend the ceremony in memory of her parents, Urmila and Puru and her sister Kirti and uncle Kadamba, all who had been seized by a cruel and merciless ocean.

Tsunami (Annivarsary)

(Sri Lanka 2005)

Chapter 2

However, due to flight delays, Rasna was not able to attend the main event in Colombo, but arrived the following day, however, she still intended to pay her respects at the Square.

After leaving her luggage at the hotel, she took an auto rickshaw to the square, and, as they drove through, was astonished at the ebb and flow of people who lived in Sri Lanka, alongside the insects and creepie crawlies who flourished and prospered in the sultry tropical weather.

She clutched the handle of the rickshaw and wrinkled her nose for its seat smelled of incense. Beside the roadside life of the city were temples, and she noticed that pink and yellow flowers were given as offering to them.

Suddenly, her auto rickshaw swerved to give way to an ambulance that sped past them, sirens blazing, reminding her of the fragile political state of the country. She thought, with sadness and pride, how her mother had taken an active part in the civil war, and how she had been one of the women of Sri Lanka who had not only altered the traditional identities of women set by society, but who had also won the respect and admiration of many by fighting for their people and country.

As they turned into the square, she expected it to be empty, but found, with surprise, that a lot of people where still walking around, as if by prolonging their stay and re-creating the tragic aftermath of the tsunami, they would somehow remain connected to their loved ones? She felt their fond memories travel noiselessly across the square and rustle amongst the leaves of ivy that grew up its walls; for them time stood still and the tragic and heart-breaking atmosphere was evident by an occasional show of tears and sobs.

Wiping her tears and thinking fondly of her family, she turned and collided into a woman who had been sobbing, and as the woman wiped her tears with her white sari, Rasna thought she looked familiar.

"Oh, I am so sorry," she exclaimed as she put out her hand to steady herself, then saw with surprise that it was Prathik, her maternal grandmother. They had not met, but her mother had not only spoken fondly of her but had proudly shown photographs of her to Rasna.

"Rasna, is that you Rasna Pethi? Oh my god you are alive! Prathik rubbed her eyes. "I am your Paat, Urmila's mother! We have not met but I recognise you from the photographs that she used to send me!"

She hugged her granddaughter tightly and kissed her repeatedly.

"Of course, I recognize you too! Mother spoke of you often when she too, showed me her childhood photos!" Rasna exclaimed as she hugged her. "So, you too have come here in fond memory of your daughter? I got delayed so missed the main ceremony but cannot begin to understand what you must be feeling, it is must be terribly sad to lose your daughter."

"Why, has what happened to her?" Prithika looked confused. "How have I lost her?"

"Paat! Did you not know? She was in the Samudra Devi crash and both my mother and father..." Rasna gulped "That is why I am here, in memory of my parents and Kirti. I thought you were here for them too?"

"Who told you that, Rasna, for your mother is alive and well!"

"What! No that cannot be possible!" Rasna cried in disbelief. "I spoke to Dad's mother and she told me that both my parents had died and that Kirti too was dead! Anyway, she would have come to London or at least called to let me know that she is safe and sound."

"She would have, Rasna, but sadly your mother lost her memory and has no recollection of the past, or even who she is. We don't know why that is – maybe seeing Puru being taken out to sea, or when she heard that you and your sister were dead." Her grandmother wiped the tears from her eyes.

"What! She thinks I am dead!" Rasna exclaimed, then looked perplexed as she added, "But if she has lost her memory how did she find you?"

"Her friend, Sudina, found her at a shelter where she was volunteering and brought her to me. Sudina had been a good friend of Urmila's for they were both in the army together and did their training together. She too lost her family in the Tsunami so had decided to join the TRO, who together with the Liberation Tigers of Tamil Eelam (LTTE) and some civilian volunteers were working together to help the victims. Imagine her surprise when she found Urmila sitting in a corner in one of the camps, clutching your dad's suitcase – again, thank God! Urmila, of course, did not recognise her friend, so Sudina thought of me. And as luck would have it, Urmila had given her my address before she resigned so Sudina could visit us after she left the army! Anyway, imagine my surprise when they arrived, Urmila holding tightly onto your dad's suitcase! For a long time she would not let go of it, I can only presume it gave her some comfort before she lost her memory, than just held on to it habitually."

Rasna could not contain her excitement. "You mean Mum is with you? When can I see her? I cannot believe it, at least not till I have seen her with my own eyes!"

"She is here with me; I thought bringing her here might jolt her memory! The doctors say that familiar objects, sound and music can help in recovery. People around us are all talking of the tsunami, and now her meeting you will help in the process of recovery, and hopefully she will be her old self again. In the meantime, do not be disappointed if there is no reaction from her. The doctor has told me not to try and force her to recall events but let it them return gradually. He also warned me that I will have to be careful as she is not mentally strong, especially when she finds out about Puru and Kirti." She touched a woman on her shoulder gently. "Urmila, look who is here, it is Rasna."

Chapter 3

A woman turned towards her and Rasna rubbed her eyes, then gasped first in astonishment then with delight when she saw that it was indeed her mother. She ran to embrace her, however, stopped suddenly when she saw that her mother was looking at her blankly. Her grandmother put her hand on Rasna's arm and shook her head.

"Hello," Urmila looked confused. "Have we met before for you look familiar?"

Although Urmila had lost her memory, she had stared to recall fragments of them which left her feeling frustrated, aware that it was the complete return of her memories that would reveal her past. However, she intuitively felt that there had been children in her life, and she had vague and fleeting recollections and images that had gradually begun to merge into reality and truth.

Some of the people standing beside her smiled as they saw a mother and daughter being re-united, which turned into despair as they knew that this was a one-off miracle and any hope of finding their loved ones alive was useless.

Rasna gave a sob and turned towards her grandmother. "How can you bear to see her lost like this every day and not be able to help her?"

"It hurts Pethi, it breaks my heart too to see my daughter like this, but at least she is alive and well, and maybe someday soon she will be the Urmila we loved. I do believe she is getting better, for she thought you looked familiar and there are times when she recognizes me too. Come back home with us and we will talk to her about Puru and Kirti. I have a few photographs too that might help jog her memory."

"Oh yes I would love to and I hope I can help Amma in some way. Anyway, I am not leaving my mother now and will take her back with me to London."

"I don't think that would be wise Rasna, for she needs to be in familiar surroundings, anyway we will discuss that later when we get home. Now, where are you staying?"

Rasna explained she was staying in a hotel, and after she had got her grandmother's address, promised to bring her luggage and move in with her grandmother immediately.

"I am so glad I came; I would not have found out otherwise that Amma is alive."

"Me too, we were told you were dead along with Kadamba, your father and Kirti, but anyway we will talk further when you get home. I will have dinner ready."

Rasna hugged her granddaughter and mother before she got into a taxi, but before they reached the hotel, they passed a crowd of people screaming and running around.

"What has happened? Oh my god, what is happening?" Rasna cried in alarm.

"This happens on a regular basis, ma'am, everyday there is a bomb explosion or some kind of violence."

The screams of people were drowned by sounds of the sirens of ambulances and the police had cordoned off the area shouting at the people to stay out of the way. They moved away quickly as no one wanted to get involved with the army, whilst others stood in shop doorways, talking nervously, but their fear only lasted for a short while, for to them the exploding of bombs was an everyday occurrence.

There was a haze of sweat on Rasna's face as she realised that Sri Lanka had a broken kind of beauty because of the political chaos in the country.

When they reached the hotel, she told the cab driver to wait whilst she collected her luggage.

Chapter 4

The street leading to her grandmother's house was wide and the trees that lined the street were large, green and shady.

As they neared the house, Rasna looked with admiration at the walls of the house that were covered with ivy that was so unrestrained and plentiful that it was cascading down the walls. There was a sprinkler that was watering the gardens that were green and luxuriant with blooming colourful flowers.

Prathika was waiting at the window and as soon as she saw the taxi pulling up, quickly opened the door with a smile. Rasna hugged her and thought how different in temperament she was to her paternal grandmother, Aadi, who was austere and unemotional whereas Prathika was affectionate and warm.

Prathika embraced and kissed her cheek.

"Come, Rasna, we go into the lounge while Jayani, my maid, will get something to drink, you are not used to this heat and must be thirsty."

"Oh, that would be lovely for I am very thirsty!" Rasna confirmed as she followed her grandmother into an air-conditioned cool lounge. She wiped her forehead and saw her mother sitting on one of the chairs.

"Mother Amma!" she cried as she ran to hug her. However, she was again met with a stony blank stare which turned into one of confusion.

Urmila heard Rasna's voice, which slithered over the smooth slippery surface of her mind. She smiled faintly for it sounded vaguely familiar, but her eyes reflected her puzzlement.

Urmila trembled and closed her eyes as there was a flicker of recognition. She had begun to recall vestiges of images which she tried to hold on to, but they fluttered than vanished. like a feather caught on a wind that had changed direction. She tried to grasp them, but they were fleeting and deeply rooted in her unconsciousness – too deep for her to consciously follow them to their origin. She was frustrated and angry that time had blocked her mind and emptied it of everything but the desire to understand and remember the past she was unable to recall.

Rasna sat at her mother's feet, looking imploringly up at her, willing her to recognise her and noticed, from the corner of her eye, that her grandmother had already laid out photos on a table nearby.

Jayani entered the room carrying a tray with plate and egg hopper on it, juggery, three teacups, a pot of tea and a jug of boiled milk. She placed the tray on the table and left the room whilst Prathika poured out a cup of tea and handed it to Rasna.

"Have this for now, Rasna, your mother had often told me that your favourite dish is murunga curry with coconut milk, -bath, milk rice and plain boiled rice cooked in in plantain leaves, which the cook is making for you for dinner!"

"Grandma!" Rasna sobbed. "Thank you, but I am still confused as to how, for a year, I was unaware that my mother was alive? Puru's mum said that her son and my mother were in the Samudra Devi crash and that she had seen their photos pinned on the wall amongst thousands of photographs of unidentified bodies! And are you sure Dad is really dead?" she asked hopefully.

"I am sorry Rasna, but your father drowned in the Tsunami after it hit the train they were on. Luckily, I think Urmila was thrown clear holding on to a suitcase and must have hit her head then, which could be contributing to her amnesia. As you know, they were coming to meet Kirti and yourself in Matara and were going to stop over in Galle when the tsunami struck."

"But why didn't you call me and tell me was alive? You had my phone number?"

"Yes, I do, but Puru's mother told us that both you and Kirti, along with her sons had died."

"I don't know why she would say that, whether it was because her sons had died, and I was alive or if she did not genuinely know? No, what am I saying, or course she knew, I spoke to her a couple of times"?

"I spoke to her too, but to be honest, the death of her sons hit her badly and I think she was grieving, but I am sure there was no malicious intent on her part."

"Well knowing her, I find that hard to believe; she is capable of anything. I can never forgive her for marrying Kirti off into a family she barely knew, and then assuring us she would look after Kirti till she was well settled.! Not only do I feel terrible about Kirti's death, but also because she was pregnant and unhappy in her last days! Even the fact she was pregnant did not please her in-laws for they were nasty and spiteful. I not only lost my sister, but niece or nephew too, but at least Amma is alive and safe. I wonder what happened to Praana and his mother?"

"Why are you worried what happened to them, the way they treated my granddaughter!" Prathika retorted angrily.

Urmila was sipping her tea listening to Rasna's voice, again finding it familiar. She willed her memory to return for she could not understand the sudden rush of affection she felt for the young girl as well as for the woman she had been staying with. She was impatient to identify what secrets her mind held, at the same time she did not want to endure more suffering, for she knew with certainty that something tragic had occurred – and what if the discoveries, if and when they came, tore her apart?

At that moment Jayani entered the room to announce that dinner was ready.

"Come, my dear, I think you need hot food and then a good night's rest!" Prathika squeezed Rasna's hand as she led her to the dining room followed by Urmila.

"Can I hold my mother's hand at least, Paat?"

"Of course, my dear, but as I said before the doctor has said to let nature take its course, so tomorrow we will look at some photos."

"No, Paat, I won't be able to sleep knowing that they might spark something, an incident, event, anything! I noticed you had them laid out on the table, so after dinner – I am famished by the way – we will go back to the lounge. I feel now would be the right time, when Amma is trying to figure out who I am for she has been watching me curiously."

"Hmm maybe you are right, Rasna. Your mum always did say you were a sensible girl!"

"I don't know about that, but Paat, the food does look delicious!" Rasna remarked as they entered the dining table "What about Mother, I would like to serve her first?"

"She is quite capable, and I am encouraging her to be so, for she is certainly not an invalid. Now eat, Rasna, and then I want to know what happened with you for your mother had mentioned that you had a young man?"

"Yes, I did, his name was Mark. He was in Thailand for a short holiday and was planning to come to Columbo when the Tsunami struck, and I have lost him too." There were tears in Rasna's eyes as she looked at her grandmother. "I went to

Thailand first, thinking I would be able to make it here in time for the lowering of the flag but there was a flight delay and…"

"Hush, never mind, child, I should not have brought up the subject had I known, but it all worked out in the end did it not? To the second I should say."

"Yes, so it did, we could so easily have missed each other. And we must go to see my paternal grandma, Aadi, and see what she has to say for herself, keeping me away from my mother!" Rasna wiped the tears from her eyes.

"Rasna, as I said earlier, I think she said that only because she been traumatised at losing both her sons, I don't think it was malice. I cannot imagine the pain of losing two sons a granddaughter and grandchild!" She shuddered. "However, you are right, her attitude was inexcusable! But you must visit her for she is your grandmother and grieving, and it is nice of you to care. She lives nearby, I am sure she will be glad to see you for it has been a year."

Once again, Rasna marvelled at her grandmother's generosity of heart. and they finished their dinner in silence, Rasna thinking both of what she had lost as well as what she had gained, Prathika silent in the knowledge that she would be losing her daughter yet again. For Rasna would surely take her back to London, however, she was content in the knowledge that her daughter was alive and would be well taken care of by her daughter.

Urmila had been quietly eating her food, feeling that there were shadows lying in wait on the edge of her mind, shadows that were pushing each other to be the first ones to come to the forefront of her consciousness. But as they drew closer and clearer, they quickly faded, and when they did, her self-confidence began to wane, and she stared around her in confusion as chaotic thoughts swam in her head.

They went back into the sitting room after Prathika had asked Jayani to bring their tea there.

"Now, my dear, before we look at the photos, tell me what happened to you during and after the tsunami?"

Chapter 5

Rasna's voice faltered as she told her grandmother that she had been with Kirti in Matara when the tsunami struck. And, as she began to relive the horror, she would begin a sentence only to abort it, then start all over again. Rasna felt that her unfolding of the account was spiralling and twisting – as if it were circling around something awful, something better left unsaid? So, she ended the struggle by giving a brief outline of the events.

She took a deep breath and in a broken voice said. "I was with Kadamba uncle after leaving Kirti, but, somehow, we got separated when the Tsunami struck. There was a group of us trying to find tall buildings. The help was late in coming, but when it did, I was taken to a camp. It was heart-breaking to see the moms who lost their young children in the tsunami, but at the same time I cannot forget the delight on a little girl's face when she found her mother or of another who found her favourite toy floating in the river!"

"And I saw that same look in your eyes when you found your mum," Prathika said affectionately. "Now let us see if we can help her."

"I think this might trigger something?"

Rasna had been rifling through the photos and picked out two, one of herself and one of a pregnant Kirti, and handed them to her grandmother, who, in turn handed them to her daughter.

Urmila took them curiously and peered at the photo of a young girl holding one arm across her stomach, and one who she thought looked pregnant. She ran her fingertips over it when suddenly a memory bubbled up – she must be related to this girl but where were they and where was the child? However, she instinctively felt that if she was told about it, the knowledge might tear her world apart... again?

Her mind tripped over itself as it caught on the sharp edges of reality. She gripped the arm of her chair to steady herself, and as she did, a name bubbled and exploded in her brain... Kirti! Her mind raced like an engine that has at last managed to catch the shaky energy that it was desperate to release. Her eyes closed as she began to remember, each memory more intense than the last, each one striking, shimmering disappearing and then triggering the next one.

Finally, she screamed as she saw the image of Puru floundering in a torrent of water before being swept away into the sea.

"Puru!" she screamed.

"Amma! What is the matter? Oh Paat, maybe we should not have shown her the photos. Paat? She has remembered something about father too."

"Wait, I will ring up the doctor, he will know how to manage this."

She left the room muttering to herself whilst Rasna held her mother's hand.

Urmila continued looking at the photograph's of Kirti, then looked confused as she said "Rasna, where are you?"

"Mother, I am here and I am fine, but Kirti and Dad are dead, they died in the tsunami a year ago..." Rasna looked at her mother's face and felt agony and heartache etched on it, and suddenly remembered her grandma's advice in not rushing the recovery.

"Oh no! Rasna, no, no, no…!" She cried. "Not my daughter and husband too? I remembered something about that but thought I had imagined it all, I was hoping I had!"

When she finally grasped the reality – that she had lost both her daughter and husband, the world seemed to collapse around her, and her grief exploded in her chest like a grenade.

Prathika meanwhile, after having spoken to the doctor, got a glass of water for her daughter, then pushed the photos aside.

"The doctor said the onslaught of her memories has been too sudden, but not uncommon. His suggestion was to let them gradually surface at their own pace, at the same time to give the recovery process a nudge when needed."

"Grandma, I did, but I don't know if that was wise. She looked so confused when she saw Kirti's photo that I told her about dad and Kirti's death. You mentioned earlier that she had a suitcase with her when Sudina bought her from the shelter? Maybe there is something in there that would jog her memory some more? Just to give her a nudge, like the doctor said." Rasna asked.

"Yes, you are right, Rasna, that is a very good idea, I'll get it now…" Prathika got up and left the room.

"Yes, I remember vaguely what happened, Rasna I am so glad you are alive and safe!" Urmila exclaimed agitatedly. "I seem to remember the words Kirti, Puru, and water death, but I cannot seem to make sense of the connection, and whatever little I do recall seems out of context. On top of which I am feeling peculiar and odd, my head feels light and my body too heavy!"

Urmila hoped she had misheard Rasna and that her husband and daughter were still alive, but if not, how could she have forgotten such a loss? Surely her love for them was so strong that she would at least have sustained it and felt their love in her heart? And, Rasna had just told her the tragedy had occurred a year ago… and yet she had felt no effect of the trauma till now.

"I should have been the one to die!" she cried as guilt filled her nose with its sad scent. "I should have died," she repeated. "I remember now what happened, but Rasna, I am glad you are safe."

She remembered clearly the Samudra Devi enfolding the coastline as it thrust forward, Urmila and Puru both excited at the promise of new beginnings, starting with the birth of their grandchild. She remembered the sea had looked serene and full of promises, probabilities, yet the same sea had taken them away cruelly, leaving behind a sense of isolation.

She lucidly saw the image of Puru floundering in water along with that of a strange woman, and both were splashing in the water struggling to keep afloat. The image was so clear she could even smell a whiff of dirty earth water! There were tears in her eyes as she remembered how the wind had whisked Puru away as the waves drowned his last word; 'Urmila' as he called out to her.

The painful memories had twisted everything out of perspective and had a fog around them.

Prathika entered the room and Rasna gave a cry as she recognized her father's suitcase

"If it is painful for me to see Dad's suitcase, how much more distressing must it be for Amma? Maybe we should give it a rest now, what do you think, Paat? And, what I find astonishing is that so many people have not survived the tsunami, yet the suitcase has remained intact!" Rasna said in amazement,

"I am sure only Urmila can tell us, but in answer to your question, no, I think it best we continue now, see how intently she is looking at the suitcase?" Prathika placed the suitcase on the floor than proceeded to open it.

"You are right, Grandma, whilst you were away, Amma remembered, but only in bits and pieces, she is beginning to put two and two together. I filled in the blanks when I saw she was struggling with them. I told her about Dad and Kirti, and I think that bit of information sparked the rest."

In the darkness outside the jasmine flowers had opened their petals and the air was filled with their scent.

Chapter 6

"Paat, are you sure that Kirti is dead, I mean the news might be misleading, as it was in mother's case?" Rasna asked hopefully.

"Rasna, I don't think that is possible, don't forget she was heavily pregnant when the tsunami struck, and, in her condition, it would have been very difficult for her to struggle against the force of the water."

"You are right, it does seem impossible," Rasna admitted reluctantly, "for her husband Praana and his mother would not have helped her either but thank God you escaped the tsunami."

Prathika was systematically emptying the contents of the suitcase, looking at Urmila, hoping for a reaction from her.

"Yes, luckily some of us escaped the tsunami, but by that time there was news about the train crash, and, how Matara, too, had been badly hit. I called Puru's mother a few days later and she confirmed that both her sons were dead along with Urmila and Kirti, and as you were with Kadamba on the day the tsunami struck, she assumed you to be dead too. Imagine what a pleasant surprise it was when Sudina came with Urmila, and now I find out too are…" Prathika wiped the corner of her eyes with her saree.

As there was no reaction from Urmila, Prathika began to shove the contents back into the suitcase. However, a letter fell out and she saw with surprise that it was sealed and addressed to her daughter. But, what caught her by surprise was that in front of the envelope were the words *"TO BE OPENED IN THE EVENT OF MY DEATH"*. She was astonished, then wondered about the contents of the letter and considered opening it.

"Ah, look a letter addressed to Urmila." She whispered to Rasna as she turned the envelope over. "It is in Puru's handwriting! Should we open it?"

But was it the right thing to do? Prathika thought. The entire world must seem trivial to a mother who has lost her husband, child and grandchild, but she had heard that most grieving people appreciated people telling them stories about their loved ones as there would be no new memories... so would this not be a gift to share with her daughter now?

"I think we should," Rasna replied. "Dad's gone and there might be something important in it, though I must say it does look mysterious."

"On the other hand, it might be meant only for your mother." Prathika said softly.

Urmila had heard them whispering and seen the letter in her mother's hand.

"Don't worry on my account, Amma. I feel strong now and can cope with the tragedies that have occurred, though I would have preferred to have remained ignorant of them! Anyway, I do recognise your father's suitcase... ah I see there is a letter from him? I thought he was joking when he told me about a couple of months ago."

Prathika handed her the envelope and when she held it, Urmila thought it felt heavy, from which she deduced there was more than a page. She ran her fingers tenderly over his handwriting, which was a bit smudged, as if by a drop of his tear? Had he been crying, and, if so, it must have been over something truly terrible. She stared at the envelope intensely, willing him to come back from wherever he had gone, and for a moment her eyes could not focus, she then proceeded to open it. What would it say?

"Amma! You don't have to," Rasna cried in alarm. "We can read it tomorrow when you feel stronger…"

"I won't be able to sleep…" Urmila looked at the white envelope that was covered with a thin layer of dust.

The words in front were written in Puru's familiar handwriting so she turned it before opening it.

Maybe it would state how much he loved her? Maybe in his youth he had done something wrong and was feeling guilty? But, even if he had, Urmila thought, he had taken care of his family. He had been so dependable that Urmila was sure that if ever there had been a crisis like, a flood or a fire, Puru would have been the first to protect his family from any kind of danger. And now, Urmila remembered that is what he had done… he had persuaded her, no nearly pushed Urmila out of the window of the Samudra Devi so she could steer clear of the wave whilst he had stayed behind to save others, and in the process had drowned.

"We will leave you to read Dad's letter," Rasna said as she and Prathika prepared to leave the room when Urmila stopped them.

"No, please stay, I want you to hear what he has to say, I am mystified as to why he would think he would die, the tsunami was unexpected and he had no health problems."

She spread out a sheet wondering at its content and began reading aloud:

Urmila, my dearest wife,
If you are reading this it means I am dead,
so, now, I think you need to know the truth.
I am too much of a coward to tell you in
person but have been living with the guilt
for too long, and as my wife, who I love
dearly, I need to confess. I love you and our
girls very much, and you have given me so
much happiness, more than I deserved. I
am so sorry for my actions and the guilt
has been like a tumour eating away at me.

I killed Sarvash, Lakshmi's husband,
unintentionally of course, for although I
loved my sister I did not like Sarvash. How
could I, for he was a much older man who
first seduced my naïve sister into running
away with him, than into marrying him!'

Urmila gasped in horror and felt disgusted as she read and reread the paragraph. Her eyebrows gradually drew into a shadowy and painful frown as she mouthed the words silently, her lips stirring strangely upon the words.

She sighed and read on aloud…

Unbeknown to Mother, I had kept in touch
Lakshmi and one day she came to tell me
that she was pregnant. I was livid, for
although she was excited about it, I foresaw
what her future would be with a baby. I
had found out a few unsavoury facts about
Sarvash, he was not only a lot older than
Lakshmi, but he was already married with
a young son! I was not only angry at him;

I was angry at Lakshmi's naivety for how could she not see through him?

I knew I could not make Lakshmi see reason, so thought would try and talk to Sarvash. I asked Lakshmi for his address, and when I did, her eyes lit up for she believed her family was finally ready to accept him.

I had no ulterior motive other than talk to him and had no intention to hurt him. If I had only foreseen the consequences of my visit, of how harmful that would be for my sister and her unborn child!

Sarvash opened the door, and there was a smug look on his face when he saw me- I felt that he was laughing at me and our family!

He was a middle-aged man, old enough to be my father. He was of an athletic build, and, reluctantly I could see that he had a crude and vulgar charm that would appeal to women, especially naïve girls like Lakshmi.

I greeted him politely and calmly then pleaded with him to leave my sister, but he just sneered at me.

'Why don't you tell your sister to leave me alone? Oh, she cannot do that now she is with child. Where will she go and who will take her in? You? Your mother?" he jeered as his lips curled upward mockingly.

He wiped his nose with the back of his hand. I looked at him in disgust and offered him my handkerchief, which he used than insolently put in his pocket!

His attitude infuriated me, so in frustration and anger, I grabbed a vase that was lying beside the photo of Lakshmi and myself and swung it at him. In a haze, I saw him fall and hit his head on the corner of the table. The blood spurted from his head and I knew instantly that he was dead.

Chapter 7

"Oh my God!" Urmila picked up another page and began reading as Prathika and Rasna looked at her amazement, not knowing what to make of it all.

'It was not like me to be violent. You know me, Urmila, I am against any kind of violence and still cannot come to terms that it was me who committed this horrible crime! And because I could not control my temper, my sister became a widow, for the thought of living without that vile man drove my pregnant sister to commit suicide… so by default, I have three deaths on my conscience.

I did not know how to handle the situation, so went back to Lakshmi and told her that Sarvash had requested me to relay a message to her - that he was returning to his first wife as he could not deal with the stress of being a father all over again.

Lakshmi was devasted, for she had been unaware of the fact that Sarvash was already married, so I left her crying and went back to her house to hide Sarvash's body in the cellar. Later that night I took his body and threw it in the river. How was I to know that his body would surface with my handkerchief in his pocket? Luckily, that piece of evidence was overlooked by the police when they found his body but was later handed over to his family with his other possessions.

But, since that day, years and years have passed and there are layers and layers of guilt piled over that one horrific memory! Sometimes I would go for months feeling normal, than I could think of nothing else but that day, and then I would feel I was going crazy! I had admitted everything to my mother, who, soon after our marriage, decided it best that I leave the country.

Anyway, moving on, Praana is Sarvash's son and his father's belongings had been given to his mother, my handkerchief was unique as it had my family's logo and my initials embroidered on it. Praana's mother took it upon herself to avenge her husband's murder, even though the police had closed the case, and later convinced her son to do the same.

After twenty years of searching their trail led to my mother. At first, Praana told her that he was Sarvash's son, and later that he had evidence that I participated in his father's death. She was astonished, not only at meeting Sarvash's son, but also because she thought there was nothing to link Sarvash's death to me, in fact, to this day, Kadamba is not even aware of it,

Praana and his mother blackmailed my mother and threatened that if she did not arrange Kirti marriage to Praana, she would report me to the police… and that is why my darling daughter was married in haste.

But now, I am afraid for my daughter, so in the event of my death, please protect her for Praana and his mother will make her life hell. I am so sorry that my daughter has to suffer for my sins, but I only agreed to the proposal because Kirti is such a good girl that whenever she puts her hand on a person or project it becomes a mark of quality. I was sure that her laughter, smile and kind nature would overcome Praana's ruthlessness.

Always yours, forgive me

Puru

Urmila gave a cry and flung the letter on the floor and paced the room, her hands covering her face with her hands.

"I don't believe Puru would do such a cruel thing, first to his sister then to his own daughter! And then he has the cheek to justify it by saying he has faith in Kirti's kind disposition! Not only has he killed his brother-in-law, thrown the body in the river but his pregnant sister and unborn child died because of his actions! And his evil actions do not end there, he goes on to deceive me for twenty years - and to top it all, to save his own skin, he puts his daughter's life in danger!"

"Mum, I am shocked as well!" Rasna said in amazement. "I cannot imagine Dad would do such a horrible thing, but then to keep it hidden for so long is unimaginable!"

Her father's behaviour and actions that had always puzzled her fell into place. His odd reaction whenever her Aunt's name was mentioned followed by being moody and irritable. His face would turn to granite and he would stare unhappily into space- and at these times no one could talk or reason with him. He would become a robot, going through the motions of doing the right thing at the right time, but, with such a sad and blank expression that she would feel that it was not her father but a replica in his place.

"Dad are you feeling all right?" she would ask, and he would take a few moments before murmuring he was all right.

But these episodes were always temporary, and the father she loved would be back, so fully attentive and jovial that it made her doubt her earlier misgivings.

She had always respected and admired her father, and never thought him to be capable of such a despicable act, however unintentional, but to so callously leave his daughter to fend for herself in what can only be called an enemy camp just so that he would be safe? That was inexcusable.

Urmila had read the letter twice and stood still, believing with certainty that if she moved, she would fall again into that deceptive void of nothingness.

A pale moon shone in the dark night and brimmed over with unspoken memories. She had loved her country and thought it to be beautiful, but what was left in the paradise for her? The person who she loved had not only perished in the tsunami but deceived her.

Chapter 8

Urmila folded the letter and sobbed with rage and frustration, Mark was missing in Thailand and Rasna was so concerned and worried about him, why should she carry her troubles as well? Anyway, at this moment she did not want to talk to anyone, she had been living with a murderer and not known it… how was that possible? Puru had lied to her to her on every occasion, told her that the only reason he had come to London was to escape any reprisal against him for his father had been an informer in the Sinhalese Government. He had told her that some people were angry with his family, for many innocent people had died because incorrect information had been passed on by him to the government. But now Urmila wondered if that was another one of his lies, for in the letter he had mentioned that his mother had urged him to flee the country because he was a murderer?

She focused on her breathing, surprised at the speed with she was recalling every little detail. She wondered what she could do to make it right for the people Puru had wronged, although it was too late for Kirti.

Sarvash's death had been an accident, but to have covered it up the way Puru had? Thrown his body overboard, then seen his sister commit suicide and the death of her unborn child. Had he felt no guilt or emotion then? She shuddered when she thought he was willing to sacrifice Rasna into that same family! That kind of ruthless behaviour was what she would have expected from her mother-in-law, not her gentle and kind husband.

Rasna voiced her thoughts.

"Mum I cannot imagine what you are going through, do you want me to sleep with you tonight?"

"Of course, Rasna. I would love that! You don't know how good it is to be with you!" Urmila smiled as she hugged her daughter.

She felt an overwhelming tiredness, and with it she felt a sense of detachment followed by huge swings of varying emotions that were exhausting.

Prathika took them to their room and first kissed her daughter then Rasna on the cheek.

"Good night, Paat."

"Good night, Amma," Rasna said sleepily as she turned on her side and drifted off to sleep, holding her mother's hand. "Tomorrow I thought we will visit Aadi, Dad's mother, Paat said she lived nearby."

"You mean Puru's mother?" Urmila thought of Puru's letter and felt angry at how his mother had participated in camouflaging Purus crime, and initiated the marriage proposal for Kirti. However, her anger was followed by compassion for her mother-in-law had lost two sons and a granddaughter. "Yes, that might be a good idea."

Suddenly Rasna sat up in bed angrily as she thought of her conversation with her grandmother, in which she had told her that her mother had died in the Samudra Devi crash.

"No, Amma, actually I don't think I want to, for not only did she lie to me, but, to your mother too! People think that tragedy makes one wiser, but the opposite is also true, and it can make one petty and spiteful. Those people have no insight other than that life is cruel, and that they alone have paid a terrible price for it. Most importantly she brought Praana and his wicked mother into our lives by marrying Kirti to Praana, who is no better than his father! And all the time Dad knew what kind of family she was being married into, it was like sending a kind gentle soul to be surrounded by enemies! What chance did she ever have?" she cried.

"Rasna, take a deep breath and relax." Urmila tried to calm Rasna and sighed. "You are right, Magal (daughter), I don't know which one of the crimes they committed is crueller… But Rasna, she is your grandmother, has lost two sons and it is only right that we call on her."

"Okay, Amma, we will call on her, but only because we will be leaving for London soon and won't be meeting her again," Rasna agreed grudgingly.

Urmila lay back on the bed, dark circles under her eyes, exhausted from the day's events and the emotional rollercoaster she had ridden.

"Mum, do you remember when we came to Sri Lanka in 2004 and I wanted to learn about our family? Once you had filled in the missing pieces, I had said that ours was certainly not a dull family, for everyone has a colourful background. Well, that was an understatement! Add Praana and my father and oh my God! I cannot believe this!"

Urmila hugged her close and stroked her daughter's hair as she rested her head on the pillow. She looked around her childhood room, but there was nothing in it to remind her of her upbringing. She only recalled the time she had joined the army, and then the subsequent events came flooding back! She thought of Kirti and her husband, and her mind began to shut down as if it could not process any more grief. Was she more disappointed in the death of her husband or his betrayal at living a lie?

As she thought of Kirti, she wondered if she could have helped her in some way? The thought was like the tip of a knife twisting and turning at her very core. If Kirti had survived she would have lived a normal life, she would dieted, danced, cooked and been a wonderful mother, but life was over for her. Urmila felt her chest constricting, as if a steel vice had wrapped around her chest.

She thought of her unborn grandchild and Puru, her time with the Tigers, and, she now understood why Puru had been so eager to come to Sri Lanka for a vacation, particularly after hearing that Kirti was unhappy although, to her and Rasna, he had dismissed those claims as being false.

She too felt responsible, for she had supported him in getting Kirti married, but had she known then what she knew now, she would have moved heaven and earth to prevent the wedding. And, as she recalled the days leading up to the wedding, knew he had many opportunities when he could have told her, and now, despite knowing Praana's background and Kirti's unhappiness, he was still willing to marry his second daughter into the same family?

What kind of man had she married? She had believed him to be honest and sincere, but he had turned out to be a shallow and selfish man. She was discovering that there were layers and layers of weaknesses rooted deep in his character, flaws that he had successfully kept veiled. He had only professed to his crime so he could absolve himself of blame, and by his confession he had transferred his guilt on to her.

She sometimes doubted Puru's wrongdoing, so had to go over the facts again and again by reading the letter repeatedly. Puru had killed Sarvesh, by default Lakshmi and her child, and in her eyes, that made him evil. She felt he was a monster, more so because he had kept everything hidden from her.

How could she not have known the heavy burden that he had carried through their marriage? Or maybe she had not known because he had not felt it to be a burden, which somehow made it worse.

She was disappointed too, for, she had felt they were not only husband and wife, but close friends too, friends who could share their innermost secrets, yet, she had not even been close to understanding him! Puru was Sarvesh's murderer, and he had moved around freely in London far away from Sri Lanka.

She wrapped her arms around her trembling body, overwhelmed with emotion. ohH

Urmila saw the sky on the point of being pierced by light as the beginnings of dawn punched a hole in the sky. A faint rose pink light flooded out seeping into the sky whilst birds sang in the morning.

'I am a murderer's wife; I wonder if that makes me an accessory to murder?" Urmila thoughts were swirling and turning on expertly on the slippery facade that her life had become after reading the letter.

The house they had lived in London, where her children had been born, and where she had been happy, now she thought of as being tainted with the sin and lies of her husband.

She had always been patriotic and loyal to her country, and when she came to London, felt that she had left a part of herself behind.

Rasna opened her eyes sleepily and asked, "Mum, do you remember where you were taken to after the train crash?" and as she saw her mother trembling, quickly put out a reassuring hand on her shoulder.

Chapter 9

"I am sorry, Mum, I should not have reminded you about that period. It must have been very traumatic."

"No, it is all right, Rasna, but, yes, I do remember now… I was taken, along with others, to a makeshift camp, but, after that, I do not remember anything, not even how I came to live with Amma!"

"Your friend Sudina, who, I believe, used be with the rebel's army with you, found you. You had amnesia by then and did not recognise her. But she did, and as you had given your mother's address to her, she took you to grandma's house, where you have been ever since."

"What about you?" Urmila asked.

"There was a makeshift camp set up at St Michelle's college for the refugees in and around Matara district."

"So maybe Kirti was taken there too?" Urmila asked hopefully.

"I don't know Mum, I only stayed there a couple of days before I went on to Colombo, but I was hoping so too, so during those two days, I did look for her but there were so many people, all frantically looking for their loved ones, hoping they would find them…" There were tears in her eyes.

At that moment, there was a knock on the door and Prathika entered the room with three mugs of tea on a tray.

"Did you two get any sleep?" she asked affectionately

Rasna got up guiltily. "Not really, Paat, but there was no need for you to bring us tea, we were going to join you downstairs."

However, both Urmila and Rasna took the tea and stared thoughtfully out of the window.

"Ah, am I interrupting something, Urmila?" Prathik looked at her daughter.

Although Urmila looked sad, she also appeared calm and determined, and Prathik felt she had the calm look of someone who has emerged successfully from an intense crisis.

Prathika put her arms around her gently and looked at Rasna.

"Rasna, you mentioned yesterday that you wanted to meet your grandmother?"

"I did but after all she had done, I don't think so! But Amma has talked me into it," Rasna grumbled.

"Rasna, that is what your father would have wanted. After all, she lost both her sons."

Rasna scowled at her mother, but much as she loved her, did not agree with her.

Prathika sensed the tense atmosphere and tried to change the subject.

"Rasna, what would you like for breakfast? Jayani is waiting to make what you like, meat, fish or chicken curry, potato curry, egg curry Dahl Coconut (Pol) Sambol, String Hopper (Appam) plain hoppers or coconut (pol) roti?"

"Oh Paat! Thank you, I love everything so will leave it to you and Amma to decide." She smiled at her, glowered at her mother, then went into the bathroom.

"And Magal, how are you feeling today? I hope it has not been too much for you, finding out about Puru and Kirti at the same time followed by Puru's letter. What was he thinking?"

"That is just it, Amma, he was not thinking! And of course, it has been a lot to take on! But at least I have found Rasna, and for that I am grateful. Would you like to come with us to see Aadi?"

Prathik shook her head. "I don't know how you convinced your daughter though, for she was reluctant to meet her. She cannot forgive her for not telling her that you were alive and well."

Urmila sighed. "And neither can I, for she told us that Rasna had died with Kadamba, but, after all, she is Puru's mother and that is what he would have wanted She is all alone without Kadamba who used to look after her, even though she ruined his life too!"

"You are a kind person and I am proud of you, Urmila, but she does not warrant your compassion, for she was the one who shrewdly arranged Kirti's marriage to Sarvash's son, just so her son could be safe! And, to top it all, although she was aware of the type of people they were, only visited her once!"

As she left the room with the empty mugs, Prathika recalled that somewhere she had read that one's weaknesses were actually manifestations of their strength. She had not thought that to be true till she saw how well Urmila was managing, and how very lonely she was going to be after she left, for Rasna would surely take her back to London.

She had supported her daughter in everything, even when she had wanted to join the rebel army to fight for a cause that she knew would be fraught with danger, complications and at the very least Urmila would be playing with danger! So, when she had left the army and returned home, she had put her foot down and was determined to get her married.

At that time Puru had seemed a perfect gentleman from a good family, but after the recent revelations about him, wished she had not been so insistent to get her married to him.

Rasna and Urmila left for Aadi's house soon after breakfast and they passed the rickshaw clogged streets. The city teemed with life and colour and Rasna was amazed at the frantic hurry of rickshaws and the grating sound of gears and hoots.

The street widened as they entered Cinnamon Gardens, where Aadi lived, and Rasna looked in admiration at her grandmother's house which had flowers cascading down the walls.

Urmila nodded at the Ramu who led them into a room with tiled floors.

"Memsahib has not spoken since she heard about her sons, but please don't be discouraged and sit with her, for she does not get any visitors these days. In the meantime, I will get some tea."

Chapter 10

Aadi was sitting in an armchair and Rasna was shocked at her appearance, for her hair was unkept and frizzled. Her once erect frame was shrunken, and the shock of losing her sons had reduced her muscles into involuntary tremors. She sat quietly, her myopic eyes glaring behind thick lensed spectacles. Rasna remembered her grandmother as being a woman of an extraordinarily strong and dominant personality, but she now saw before her a crumpled and broken woman.

Her arms gripped her armchair and she looked at them with a calm smile as if she forgave them for being alive. Urmila's enforced complacency began to turn to rage as she recalled Aadi's abuse towards her family. She felt so enraged that she began to welcome the stimulus of a fight and the openness of behaving exactly as she wanted to.

"I don't think she recognises us, Amma!" Rasna whispered.

"Hush, I know, Rasna, but don't forget what Ramu said."

Aadi looked at them with tight-lipped disapproval, and both Rasna and Urmila felt her cold welcome, and, as she looked away, Rasna felt she was turning all that they had suffered into a travesty.

Rasna lowered herself into a creaking chair while a Myrna bird sat on a tree that overhung the terrace. It let out a series of whistles than took off in alarm.

At that moment. Ramu brought in a tray with tea and fritters and placed it on the table and withdrew.

Afternoon dwindled into afternoon and they sat in silence; Aadi in grief, Rasna full of resentment, Urmila trying to kerb the feeling of intense hatred that she felt for her mother-in-law. She ran through the list of people Aadi had wronged, starting with her own daughter Lakshmi, imparting wrong counsel to Puru, destroying Kadamba's marriage by trying to control them and last, but not least, keeping her away from her daughter.

This silent internal battle amongst the three was only revealed by scowls and frowns. Aadi sat upright, hands folded on her lap, sometimes, she would look at them than start crying, tears running from eyes that were sunken and had dark circles under them.

There was a fusion of tension and emptiness in the room, and the air was taut with unspoken thoughts. Life had a way of throwing unexpected things at people, and each became preoccupied with their thoughts, dealing with their tragedies in their own manner.

Rasna sat looking sadly out of the window, twisting the ring on her finger, the ring that Mark had so lovingly given her. She winced at the strong wave of resentment she felt towards Aadi, for she was by nature a quiet and gentle girl. Therefore, she felt ashamed of her strong reaction, realising that everybody carries with them some baggage, some possibility of destruction or even malice? Everybody had some prejudice or weakness through which the finger of hate could penetrate, and she could not but help think that Aadi had found them most people, starting with each of her children.

Urmila thought of Puru, how he and his mother had callously sacrificed her daughter by marrying her into Praana's family just so they stayed safe!

Kirti with her small, beautiful face, delicate petite figure and sweet smile - how beautiful she had looked on her wedding day, wearing a crimson sari that was embroidered with gold.

She shook herself and got up as Rasna turned from the window.

"Amma, I think we should leave; we are only making her uncomfortable."

"You are right Rasna, but we have done our duty, for your father's sake. She looks so sad…"

"Mum, you are so naïve! I thought you would have realised it by now. If ever there was a kind bone in her body she would not have behaved as she did! And as for Dad, after what he did to his sister's husband and then to Kirti, he does not deserve our sympathy either!"

"I know child, but no one should suffer like her."

"Mum, you are forgetting, you too have lost your husband, daughter and grandchild, but you are not bitter! You would not behave as she has done!"

"Rasna, one changes as one gets older and we become dependent on our children, and women specially, find it difficult to adapt to tragedy, therefore are less accommodating to any change of circumstances. Anyway, let us go home, Amma must be waiting."

As they got up to leave, Aadi who had not acknowledged their presence, felt there was no need to bid them farewell.

As they walked out Rasna remarked, "My, I am glad that is over, Amma, she is rude, she could have at least been civil to us!"

"Me too, I think you were right, Rasna. It has made no difference to her that we came. In fact, she hardly noticed us, though at times I felt her eyes were shooting arrows at us under those fiery brows of hers! Must have been my imagination."

"It was not your imagination, Amma, for I noticed it too. She is a very cold woman, Amma, not at all like your mum!"

"No, thank God for that." Urmila turned around to find that Ramu had followed them and was trying to get their attention. "What is it, Ramu?"

"Memsahib, Aadi does know what is going on, but soon after the tsunami an Englishman came and said he was looking for his "Indian Princess'. I think he meant you, Rasna memsahib?"

Rasna looked at him in amazement. "Mark, Mark was here?"

"Yes, that was his name, Aadi memsahib told him you had died, we all thought you had died with Kadamba. Anyway, he was heartbroken, but did not want to believe it, so left his phone number and address in England." Rasna ran to hugged him and looked at her mother with shining eyes.

"Mum, that means Mark is alive and well! Oh my god, I will phone him as soon as we get home. We have to book out tickets for London as soon as possible, Amma, I can't wait to meet him!" Rasna's eyes were shining with excitement" Ramu, you did say he was alive and well?"

"Yes, he was alive and well, except for a broken arm that is!" Ramu smiled and handed her the piece of paper he had kept safe, for he was very fond of Rasna and had also hoped she was alive and well.

Rasna jumped in excitement and hugged Ramu again than embraced her mother.

"Oh Ramu, thank you so much! Amma, did you hear that, my Mark is alive and well! I can't wait to talk to him, he will be shocked and surprised." Suddenly a thought occurred to her. "Oh my God, Amma it has been a year since the tsunami, he might have got married or found someone else."

"Calm down Rasna, one thing at a time. Ramu, can you get us a taxi please?" Urmila tried to curb her daughter's excitement. "This is great news, Rasna, but I don't think he would have married or got a girlfriend, for coming here to look for you, then leaving his phone number just shows how much he really loves you."

As Rasna sat in the taxi that drove down the road in a whirl of grey dust, she clutched the piece of paper tightly, for it was proof that Mark was alive

Chapter 11

As they drove home from Aadi's house, Rasna felt as if the colours of the flowers glowed more vividly. their scent was stronger, and the chirping of the birds was sharper. And this was only because she had just been informed by none other than Ramu, her grandmothers' servant, that Mark was alive and well, and had been in Colombo on 28th December 2004. He had given her a scrap of paper with Mark's mother's phone number which Rasna clutched it tightly.

As they neared the house, she saw a servant sweeping the veranda, brushing the dead flowers and leaves into a corner.

Rasna ran upstairs to call Mark, and Prathika, who was sitting on the sofa in the lounge, looked at her disappearing figure curiously and gestured to a seat beside her.

"Urmila why don't you come and join me? Is everything okay, I saw Rasna running up the stairs? It is teatime, and I am just waiting for Jayani to bring me some tea."

"Everything is fine, Amma, in fact it is better, it is wonderful, for Rasna just found out that Mark is alive! He came to meet her at Aadi's house on 28th December of last year, but of course she told him, like she told us, that Rasna had died in the tsunami! Mark did not want to believe it so left his mother's mobile number, just in case, and left it with Ramu."

"That is good news, Urmila! I am so happy for her, she is such a good girl she deserves some happiness, but yesterday I overheard Rasna saying that she was thinking of booking two tickets for London?"

Jayani came in with a tea tray and placed it on the table, and after she had left the room, Prathika poured a cup and handed it to her daughter.

"Yes, you must have, for I was thinking of going back with her, of course I will miss you, Amma." Urmila took a sip. "Why? I can tell that something is bothering you?"

Prathika added sugar to her cup than stirred it with a spoon thoughtfully. "I did not want to say this earlier, but ever since Rasna has been staying with us, it has been at the back of my mind. Today I think I must speak out."

"Amma, you are worrying me, I thought you did not mind my going, you actually approved of it. You know that it is because of her, and you of course, Amma, that I regained my memory, though sometimes I wish I had not! Don't get me wrong, I love Rasna and am thrilled she alive and well!"

"Urmila, how can think that!" Prathika said crossly. "You know I love her and was glad you were going with her. I have loved having both my girls staying with me, and will miss you, but was just thinking about your life in London. And, I am not saying this for selfish reasons, but because you know I love you dearly. Rasna will go to work during the day, and with nothing to do, you will miss Puru and Kirti even more. And now that Mark is back in the picture, they will have a life of their own, whereas if you stay back with me..."

Outside, a faint light was swimming through the trees as the sun gently plunged into late afternoon.

Urmila sighed. "Yes, you are right, Amma, I had not thought of that, we just found out a little while ago about Mark. But I was so happy to be with her for she is all that I have left, apart from you of course. I had envisioned a traditional wedding for her, with a wedding feast., where guests washed hands in small bowls of iced water and the uniformed servants served guests in bowls." Urmila sighed "No, what am I thinking? I am only glad she is alive and well, and I know she will be happy with Mark."

"What we want for our children, and what they want for themselves do not go hand in hand, but at the end of the day their happiness is all that matters. But think about it, we don't know what the situation with Mark is." Prathika said wisely.

At that moment Rasna ran into the room, her eyes sparkling with excitement, and first hugged her mother than grandmother. "Mark is alive, Ramu had told us but I had to hear his voice before I could believe it! He says that in his heart, he knew that I was alive and to come as soon as possible and I cannot wait to see him too. I am going to book our flight to London."

As Rasna turned to leave the room, Urmila spoke with a tremor in her voice.

"Rasna, just book the ticket for one…"

"What are you saying, Amma, you are coming with me!" Rasna replied angrily.

"Rasna calm down," Prathika intervened.

"No, I won't, Paat, you want your daughter to live with you, well I want my mother to come with me."

After Rasna's anger had subsided, Urmila tried to explain. "And not only will I be with my mother, Sudina is coming to stay with us, for she lost her family in the tsunami. I would like to be there for her, we both would, we have a lot to thank her for, for had it not been for her I would still be rotting in some shelter. In fact, I am going to try and persuade her to stay with us permanently, or at least for a while. And, I promise I will come and see you once you are settled."

Reluctantly, Rasna agreed, knowing her mother would be safe and happier in Sri Lanka with her mother and friend.

They had been talking till the onset of darkness- the light had faded rapidly, and it had become cool as a gentle breeze rustled amongst the trees.

Before going to bed, they had dinner of murunga curry with coconut milk, Kirti-bath, and plain boiled rice that was cooked in plantain leaves which they ate in a quiet subdued manner.

The next morning, Rasna made the booking for London, and the days flew from one warm day to another, till the day of departure came.

Morning came as usual and the scent of orange blossoms flowers drifted in from the garden.

Urmila felt her heart would break, and for a while Rasna's decision wavered as she saw her mother's unhappy face. However, she was happy in the knowledge that her mother was alive and safe and would surely be happy here.

They had wanted to come with her to the airport, but she could not bear the agony of a prolonged goodbye, so quickly hugged them, then got into the taxi which was to take her to Mark.

Prathik and Urmila cried softly as they stood and watched the taxi disappear round the corner to the airport where Rasna would take a flight to London.

They had gone to bed soon after, and although, Urmila was happy for her daughter, she was woken by a nightmare and she sat up in bed, wiping the sweat trickling down her forehead. The nightmare had begun pleasantly enough with golden sand shimmering in the sun whilst gentle waves rippled across the sea. On the edge of the shore were palm trees, their branches swaying in the breeze, however, against the backdrop of tranquillity and calmness she heard the crackle of gunfire and screams of children.

Although the intensity of the dream had subsided, she felt its echo around her – the noise of a fighter jet flying overhead followed by a deafening explosion. the vibration of the earth as it was hit with the impact of the bombs, the images of the twisted bodies, house beams and tree branches were all entangled in her dream. And amidst the chaos she saw a vision of a tall and beautiful woman beside her, both dressed in camouflage attire wandering in a forest. ohH ohH ohH

ohH And as her memories suddenly materialised and mixed, the horror of it all hit her. Beginning with her joining the army, the carnage she had witnessed there, the tragedy and loss she had suffered at the hands of the tsunami, and finally the content of Puru's letter!

She squirmed and kept her eyes closed, needing to fall back to sleep but not being able to do so. She lay in bed holding in her pain, learning, as everyone does at one time or another, that hostilities, be they old or new, should not dictate their present, and whilst one part of her past belonged to rebels and causes, the other belonged to her family. She was astonished at the quick pace with which she was recollecting her past, for the blockage in her mind seemed to have cleared and she was remembering everything with a clarity that surprised her.

She turned her head and thought of the time she had signed up for rebel military training and the subsequent events that had led her full circle back to Sri Lanka. Urmila, once having made up her mind to join the rebels, had tentatively broached the subject to her mothe

Sri Lanka 2004

Chapter 12

"Amma, the more I listen to the rebel message, the idea of an armed struggle appeals to me, and it seems to be the only likely reaction, and maybe even solution to the conflict in Sri Lanka. I think, that if we are going to be killed or driven from our home, shouldn't we at least put up a fight?"

"No, you are not going to join the Tamil Tigers, Urmila, and that is the end of the matter!" Prithika had tears in her eyes

She was a pleasant looking woman with twinkling eyes and a sweet smile however, her once strong personality had been drained away by years of caring of her now dearly departed husband.

"You are wrong, Amma, you are only saying that because I am a woman, and because you come from a generation who thinks that a woman should obey her husband and be at his beck and call! You always place a woman in relation to a man – as a wife, mother or daughter!"

"Urmila, you know that is not true. I only have your interest at heart, anyway, things are not as bad as you think."

"Only because you do not get to see broken glass on the roads, as the ambulancemen have become efficient in gathering bits and pieces of human life after a bomb has blown up, then moving it out of sight with practised hands. They think and hope that people, like you, will believe that because nothing is visible, there is no problem."

Urmila drank her tea and toyed with Kiri-bath whilst the air was tense with unspoken thoughts which Urmila broke.

"You know that each house has already received a letter ordering that one child, be it girl or boy, should become a fighter. And besides, I cannot bear to see my friends being dragged from their cars and abducted, the homes, offices and shops are being ransacked by Sinhala youth who are looking for us, anyone from Tamil ethnic minority. And what is the government doing to protect us… nothing!" she exclaimed as she heard sirens and ambulances sweeping past.

She looked out of the window where the dawn was trying to push through the sky, whilst a faint rose pink light flooded it, gradually covering the horizon

"I understand your feelings, Urmila, believe me I do, but I cannot let you join the rebels!" Prithika, had replied firmly, pursing her lips. "I will keep you hidden, if need be."

"Amma, that is what Mangai's mum did, and look what happened to her! She was our neighbour and her mother only let her out during the night and hid her in the basement during the day but still…"

"Yes, I know Urmila, but Mangai came out during the day once, and Shobana, a Tamil woman who lives in the house next to Mangai's and whose daughter had been kidnapped, saw her and reported it to the Tigers. The next day they came and took her away, and to this day I cannot forget the cries of the mother as she begged them not to take her daughter!"

Chapter 13

“**Y**our daughter will be returned to you, they had said, and true to their word, she did come home, but only as a dead body that was wrapped in a red tiger flag! I do not want the same fate to befall my daughter!”

Urmila sighed. “This is only one example of the many betrayals that are ripping the Tamil society apart. Shobana could not bear to see Mangai safe whilst her daughter had been forcibly kidnapped.”

“That is why, Magai, please listen to me! Plus, you know that our society is very traditional, and parents do not want their sons to marry ex-fighters. You should be thinking of marriage instead of joining the rebels!”

“Amma, I am too young to marry, and anyway, if I don’t join now, Shobana or somebody like her will report it, so it is only a matter of time before I am taken forcibly.”

Finally, Prathika had relented, but only because she knew her daughter was too stubborn, and she would have joined despite her mother’s objections.

Urmila had joined the rebel tigers, and Prathika received occasional letters from her in which she was informed that she was safe. She had met a nice woman called Sudina, whose friendship she had come to cherish They were selected for military training and sent to an all-girls' camp called the Freedom Bird.

The letters were detailed, explaining how their training was very demanding, how the day would begin with a two-hour exercise regime followed by commando. In the afternoon they had firing practice and lessons in explosives and camouflage. And when they were told they were ready for field action, they would roam the jungle dressed in the universal guerrilla attire, Khaki pants, and bandanas with casually slung grenade launchers from hips up onto their shoulder.

With their rifles on their shoulders and cyanide capsules clasped between their teeth, they would wait for the enemy soldiers. Their orders were to shoot, and they had been ordered that if caught they were to first puncture then swallow the glass capsules that hung on a thread around their necks, for as a Tamil Tiger guerrilla, there was no honour in being caught alive. They were surrounded by bombing and artillery shelling, day and night; and their activities were restricted by long curfews. They spent many days in their home-built bunker with hands over their ears, trying to block out the sounds of gunshots and explosions.

However, Urmila had soon became disillusioned with the cause for she saw it had become increasingly cruel, their only thought was in protecting its leaders and were willing to endanger innocent civilians. From kidnapping youths, the rebels were even going so far as to snatch children from the parents so they could train them to become fighters – innocent children who often had to face a useless and sometimes torturous death. So maybe what they were doing after all was not any better than the actions of the enemy soldiers?

She began to question why she, or any other woman, had enlisted in the cause… was enrolling in the cause an indication on the part of the women, herself included, to prove that they were equal to men, to escape being raped by the military or was it genuinely a commitment to die for the cause? Whatever the reason, it was difficult for anyone to associate the gentle faces of the female suicide fighters with massacres and suicide bombs that resulted in the innocent dying.

After months of roaming the jungle, Urmila contracted malaria and the illness had left her broken, both physically and emotionally, and amid the chaos she was grateful of Sudina's friendship. They had been roaming the jungle one day when Urmila turned towards her friend.

"Sudina, thanks for looking after me during my illness, but I have had time to think. I am going to resign, why should we fight a war that cannot possibly be won and watch the innocent dying, sometimes by our own hands? I hate to admit it, but my mother was right!"

"You would have done the same for me too and I too do not like to kill the innocent too, but Urmila please don't resign! To be honest, I don't think I would want to stay without you."

"Then why don't you resign with me? Give it all up, admit we were wrong. Now that I look back on my decision, I think I see a bit of recklessness and selfish teenage rebellion on my part that made me want to join the rebels."

"Maybe you are right, the leaders glamourized the cause in order to recruit people, but it is too late for me, for I cannot go back for my family; they have disowned me!" Sudina had shaken her head sadly and when they said goodbye had tears in her eyes.

"I am so sorry Sudini, you never said anything about it," Urmila scribbled on a piece of paper. "This is her address, so you must come and see us as soon as you leave the army. In the meantime, look after yourself."

They embraced and Sudina had tears in her eyes as she waved Urmila goodbye.

As Urmila travelled home, she was unsure of what her future would hold for she had severed all ties with the tigers, and the only emotion she felt was relief, as if she were no longer capable of experiencing happiness or sadness.

Chapter 14

As soon as she saw her, her mother ran towards her, arms outstretched. She embraced and held her tightly, all the while sobbing.

"Thank god you are all right!" she repeated as she ran her hands down her face.

Urmila, however, was thankful that her mother had not turned her back on her.

"'Amma, I thought you would be angry with me and since I joined against your wishes you might not want to have anything to do with me," she said, finally.

"How can you say that! You're my daughter, Urmila," Prathika replied. "I'd never give up on you."

"My friend Sudini, I mentioned her in my letters, her family disowned her, so I thought maybe you too…?"

Prathika did not say anything but hugged her tenderly. "Sudini sounds like such a nice girl for you mentioned her often in your letters. What kind of parents would do that to their daughter? But I am glad you are safe Urmila, that is all that matters to me."

Urmila had been home for a few weeks and she was enjoying the peace and quiet when one day her mother called her….

"Urmila, before you joined the Tigers, I had mentioned that most-parents do not like their sons to marry ex-fighters, however, I hoped you would one day be back home so had mentioned about you, my daughter of marriageable age, to a few of my friends. Anyway, one family saw your picture and have agreed, should you come back, to take the matter further. In fact, they are so interested that we have already had the horoscopes analysed by our priest. They are a good family, and Puru the boy, is prepared to take the matter further, however, the only downside is that he will be moving to London."

At first she had been averse to the thought of marriage, but when she met Puru, he had seemed a kind and gentle person, the complete opposite of his mother, who had a sharp edge to her combined with a steely determination. But since they would be leaving for London soon after the wedding, Urmila did not consider that to an issue, so, once she had approved, the marriage formalities began.

The wedding arrangements were long and complex, and the agreement was first set out verbally then written. They then went to Puru's house where priests from both sides exchanged the marriage agreement which was then placed on a plate that had bananas, coconuts, and betel leaf. The bride and groom then exchanged gifts; she got a beautiful silk sari from her in-laws' side whilst Puru was presented with some clothes and money by her mother.

A few days before the wedding, Urmila's family performed a ceremony called Paalikali Thalippu/ Karappu. With the sounds of music, special clay pots were decorated with sandalwood paste and kumkum powder, whilst a little bit of curd and nine types of grain were put in each pot, which, on the first day after the wedding the bride and groom threw into a nearby pond. It is believed that the fish in the pond would eat the grains contained in pots and bless the couple.

On the wedding day, Urmila wore a heavy silk pink sari with a gold border, oiled her long black hair which she than coiled into a bun. As a finishing touch to her ensemble and on a whim, she decorated her hair with white and pink flowers.

As Puru entered the room where she was seated, she looked at him in admiration from under her long lashes, for he looked handsome in a long white shirt with a white and gold turban perched on his head.

Soon after the wedding, they had left for London, where he got himself a job, and soon as they were well settled had two girls, Kirti and Rasna.

Puru was a firm believer in tradition, and both girls had been brought up with traditional values. As soon Kirti turned twenty, Puru insisted she have an arranged marriage, and soon after his mother told him that she had found a suitable boy. They had gone to Sri Lanka for what was supposed to be a family holiday, but Kirti's marriage was quickly arranged and organised in such haste that and many of the rituals were omitted.

London (2004)

Chapter 15

Which is why Urmila and Puru were hoping that for Rasna's wedding, the ceremony would be performed conventionally.

Urmila was an attractive woman with warm kind eyes, but her forehead was wrinkled with worry. Her hair, which was touched with grey, was first plaited, then pinned into a bun at the nape of her neck.

Urmila sighed as she went to the kitchen, aware that Rasna did not want to marry, and although she was not sure, Urmila suspected that she was seeing someone.

Rasna, meanwhile, had woken up in the morning, yawned, and thrown back the bedclothes. She went to the window to open the curtain and as she did, found that there were snowflakes swirling in the sky.

They whirled through the sky, blurring everything, and the landscape looked as if was a canvas on which the paint had not dried, but was oozing and trickling down from the heavens.

However, as it was bitterly cold, Rasna drew the curtains back over the windows again to keep out the cold, then ran back to bed and pulled the quilt over her just as her mother entered the room.

"I see you have not even started packing!" Urmila exclaimed as she entered the room. Her eyes flashed angrily as she saw the empty suitcase lying beside the bed. "Tomorrow we leave for Colombo and I need to know if you need anything… Rasna! I am talking to you!"

"Mum, I have told you before, I do not want to go! Beautiful as the country it is, I have heard about the civil war and… Oooo it is so cold!" Rasna unfolded herself from the position she was curled in, rolled her legs over her bed, then got up and stretched.

Her room was large, and against one corner of the wall was a desk and the other side was taken up with books on bookshelves.

She ran her fingers through her hair then looped one of the loose strands over her ear.

"I am going for a quick bath, Mum." Her dark eyes glittered with annoyance as she turned to look at her mother's confused expression.

She ran into the bathroom and emerged later wearing her favourite black jeans and a turtleneck pink cardigan that emphasised her slim figure. Her black hair, that usually cascaded down her shoulders, was wet, and her olive skin enhanced her large black eyes.

She sat down at the dressing table and began drying her hair vigorously with a towel then threw it peevishly on the bed.

"Mum, were you involved in the civil war?"

Urmila looked taken aback. "Who told you about that? Your father? I told him not to!"

"Mum, please don't get angry at him, it was Kirti, who of course could only have heard from Praana. But Mum, why don't you want us to know? I think it was admirable of you, that despite knowing the status of a woman, you had the courage to break out of the boundaries set by our society for women."

"That was the past and neither here nor there, I do not know why you are making such a fuss about going, Rasna. Your father wanted to go in April, and now that he has agreed to travel in December, you have changed your mind! I cannot keep up the two of you. Anyway, it will be a good holiday which we all need, especially your father, for he works too hard," Urmila said in her charming soft voice- but her lips were closed firmly together.

"I think you know why Amma… it's not only that I cannot miss my assignments but also because I am sure you have planned to get me married! Kirti hinted as much, and like I said, that place is dangerous, I do not know how you left your daughter there, alone!" She drew herself up with injured dignity.

Kirti was her elder sister and friend and they had been inseparable – of the two of them Rasna had been the tomboy, good at sports, ready to try anything new, surfed, in fact loved any kind of water sport. Kirti, on the other hand, was like a flower, lovely with skin that was soft. She had a lovely temperament and an infectious laughter that was always on the verge of erupting, but although she was shy and gentle, all girls in her college wanted to hang out with her, because not only was she cool and pretty, shewas stylish and only wore the latest trends in fashion.

Rasna's eyes flashed, and her olive skin face was flushed. She could envisage the type of boy that would be chosen for her, not handsome and with no personality, holding down a dull job. There would be no future for her to but to retire on his meagre pension. And she shuddered to think how they would arrange their first meeting, it would be akin to that of a cattle market, with her being the prize cow!

"I have told you many times, Rasna, that is not the case," Urmila said hesitantly, for she knew Rasna's disliked any attempt of match-making "We realise you have your degree to complete. There is nothing for you to worry about, for we only want what is best for you." Urmila tried to assure her daughter, sighed, then put her arms around her. "But let me let you something as a parent… All we want is that our children have a secure and successful life."

"Mum, that is sweet and believe me, I do understand," Rasna exclaimed, "and Mum, please do not try to convince me that all parents have the success of their children in mind, what about all the children who are recruited by the LTTE? Forcibly, I must add! Where are they then?"

"The word you have to keep in mind is 'forcibly', but who told you about LTTE, and why does your conversation always go back to the political situation in Sri Lanka? Every country has its problems."

"Mum, everyone knows about it, it is in the news and the world is involved and concerned. Anyway, the main reason is I do not trust what you have in planned for me."

"And I have told you so many times that is not the case, we have not planned anything!"

"That is what you said when we went last year for a holiday and poor Kirti… Grandmother arranged her to meet Praana and within a week she was married!"

Rasna missed her sister – their shopping sprees, giggling in the night, sharing secrets!

"Don't answer back, young lady!" Urmila replied in anger. "And what do you mean, poor Kirti? It was not a forced marriage and Kirti did not refuse, in fact she was happy, still is and why not? Praana is a good boy and comes from a good family."

"And how do you know she is happy, Mother? Kirti was not pleased with the proposal, but she did not voice her doubts for she is a kind girl who would not oppose your wishes. And anyway, everything was arranged and happened so quickly that made it impossible for her to protest, what is worse is that since her marriage have you ever bothered to find out if she was happy?" Rasna choked, trying to hold back her tears.

Chapter 16

"Rasna, what are you trying to say? Tell me!" Urmila stared at her in confusion. "Is Kirti okay?"

"That is what I am trying to say, although Kirti does not want me to mention it, she is not happy with Praana, or with his mother for that matter. I do not understand why both you and Grandmother believe him to be a nice boy from a good family. And, even if he is from a good family, does he have the qualities of a good husband? No! His name means to give life, but he has drained it from my sister's! Kirti told me that he thinks that everyone has their place in the world, and you know what that means. He expects Kirti to prepare his meals, iron his clothes and…"

"They are educated and rich people who can afford to have home help."

"Well, she does not, Mother and even if she does, she is still supposed to look after everything. How could you be so cruel and leave your daughter in a strange country with strange people?"

"And if she is so unhappy, then why have you not mentioned it to me before? And you know how sensitive Kirti is, some people have skins that bruise easily. Why, that girl has a soul that I can only call raw and tender! And as for Colombo being strange, don't forget it is your motherland!" Urmila looked furious, and then suddenly had tears in her eyes. "What has Praana done to make her so unhappy?"

"I agree, Mum, Kirti is sensitive, but there is just so much that even she can take! But she is kind and gentle and she made me promise that I would not tell you, only because she does not want to worry you. I only mentioned it because you seem to think that my going to Sri Lanka will solve all problems. Anyway, please don't tell Father."

"I do not know what problems you are referring to, Rasna, but why didn't you tell me?" she asked again, but when she looked at Rasna's angry face hurriedly added, "but if that is the case then shouldn't you be with your sister? She is expecting and..."

"Mother! Do not try and blackmail me emotionally! I am delighted and excited that I will be an aunt, but I have my studies and..." Rasna replied sulkily. "And anyway, why would I want to get married? Just so that I stay at home the whole day, have no money, ask my husband's permission for everything, one who could turn out to be a jealous man, and I have not mentioned the in-laws as yet! No thank you!"

Urmila sighed and patted her daughter's shoulder smiling warmly.

"Rasna, why are you so cynical about arranged marriages? Some have happy marriages; look at your father and me. There are good times, a shoulder to cry on, someone to laugh with." However, when she saw her daughter's face, quickly added, "Maybe you can consider coming later. I will talk to your father and explain. Does that sound better?"

Rasna nodded her head.

"Good, now where is your father? He should have been home by now but..." She left the room, muttering under her breadth.

As soon as she had gone, Rasna hurriedly rummaged in her handbag for her mobile, then dialled Mark's number and waited impatiently for him to answer.

Mark was studying law with her, and they had become close in the last year. In fact, they had become so close that they planned to go into law practice together after they had finished their degree, which would be soon.

Mark was tall, blond, with muscular shoulders and a slim waist. But not only was he a handsome man, he was decent, kind, and affectionate, a man who was strong and who she could depend on.

They would often do their papers together, then afterwards go for a stroll, a coffee or hamburger. They always laughed a lot and gradually their relationship had grown stronger, for they had the same taste in music, films and books, and Mark loved Rasna's quick wit and her warmth of spirit and friendliness.

As soon as she heard his voice she exclaimed.

"Mark, I need to see you today if possible."

Her voice sounded so agitated and tense that Mark was worried. "Of course, my princess, but won't it be difficult since you are leaving tomorrow?"

"It will, but I will come up with some excuse that I have some last-minute shopping, how about you? You too are leaving soon for Thailand."

"Ah, yes, Phuket. I am looking forward to that trip, my parents have told me so much about the emerald green sea and waterfalls, but I only wish you were coming with me." He sighed than added, "But of course I would love to see you today, you sound worried, are you afraid your parents are going to get you married?" Rasna could hear him chuckling.

"Mark, it is not a joking matter! You know what happened to my sister and I do not want the same thing to happen to me!"

"I know and I am sorry. How about we meet at 5 p.m. at the café round the corner?"

Rasna heard footsteps approaching so quickly whispered "Okay" and hid the phone under the pillow.

Her bedroom door opened, and her father entered, wearing a white sarong, followed by her mother. He held a cup of tea in one hand and a slice of cake in the other.

Here we go again, Rasna thought as she looked at them.

"Young lady, your mother says you don't want to come with us to see your sister but prefer to stay here?" her father roared as he turned his ferocious anger on her. " Is that true?"

There was an edge in his voice and Rasna cowered. However, she was a strong and rebellious girl, so stood up straight, her head flung back defiantly, tears of frustration in her eyes.

"Only because of my exams and…"

"No, that is no excuse for I planned this vacation knowing full well you can take a few weeks off. You are far ahead, and you can always study there. Your mother explained that she thought we were going to get you married? Hah! Wherever did you get that preposterous idea?" He chuckled then murmured, "I wish!"

"I knew it, Mum, that is what Father wants and…!"

"Hold it, young lady. Firstly, you were not supposed to hear that and secondly, I said that only because until a daughter is married, she is always a burden… in a good way of course. And anyway, there is no proposal for you and no boy there waiting to marry you! Now, does that satisfy you?" Puru said brusquely as his eyebrows shot up.

"You said the same about Kirti and…!" Her father's tone sparked a tone of rebellion in Rasna.

"Will you stop harping on about her! Your grandmother had arranged a match which we knew nothing about!"

It was on the tip of Rasna's tongue to voice her concern that is what grandmother would have arranged for her too, but decided it was best not to antagonise her father any further.

"Now your mother has suggested that you will come a week later and that seems reasonable. However, for now… come, Urmila, have we finished our packing?"

"Thanks, Dad!" Rasna said with relief then hugged her dad warmly.

"Only a week later only, mind you, for we will only be there for three weeks. Though I cannot understand why you would want to come after the holiday season!" He winked at his wife and left the room, followed by Urmila.

As soon as they had left, Rasna sat on the bed and put her head in her hands wearily. Initially, she only had had a niggling doubt that her parents wanted to marry her off, but her suspicion was confirmed by her father's attitude; the way he had looked at her mother and winked.

She looked at her wristwatch impatiently. She needed to talk to Mark and it when it seemed that time was passing slowly, she took a book from the bookshelf and began reading.

Finally, as soon as it was 4.30, she ran downstairs, opened the cupboard, and took her coat off the hanger. She was pulling the gloves over her small hands when her mother called out to her from the kitchen.

"Rasna would you like some…?" she came out of the kitchen rubbing her hands on her apron then looked surprised as she saw her daughter wearing her coat and gloves. "Are you going out?"

"Yes, I need a few things to send to Kirti and…."

"You are leaving it late, I must say. The shops will be closing soon. I am sure that can wait till tomorrow, our flight is in the evening. It is snowing outside and… Anyway, you can bring it yourself, she might appreciate it more!"

"No, Mum, it is better I shop now for I do not want to leave it till the last minute. I thought something for the baby too…"

"That is very nice of you, but you better hurry and don't be out too late." Urmila smiled affectionately.

She was extremely fond of her daughters and would do anything for their happiness, and the fact that she had been the cause of Kirti's unhappiness brought tears to her eyes. She had not stopped thinking about the matter since Rasna had mentioned it and was now impatient to be with her.

"Thanks, Mum. I won't be late, I promise."

Rasna opened the door to a gust of snow.

"Rasna, don't forget to take an umbrella…!" She heard her mother's voice. "It is snowing outside, Rasna, you do not have to go."

"Okay Mum, but I do I have to send something for them." She quickly ran back, took her umbrella, unfurled it and quickly ran to the bus stop. The café was only a few stops away and the bus would drop her exactly opposite. She stood huddled, waiting for a bus, and saw that in the bus stop was crowded with people who were also bundled up against the raw wind.

The light snowfall had stopped, and thin rays of afternoon sun had appeared from under an oppressive cover of stormy and wintry clouds.

She stood shivering and huddled under the bus stop; strands of her loose hair danced in the wind when she heard the toot of a car.

At first, she ignored it, for she was used to men seeking her attention, but when it continued, she looked up and her heart beat faster as she saw Mark's blond head.

Chapter 17

Smiling, she quickly ran to the car.

"Quick, get into the car." Mark opened the car door.

Rasna's face was flushed with the cold and seeing her, Mark's heart skipped a beat. He quickly reached across and encircled her waist, and, for a moment Rasna rested her head against his warm shoulder.

"I thought we were meeting at the café…" Rasna's liquid eyes looked up and they exchanged a long tender look. She kissed him lightly and he felt as if a delicate exotic butterfly had landed on his cheek.

"I cannot have my Indian Princess running around in this weather now, can I?" He looked at her with a sly wink that told her how beautiful she looked.

He chuckled, lightly kissing her forehead before withdrawing his arm and concentrating on the road ahead. He drove fast and he opened his window slightly before placing his arm on the window ledge.

"Mark, it is freezing, and you will catch a cold!" Rasna exclaimed as she saw the wind rustling through his wavy hair.

"You are right, but I like the wind and the café is just round the corner!" Mark turned his head from the road to smile at her.

"That is only because you are in the warm car… try standing out in the snow and liking it!" Rasna snapped.

"My my, we are touchy today!" Mark turned his head towards her and smiled disarmingly, his eyes milky with love.

The warmth in Mark's eyes and the short distance between them brought a flush to Rasna's cheeks and she felt herself slipping and falling emotionally - wondering if this was love?

They drove in silence and every few minutes Rasna would turn her head admiring his good looks and his strong muscular shoulders.

"Here we are, now all I have to do is to find a space to park!"

For the next few minutes Mark concentrated on turning and reversing his car in the small space he had found. After he had successfully parked, Rasna undid her belt and was going to open her door when Mark stopped her.

"No, wait don't get out yet." Mark quickly ran to her side of the door and opened the door. "I have an umbrella and…"

"Mark, please don't fuss so! I too have an umbrella …" She laughed and pushed her hair back from her face.

"Right, let's run for it, I am starved!"

Mark reached for her hand and tucked it in his arm and hugged it close to his body as they ran into the café.

The restaurant was busy, and as soon as they found a table. Rasna took off her coat and placed her purse on the table.

"I'll go and order, Rasna, the usual?" Mark's eyes twinkled Rasna had seated herself at a table, elbows on table. "Yes, Mark, you know what I like! Especially their coffee."

Rasna marvelled at how handsome he was and admired the easy and graceful way he moved. He was tall, slim, with warm green eyes, and high cheekbones. His face was tanned and rugged and there were laughter lines around his eyes. The white shirt that he wore emphasised his broad shoulders and tapered down to his slim waist. His blond hair fell over his forehead and Rasna loved his charming habit of blowing his hair back from his forehead when he was tired.

Having ordered, he strolled back, sat down, pulled his chair forward and folded his long, graceful hands on the table. He looked into her dark liquid eyes tenderly, and it was as if they had drawn a curtain around themselves, and their voices were slow and soft as they spoke.

"I have ordered coffee first, Rasna, it is so cold, you must be freezing! Now, what is troubling you, my Indian Princess? I thought you were looking forward to going to Colombo to see your sister?" His expression turned from one of amusement to deep concern.

He ran his hands through his wavy hair before they reached into his pocket bringing out a packet of cigarettes. He took one out, lighted it and inhaled deeply, looked at Rasna worriedly, then reached out and took her hand which had been resting idly on the table.

Rasna had her hair pinned back and the style emphasised the smooth lines of her neck, the curve of her chin and the depth of her dark eyes. Hers was the face he had dreamt of since childhood, the face he had fallen in love with as soon as he had seen her.

She felt herself sink into his warm company and the sound of his gentle voice - for he had a remarkable natural limitless enthusiasm that embraced all things and people. He had a sense of humour and even had the rare ability to laugh at himself!

Mark reached out and took her other hand which had been lying on her lap and knitted his fingers around hers.

Chapter 18

"Mark, I don't want to go with them, but remarkably, father has agreed that I join them a week later. So, if you are not too busy, we can spend time together before you leave for your vacation to Thailand?"

"I would love that, and to be honest, I am not looking forward to my vacation, I feel that you might need me."

"Come on Mark, how can you pass up a chance to see the white beaches, emerald sea, the waterfalls and not forgetting the snorkelling! You have been raving about it for I do not know how long! And you would be escaping this horrible weather!"

"Oh, I am sure it will be beautiful, and it would be nice to be away from this weather, but I would rather go with you." He gripped her hands tightly.

At that moment, the waiter came with two cups of coffee.

"Would you like to order now, sir?"

"No, it is all right, I have already placed our order, Rasna I thought you would like hamburger and chips, would you like anything else?"

"But… no, that will be fine, Mark." She took a sip of coffee, then remarked "Hmm, very nice, I love the coffee here!"

"Glad you like it, Princess, but you know that I have to leave for Phuket on the 22nd. It is a 13-hour flight so will arrive on the 23rd but it will be great to spend time together, but how did you convince your parents?"

"I told them that I had too many assignments to complete as it was my last year, and, anyway, my sister is not due for another two weeks so I can shop around for the baby. Kirti sent a list as long as your arm! And of course, my parents do not know about you, else…"

Mark frowned as he concentrated on what she was saying. He always listened with interest, for when talking to him about them, she was always frank and candid.

"Oh, so why don't they know about me, Rasna?" His eyes twinkled. "Jokes aside, why have you left things till the last minute? I mean, vacations are planned well ahead, and you have even left the shopping till the end!"

"Actually, it was Dad who persuaded us to go now, even though the original plan was to go in April. It is our new year then and the baby would have been six months, delightful age. But Father could not get holidays, so we decided to go in December; well, he did. But I have been undecided, although my parents thought I would meekly do as I am told, I know they might have the same in store for me as Kirti."

"I met her once and thought she was a kind, affectionate girl. So why are you convinced now that they don't have a proposal organised for you?"

Mark laughed and Rasna loved to hear his laughter, for, when he did, his eyes brightened and crinkled at the corners.

"No, that is just it, although they assure me they have not, I don't believe them, it is small things, their body language etc."

The waiter arrived and placed the food on the table, and as he left Mark remarked.

"Rasna, maybe you are imagining everything, and they really do not have an underlying motive? Anyway, would you like another coffee?"

"Mark I am not imagining it!" she cried impatiently. "But I might have another coffee, later though." She took a bite of the hamburger then dipped her chips in the sauce.

Mark smiled warmly for he had not met anybody quite like her. She was affectionate, warm, generous and considerate. Not only did she have a nice disposition, but she was also a beautiful girl with a dark, sultry and exotic beauty.

Mark loved her deeply and whenever he thought his love had reached its peak, he would get a peek of an additional loveable side to her personality which deepened his love.

"Mark, penny for your thoughts? How come you are not eating the hamburger?" There was a twinkle in Rasna's eyes as she wiped her lips with the napkin.

"Actually, I was thinking about you, so they are worth more than a penny! And you know me well; I love hamburgers so will have it now!" Mark smiled disarmingly.

"Mark, will it not be boring to travel alone to Thailand? Oh no, I forgot, you are going with your friend."

"I was going with John, but he rang me this morning saying that he had a family emergency so would not be able to accompany me. I was sorry to hear that for he is a fun person to be with. I did think of cancelling but…" Mark frowned "And my parents do not want me to cancel either."

"Oh, I am sorry to hear that too, I hope the crisis is over!"

"No, I am afraid not, he is going to lose a lot of money but anyway, since you are not going to Colombo, do you want me to cancel too? I would love to spend more time with you." Mark grinned.

"Of course not, I would not dream of asking you to.. But if you are not going to be here, I might as well go with my parents. Thing is, I do not want to go to Sri Lanka at all, not in a week not now, not ever! Well maybe sometime to see Kirti."

Mark pushed his plate aside and leant forward.

"Rasna, I cannot let you go before letting you know how I feel. You know how much I have come to love you and I hope you feel the same …"

He took a small black box from his pocket and placed it on the table. Rasna looked puzzled then gasped when he opened it, for lying on the velvet cushion was the most beautiful emerald ring, smouldering fire.

"Mark that is beautiful! What…?"

"This has been in our family for generations, but I have been thinking for some time now, Rasna, will you marry me? I know this is not the right place or time but since we are leaving…"

"I beg your pardon, what did you say?" Rasna whispered.

"Hey, do you want me to go down on one knee and all that? I will repeat my question… will… you… marry… me?"

Chapter 19

"Oh gosh, Mark!" Suddenly a wave of shyness swept over Rasna and she looked down at the table, her lashes like wings on her cheeks.

"My Indian Princess, I have always dreamt of somebody like you, your beautiful eyes that sparkle like moonlight on a deep and silent lake, someone who loves me… you do love me, don't you?"

She smiled gently, for he could spin words and had the ability to take a word or phrase and turn it around till it shone like a fine jewel that was sparkling in the box.

"Of course, I love you too but you know that…"

"Hush, my darling, don't say anything. In fact, whatever your answer maybe, keep this ring, something to remember me by."

"As if I can I ever forget you!" Rasna whispered. "Oh, but I can't take it… it is so beautiful…"

Mark took her delicate hand and placed the ring on her finger where it sparkled and glowed.

"I understand, Rasna, you don't have to wear it, but please keep it with you."

There was a pause in which Rasna tried to find the right words for she had not expected Mark to propose.

"Okay, I will, Mark but isn't it too expensive?" She turned round, innocent eyes on Mark.

"Nothing is too expensive for my princess!" Mark laughed." And like I said, it has been in our family for generations…it is waiting for my bride."

"Oh Mark, I do love you!"

Rasna started crying softly and Mark turned his chair towards her and took her hand in his. He took his handkerchief, held her chin and gently wiped her tears.

"And is that something to cry about? Am I that bad?" He grinned impishly.

"Oh of course not and I would love you to meet my parents and bring this out in the open!"

"But since they don't know about me it would come as a shock to them."

"Noo! Actually, I did not think about that, maybe I should gradually introduce you?"

Mark put his hand under her chin. "Yes, that is a better idea, you thought I was not serious enough or did not love you. Is that why I was not mentioned? Anyway, you do believe now that I love and want to marry you?" he asked gently.

He put his hands over hers, his eyes revealing the strong emotions that he was trying to control.

Rasna nodded her head slowly. She smiled wistfully and touched Mark's cheek tenderly. "But it is not easy to disclose the depth of my love to my parents for they are very traditional and have set their eyes on my marrying somebody from Sri Lanka. But I have spoken of you often to my mother, indirectly of course."

"If they are so old-fashioned, then, maybe you should tell them about me before you go? That way, they need not put themselves in an awkward position by arranging your wedding and you doing a runner!" Suddenly his eyes clouded. "Don't tell me you are going to give in to them like Kirti. if so, I hope it is not because you don't love me?"

"Oh Mark, please don't say that! You know I love you," Rasna cried. "I want to tell them too but have been waiting for the right moment to break it to them gently. Anyway, I have spoken to Mum, and she knows you are a good and decent person."

"I am sorry Rasna, but that is not good enough, did you speak to your father?" Mark looked disappointed. "I had thought of flying down to see you in Colombo from Pukhet for I have heard much of Sri Lanka's beauty and the hospitality of its people. And if there must be a marriage, I will be there to stop it so… or it will be to me they marry you too!" Mark said firmly.

"Mark!" Rasna put her hands over her ears. "I love you, but your ideas, thinking and logic, thrilling as they are, are too implausible. I mean, imagine me getting married in Sri Lanka!"

"Sorry, darling, it is just that I want to start my life with you as soon as possible, and the thought that it might not be so scares me."

Rasna reached out her hand and touched his arm reassuringly.

"Believe me, I feel the same. I would love to tell them about us, maybe I will once we are in Sri Lanka, for my dad is always in a good mood there; his mother pampers him!" Rasna grinned then ran her fingers through her hair. "The downside to that is that it might be too late."

"Why didn't you tell me all this before?" Mark asked.

"Because everything has been in haste, I believe my dad's vacation has just been finalised. The way my mother, when she was planning the holiday, was that he might or might not go, but in the end whatever the case she was definitely leaving to be with my Kirti!

"I still think you should try and talk to them when you get home. And if they are difficult, all you have to do is come and stay with me or with a friend, if you like." Mark smiled tenderly. "Look, if you want, I can come with you and I can explain that my intentions towards their daughter are honourable!"

"Thanks, Mark, that is kind of you, but I think this is something I have to do on my own. I know they will be angry, and I don't want them to humiliate you in any way."

"Now you are being nice! Shall we go?"

As soon as Rasna nodded, with one swift movement he had crossed the space between them. Then taking both her hands he gently and slowly drew her to her feet and held her close. With one arm, he encircled her waist whilst with the other he tilted her face towards him, then gently kissed her,

"Now promise me, no more crying?" he said softly as he put his hand around her, his eyes soft and warm.

Rasna nodded but failed to take her eyes from his for they were like magnets and she felt their magnetism pierce her heart.

They ran to the car, for although the snowfall had stopped, the wind had picked up its velocity and it had become even more wintery and bitter.

Rasna shivered and as soon as she had tied the seat belt, remarked:

"Oh, how I hate this arctic weather! Gosh! You must be looking forward to your holiday."

"In a way I am, but you too are going to a tropical and exotic place. But Rasna, I was serious when I said earlier that I will not go ahead with my travel plans until I hear from you. Promise you will speak to your parents tonight?"

"Yes, I promise, and Mark, please remember to keep your mobile on, I will need to speak to you anyway for I don't know how they are going to react!"

As they reached the end of the road, Mark asked her for direction for he insisted in dropping her home.

"You don't have to, Mark. You can drop me at the bus stop. I can walk from there and…"

"No, I will drop you outside your home," Mark said firmly.

As soon as they neared the house, Mark slowed the car, braked, and turned towards Rasna. He kissed her tenderly before he got out and opened her door.

"Don't worry and good luck!"

He drew her to him and Rasna put her arms round his neck. For a few minutes, they stood in silence as the tears glided down Rasna's cheeks.

"Rasna, your skin smells of honey!" Mark murmured as he nuzzled her neck then drew back sadly. "Good-bye, my darling!"

When he kissed her cheek, his lips became wet with her tears and their salt stung him.

"Bye for now, Mark." Rasna lifted her cheek from his shoulder and they looked deep into each other's eyes.

She reluctantly removed herself from his arms, turned and waved goodbye, her heart thudding painfully at his departure.

The sky was stormy and forbidding and she shivered, clutched her coat tightly around her as she entered her house.

Chapter 20

"Rasna, is that you? We are in the sitting room," Urmila called.

Rasna walked into the room apprehensively, looking at her wristwatch. She was not late, but her mother's voice sounded ominous.

"Did you buy the present for Kirti,Rasna?"

Puru raised a sardonic eyebrow as he turned from the window. Outside there was the sound of the wind as it blew across the trees, making a horrible sound – as if their branches were screaming in pain.

Although he said nothing, Rasna felt he was trying to control his anger for his hands were clenched into fists. But why was he so angry?

"No, I did not, I could not find what Kirti wanted. By the time I reached the shops they had closed, you were right, Amma, I left it too late…" Rasna's voice faltered.

"You, my girl, are a liar!" Puru roared "Let me get to the point… who was that boy who brought you home and had the audacity to put his arms around my daughter! Who is he and where have you been all this time?" Puru's usual pleasant face had hardened into a glare and his voice cracked like the lash of a whip. "Were you with him all this time? Lying to us by saying you were shopping?"

Urmila remembered the occasional rages of the past so quickly interrupted.

"Don't assume, Puru. It might have been the brother of her friend she had met who was kind enough to give her a lift in this horrible weather." She looked imploringly at Rasna.

"Urmila don't be silly! Why would the brother of a friend put his arms around Rasna?" His tense face became a mask of anger and his cold eyes studied her intently.

Rasna mentally reproached herself for being so careless, but she had been so unhappy at leaving Mark that she had completely forgotten they were standing outside her home. And although she had been steeling herself to break the news about Mark to her parents, now that that it was out in the open, she felt intimated by her father's attitude.

Her hands were shaking for she hated any kind of confrontation and had always tried to avoid them.

"Dad, that was Mark. Mum, I have mentioned him to you often. He is a genuinely nice boy and…" As her voice wavered, her father barked at her.

"And what does that have to do with the fact that not only does he bring my daughter home at night but puts his arms around her!" Puru's voice edged on anger and frustration.

"Dad, Mum, Mark is a very decent and good man… in fact, he wanted to come in himself and explain to you that his intentions are honourable and…."

"Rasna! What are you talking about? What intentions? And what are you holding in your hand?"

Puru looked fiercely at his daughter then turned towards Urmila.

"I don't understand her Urmila, but can you make any sense of what your daughter is saying?"

"No, I cannot." Urmila floundered, however, there was a slight smile on her lips for Puru only referred to Rasna as her daughter when he was angry. "Now, Rasna, start again and tell us what he meant."

"N-Nothing," Rasna stuttered. "Dad, and please believe me, Mum, I wanted to tell you a long time ago, but the time never seemed to be right. Anyway, we have been going out and today he asked me to marry him!"

Urmila and Puru both looked incredulously at Rasna then after a moment's silence her father spoke.

"And I hope you had the good sense to decline for you know that is something we would never give our blessings too?"

"Dad, you don't understand, we love each other and..." There were tears in Rasna's eyes.

"Now stop that nonsense immediately!" Puru turned towards Urmila. "Now, Urmila, prepare Rasna to get married to Annama. He is Praana's cousin, has a steady secure job and is a good Tamil boy. Your grandmother says he is dependable and will make you happy. Now you know why I wanted her to come with us and get her married... I knew she was up to something! And you, Rasna, are you going to be a good obedient daughter like your sister and get married to the boy your grandmother has chosen for you? And as for love, you will get to love him."

"I knew it! Dad, you promised that was not your intention, yet you know the name of the man you are planning to marry me off to! All this time you were not being truthful and honest." Rasna cried.

She felt her lips tremble and the tears flowed from her angry eyes as she ran out of the room to her bedroom, slamming the door behind her. She flung herself on the bed and was still sobbing when her mother gently opened the door, entered, and sat down beside her. She gently stroked her head.

Rasna shrugged off her hand and sat up. She glared at her mother furiously then began sobbing like a little girl. She made a dive for the drawer where she kept her tissue box.

"Mother, how could you? You promised, but downstairs you did not take my side..." Rasna blew her nose noisily.

Urmila sighed, hugged her daughter then looked worried. She wished she knew what was best for her and what the future held for her. She waited for her daughter's sobs to subside.

"How do you know Mark? I thought you wanted to be a career woman and have a practice one day?"

"Mother, have you forgotten? I have mentioned him many times. We are finishing our degree in law together. And one day I want to have my practice, with Mark of course." Rasna's face was awash with misery and her eyes looked miserable. "If I get married in Sri Lanka, I will be stuck in the house."

"Oh yes, I remember now, you did mention him." Urmila gave a slight nod. "But it is not necessary that you sit at home all day after marriage in Sri Lanka. You can have a career there too, you know."

"How could I when you are not even letting me complete my degree? And, Mother, Mark really is a nice person. Very decent and good. At first we were just good friends, but we like the same things, music films etc. and I don't know, somehow along the way I fell in love with him. When I realised that, I tried to nip it in the bud for I knew it would only bring pain to you. I am surprised that he loves me too, despite the entire negative signals I put out." Her voice was thick with tears and her eyes glistened.

Urmila sighed again. "How do you know it is love and that it will last? It takes time to peel back the layers of personality of a person to discover the real one. Rasna, I know you think you are in love at the moment, but you are very young, and your father is a very wise man. What you are feeling may only be infatuation that will only last for a while. Is it worth losing your family over that? And why didn't you tell me how strongly you felt about him? Though it is my fault too, I should have been able to see the signs...." Urmila murmured.

Rasna's normal reserve began to crumble, and she blurted:

"Oh mum, it is not your fault, I was afraid of your reaction and of course not! I do not want to lose my family. I was hoping you would meet Mark and see what a nice person he really is. And I did try to suppress the feelings I have for him... honest!" She started sobbing uncontrollably.

"And do you really believe he truly loves you?"

"Yes, he does. Look, Mother, he wants to marry me and gave me this today. He says all he wants is my happiness, even if it means sacrificing his! Now if that isn't true love, I don't know what is."

She took out the small black box from her bag, opened it and showed the smouldering emerald ring glowing on the red velvet cushion.

Chapter 21

Urmila's eyes widened as she saw the ring.

"Does that mean you accepted his proposal without talking to us first?" Her voice sounded low and sad.

"No, Mother, I did not accept. He knows that I will be going to Sri Lanka where I might get married. But he is going to Thailand and was insistent I keep the ring even if I cannot marry him. Now wasn't that nice of him?"

"It was, but I hope he realises that marriage with him is out of the question. He is not Tamil and that is especially important to your father."

"Dad is comparing me to Kirti, but what good has marrying a Tamil done for her? She is unhappy with Praana, and I know that Mark would never make me unhappy."

Urmila got up and looked down at Rasna.

"The best and only thing for you to do now is to come with us…"

"After what Dad has just said! Never!" Rasna replied vehemently. "I had actually decided to come with you, but after Dad's attitude and the fact that there is Annama waiting for me, no thank you!"

"And have you forgotten how much Kirti needs you? She will not talk to me, but she will to you. It will mean a lot to her if you are there."

"If she knows that you have planned the same thing for me, I can assure you, she will not want me to come."

"Nothing is more important to me than your happiness, Rasna. I will try and talk to your father. I am sure his anger has subsided by now. And about that boy he says has for you, well that is the first I have heard of it! Either he has not told me, which is unlike him, or he was only trying to scare you!"

"Well, it worked, Mother, and I don't think he was trying to frighten me. He knew the name of the person, what he does and even that he is Praana's cousin!"

"Rasna, you may have something there. Maybe he did not tell me because he knew I would take your side. Let me remind you again that it was at your insistence we changed our holiday dates from April to December. I don't know what has got into your dad, but he now insists on going in December, but I will stay back with you. Your father will like that."

"No Mother, that will not be necessary, as for going at this time, actually it was Kirti who insisted you be in Sri Lanka for the birth of her child. And, at present, she needs you more than I do, the baby is due anytime next week."

"Let me talk to your father again." Urmila wrung her hands. "But if and when you do talk to him, keep in mind that you must not mention Mark again, for that will only trigger his bad temper- again!"

"I won't, but Mother, when you speak to Father, could you tell him how unhappy Kirti is, and all because she wanted to please him? Does he want me to be unhappy too?"

Urmila looked at Rasna wiping her tears with the back of her hand, and she looked so like a little girl in her ponytail and jeans that Urmila's heart melted.

"I'll try and make him see sense, Rasna, but I don't promise."

She patted her daughter's head then quickly left the room so that Rasna could not see the tears that had welled in her eyes.

As soon as she left Rasna quickly took her mobile from under her pillow and dialled Mark's number, was surprised there was no answer. She left a message giving details of what had occurred and asking him to get in touch with her as soon as possible.

She sighed and, on a hunch, decided to check her messages, and was surprised that Mark had already left a message on her voicemail that he was in hospital as his parents had been involved in a car accident, and that he would try and contact her as soon as he could.

Rasna groaned and flung herself on the bed again as she heard her parents' raised voices downstairs. She stared at the ceiling, her arms under her head. She already missed Mark and wished she could be there in his time of need and hoped that his parents would recover, for she knew how much he loved them.

Her mind went over the conversation with her father, trying to rationalise the situation, but which only resulted in a splitting headache.

After a while, the angry voices downstairs subsided, and she heard her mother's footsteps climbing up the stairs.

Rasna sat up eagerly as Urmila opened the door and entered.

"Well, Mum, what did he say?" she asked eagerly.

"I am sorry; you know how stubborn he can be. He is adamant that you come with us and nothing we do or say is going to change his mind!" Urmila sat on the bed, looking miserable.

"Oh, what a mess!" Rasna put her head in her hands. "So, there is a marriage planned for me. Is it Grandma again who has…?"

"I did explain to him about Kirti, but he would not hear of it. And as I did not have the details as to the cause of the unhappiness, and it was only your word about it, well, he is now convinced that it is only a plan you and your sister thought up!"

"Mum, what am I going to do?"

It was on the tip of her tongue to ask her whether she could lend her some money for her flight to Thailand, but by now she understood fully that Urmilas's loyalty, like that of most Asian women, lay with their husband, and Rasna was too kind a girl to put her mother in a situation where she would have to make a choice.

"Rasna, dinner is ready. I suggest you have some food and have a good night's rest. Things always seem better in the morning, and the packing can wait for the flight is in the evening." She smiled tenderly.

"Mother, how can I eat at a time like this? And I do not want to face Father," she said sulkily. "He is so angry that we both might say things we may regret later."

"Why, my Rasna, my little girl has grown up!" Urmila smiled gently. "Don't worry; I'll bring up some food."

"Mum, you don't have to. I can always go down later after Father has eaten and…"

"Puru will still be around for you know how he likes to potter around after his meal."

She left the room and Rasna thought she would try to call Mark again, before remembering that he would be in hospital where mobile phones had to be switched off. She would have to wait for him to contact her.

She sighed, collected her clothes, and went to the bathroom, hoping a hot bath would refresh her.

She came out half an hour later, wearing a simple white cotton shirt and jeans. As her hair was still wet, she sat on the bed towelling it then twirled her hair so she could pin it up.

Urmila entered with a tray, set in on the side table and sat on the bed.

"Your favourite dishes, Rasna. I am sure you will feel better after eating."

Rasna wrinkled her nose as she smelt the aroma arising from the tray and remarked.

"Mum, you are right. I am starving! I could eat a horse!"

"Sorry, my dear, I do not know how to cook a horse!" Urmila smiled tenderly and there was a twinkle in her eye as Rasna dug into her food despite having had a snack earlier with Mark.

"And as usual your cooking is delicious! I think I will forfeit marriage just to stay with you!"

"Just for my cooking? You mean your mother has no other qualities you love?" Urmila's eyes glistened.

"Oh, Mum, of course there are! Loads and you know I love you very much, please don't cry."

"Don't worry; I know it was one of your pranks." Urmila smiled as she wiped her eyes than patted her daughter's head. "But you will be and getting married at some point, and I will miss them!"

"Mum, I thought we were not going to talk about that? Rasna snapped.

"No, of course not, I was only thinking how lonely I will be with you gone, that is all. Anyway, marriage or not, I know you will be moving out to work or start your practice."

"Hmmmm…" Rasna licked her fingers as she finished her dinner.

"And anyway, seeing your table manners I do not think anyone would want to marry you!" Urmila could not resist saying with a smile as she picked up the empty tray. "Now, I suggest a good night's sleep. Good night, Rasna."

"Good-night Mom, you are the best….!"

Rasna checked her mobile and when there was no new message from Mark, fluffed her pillow, switched off the light then lay down on her side, a smile on her lips as she recalled her mother's joke on her table manners! However, the smile left her lips as she recalled her father's attitude.

The thought of Mark bought a twinge of ache it for seemed impossible they would meet anytime soon for events were spiralling out of control.

There was a tiny tear running down her cheek as her dark lashes curled like butterflies to rest on her cheeks.

Chapter 22

Urmila smiled tenderly, then quietly shut the door behind her as she went downstairs with the tray, looking thoughtful. Although she had tried to make light of the situation with Rasna, she knew how stubborn and ruthless Puru could be.

After having deposited the empty tray in the kitchen she entered the lounge to find Puru sitting in an armchair, his glasses on his nose and reading a newspaper, the lamp in the room casting a faint glow over his face.

As soon as she entered, he peeped at her over his glasses and the newspaper.

"And how is madam? Did you manage to talk to her and make her see sense?" he asked irritably. "I cannot, will not, tolerate such rudeness from my daughter!" He put down the paper angrily, took off his glasses and started polishing them vigorously.

Urmila sighed and sat on the sofa, and it was sometime before she spoke, choosing her words carefully.

"Puru, Rasna is a good and sensible girl…"

"How can you say that? Ha! Wanting to be with be that Englishman and doing I do not know what! Didn't you teach her any of our values?"

"Of course, I did, we did together. But love has a way of disregarding principles, and just because he is not Tamil does not mean he is not a good and decent person. You have always been proud of Kirti and Rasna, even though you do not show it."

"Yes, that is true; I was… am," Puru admitted grudgingly as he tried to keep a grip on his temper. "Nevertheless… I will not be spoken to like that by my daughter!"

"Your daughters always wanted you to be proud of them and want to earn your affection. It is this feeling that encouraged Kirti to accept the marriage proposal that you suggested!"

"Exactly my point! She trusted and had faith in me for Praana is a good boy and she knew we only had her best interests at heart. And now she is well settled and happy."

"I don't think that is true, Puru. You know what we were talking about? Kirti told Rasna how unhappy she is and that Praana is not a good and decent man at all. And that all the politeness and charm you saw were actually all a pretence …"

"What are you trying to tell me, woman! And you believe what Rasna told you? My god! Don't you see? She is trying to pull the wool over our eyes by saying that Kirti is unhappy thereby showing us that an arranged marriage is not a good idea! And even if that were true and Kirti is not happy, why didn't Kirti tell my mother who would have told me? But you have a soft mother's heart and would believe anything your daughter says!"

Puru snorted and picked up the newspaper he had thrown on the table earlier.

"Puru, after all, how do we know for sure Kirti is happy? We have left her in a strange country with a strange man who is…"

"You seem to forget my mother is there," Puru remarked drily, however Urmila saw a fleeting look of fear in his eyes and wondered at it. "Everything is all right there, and I am sure she is well looked after and Praana is not actively involved in anything untoward."

"How can you take this so lightly?" Urmila cried. "And everything is not all right in Sri Lanka, you know that. You told me it was at your mother's insistence that you came to London after Black July. Was there another reason too?"

"No! That was a dreadful day when thousands were killed…"

"Puru, please don't change the subject! I know Kirti, do you think she is the kind of girl who would confide in anyone, even us, leave alone your grandmother whom she barely knows?"

"Urmila, I don't want to talk about Kirti anymore! Even if Kirti did not confide in her, Amma would have mentioned it had she sensed something was wrong."

"Are you sure she would want to do that? Don't forget it was she who introduced and suggested Praana for Kirti, so might feel uncomfortable to admit that she had been wrong"

"Urmila, I said I do not want to talk about Kirti. Now, is Rasna coming with us?"

"Puru, don't doubt your daughter. She was planning to come with us tomorrow as originally planned at Mark's suggestion. She is not blindly in love; he has been very kind and considerate. He knows about Kirti and how she needs Rasna to be there, and not only did he want to come himself to talk to you, he has given her a lovely ring as a symbol of his love. And before you say anything, it is not conditional. It is only an expression of his love, whether they get married or not. Now I do not of any man who is that considerate. He could have taken advantage of her feelings at any time…"

Puru glared at her.

"And whose side are you on?"

"I am not on anybody's side. I am just trying to explain the facts as they stand to you. Praana, a Tamil boy is making Kirti unhappy, whilst an English boy is making Rasna happy! Would you rather she be unhappy? I think you are being too harsh on her. The only thing Rasna is concentrating on now is to complete her degree and then further a career in law, another thing Mark is supporting her on. And I understand how she feels because I wanted the same, but my mother got me married instead!"

"There you are! My point exactly! You are happily married with two lovely daughters. And anyway, you did not have a career, but you did join the rebels, something unheard of…" Puru said triumphantly, throwing down the paper again.

Urmila clenched her fists, angry at the way Puru always shut of her needs, her emotions.

"Yes, and that is where I had a taste of freedom and independence. I am blessed with two daughters and you have been nothing but kind to me. But there has always been a void in my life… that I could have waited, got a degree, a career…" Her voice trailed off wistfully.

"Why do you feel that you have missed out on pursuing a career? You are my wife and as such it is my duty to provide for you, which I have done, and you have not gone without anything!" Puru snapped.

"You are right and thank you, and you are also a very good husband and father, but it is not the material satisfaction I needed, but the mental stimulation to express my individuality; not one that society has bestowed on a woman i.e. daughter, wife, and mother! And that is exactly what Rasna is trying to break out of!"

"Oh, come on, Urmila! You could have continued with your studies, done a course or something. Don't blame everything on me!"

"No, Puru, I don't think you would have allowed me to." Urmila sighed. "Anyway, you know I had Kirti shortly after we were married and you told me, in no uncertain terms, that my place was in the home, and I agreed, for the welfare of children is most important. But if Rasna wants to pursue her dream, why not let her before she is tied down to family duties?"

"My duty as a father, and my father before me, is to see that my daughters are married and settled and thus safe from a man's exploitation. You know what kind of men I mean, those who prey on a girl's vulnerability!" There were tears in Puru's eyes.

Chapter 23

"You are thinking of Laxmi, aren't you?" Urmila asked gently.

Laxmi was Purus' sister, and although Urmila had only met her once, she been impressed by her sweet innocent beauty and charm. She had therefore been surprised when she was not at their wedding, and when she asked Puru, the only reply she had got was a murmur, and the look on his face was so pitiful that she did not pressure him for an explanation.

Gradually over the years, although Puru still did not like to talk about Lakshmi, she learnt that Lakshmi had eloped with Sarvash, a Sinhalese man who was not only old enough to be her father, but one who was already married with a son.

When Laxmi eventually discovered the truth about Sarvash, she had felt humiliated and betrayed. The details in between were sketchy but the next thing she heard was that a stranger had told the police that he had witnessed the suicide of a young pregnant girl, who the police later identified as Lakshmi.

She learnt that Lakshmi had gone to Lover's Leap and jumped awkwardly, partly due to her despair and partly due to her condition, her feet skidding in the damp moss of the ravine.

"I saw her jump, but it was too late to help her, and as she flew down the ravine, her hands floundering and clutching in space, her scream echoed through the valley. The next thing I knew, she was being swept away by the river's current, though she came up for a moment floundering in the water and that is when I saw her black hair caught on the wood that was floating in the river."

Urmila remembered that it was called Lover's Leap because an English woman named Marina had jumped there when she discovered her lover was being sent back to England.

"Puru, you should not feel guilty about Lakshmi, for not all men are like Sarvash!"

"Urmila, I don't want to talk about Laxmi. What she did was unforgivable, however tragically it ended, I am that Rasna too is going down that path."

"How can you compare a young, decent and handsome young man to an old man who encouraged Lakshmi to leave her home? That in itself should tell you what kind of man Mark really is."

"Hah, you would say that wouldn't you?

However, he knew she was right, and there was not a day when he did not recollect Laxmi's twinkling eyes and impish smile that had endeared her to everybody. Nor could he stop blaming himself, for was it not it his duty as a brother to ensure his younger sister's safety? And he had failed miserably, and only his mother knew the complete truth!

Urmila saw his guilt-ridden face and realised that Lakshmi's tragedy was the reason Puru's was so overprotective of his daughters. She sighed, thinking it was best to drop the subject for now, but address it later, when he was in a better mood.

"I have finished your packing, could you just check and see if I have missed anything? I am going shopping tomorrow so..."

"Aren't you leaving it a bit late for that?" Puru replied gruffly. "You just told Rasna off because of that! Anyway, if I need something, I can buy it from Colombo. Sri Lanka is not a village, you know!"

"That is not what I meant..." Urmila replied uneasily. "In that case I think I will go up to bed, I have a terrible headache... oh and don't forget to check the doors before you come up."

"Migraine playing up again. Urmila you should learn to take things easy and not get so worked up. And yes, of course I will check the doors before I come up. Now don't worry and good night... you better tell Rasna she is coming with us!"

After Urmila left the room, Puru laid the paper aside and sat looking out of the window into the night for the curtains were not drawn. His conversation with Urmila had not only opened up old wounds, the hurt and guilt he still felt about Laxmi, but revealed the fact that Urmila, through all the years of marriage, had not been entirely happy with him as he had thought.

He swallowed as he thought how hard he worked for his family to see that Urmila lacked nothing. He had been willing to work nights and even did two jobs sometimes to see that Urmila did not have to go to work.

And when his daughters were born, he had thought that nothing was good enough for them, but it seemed that he had been mistaken all along.

He sat awhile, musing over past events, how he had not wanted to come to London but had felt he had no choice but to flee the country. What he did not realise was that whilst everything and everybody around him had changed with the times, he had remained the same.

Finally, he gave a sigh, got up checked the doors, switched off the electricity and went to bed.

Chapter 24

Rasna opened her eyes the next morning, to find her mother smiling tenderly down at her.

"You know, Rasna, you look like a baby when you are sleeping!" She ruffled her daughter's already tousled hair.

"Mum, what time is it?" Rasna hurriedly threw off the bedclothes and perched on her bed, rubbing her eyes.

"Time for you to get up! Here, I got you a cup of tea." Urmila said as she handed her a mug." Careful, it is hot!"

"Ouch! You are right, it is very warm! Mum, you are the best! Thank you!" After blowing on the mug, she gingerly took a sip. "Mum, you spoil me, but I love it!" Her eyes twinkled then clouded as she recalled the previous evening's events.

"Mum, come sit next to me, did you talk to Father?" she asked anxiously.

Urmila took a sip from her mug and sat on the bed.

"Rasna, I did, but I don't think he is going to change his mind. He insists you come with us and not a week later. And, you know there is a reason why he behaves the way he does. He is upset because he actually wanted to spend time with his family in April; it has always been his wish to spend Sri Lankan new year back home."

"Is that the religious festival you mentioned earlier?"

"Yes, it is called Aluth Avurudu, and it is an especially important one too. It is our new year, celebrated in April after the harvest has been collected and the trees are in full bloom. A time when homes are freshly painted, anyway it is a happy time for festivities when a family should be together. And you would have loved it too, when temple bells ring, a time when everything must be done in a specific manner and at a specific time…"

"You know, Mother, that I think all rituals to be superficial. And if Father is that keen on it, we would have observed it in London, but I do not recollect our ever having celebrated anything of the sort."

"That was because your father was always busy working, and to be honest, it is not quite the same thing, I mean the atmosphere, being with his family etc. And of course, he misses Kirti…"

"Hmmmm." Rasna did not sound convinced. "So, in a way it is better we are going in December. And did you speak to him about Kirti?"

"Yes, but he somehow cannot believe that to be true, says his mother would have informed him if anything was amiss as she has been to see her. However, even though he does not show it, I think he is worried for he is the one pushing insisting we go now."

"Hah! That cannot be true about grandma, for number one, she would never admit that anything was wrong because she arranged the wedding, and number two, she has not been to see Kirti! Well, she did go once, but only for a couple of minutes. I have a feeling she knows something unpleasant about Praana, for she only visited at a time when she knew he would be at the office. Mum, don't you see, we must do something to help Kirti?"

"And she is having her first baby alone! You know, Rasna, we have a tradition that the girl comes to her parents' house for the duration of her pregnancy!" Urmila wiped her eyes with the corner of her sari. "Rasna, don't you think she needs you more than ever? More than me because she can confide in you… please do not make things any more difficult! I am so excited at being a grandmother, to go shopping in Pettah and knit baby clothes and…"

Rasna took her mother's hand and held it against her cheek for it broke her heart to see her mother in distress.

"Amma, please don't cry! I promise not to make things difficult… and you will go to Pettah to shop, in fact I will come with you." Her voice quivered. "But what about the boy Dad mentioned?"

"Don't worry, Rasna, I think he only said that to frighten you and was said on the spur of the moment."

Rasna felt torn between her love for Mark, her love for Kirti and her duty towards her parents.

"Mark left a message saying that his parents were involved in an accident, and I have not been able to speak to Mark to find out how they are. Both Amelia, his younger sister and Mark are with them at the hospital. I would have loved to visit them at the hospital and stay back."

"I don't think that would be possible, you can always ring and find out how they are. If your father did not know about Mark, he might have considered it, but now," Urmila answered sceptically. "And anyway, Kirti told me she got the dates mixed up for the birth of her baby, so the sooner we all go the better."

"Oh dear! Trust Kirti to do that!" Rasna placed her mug angrily on the side table, her eyes glistening with tears of frustration.

Urmila looked at her daughter sympathetically, wondering why her husband could not understand that marriage was supposed to bring his daughter happiness and not misery.

"You are a good daughter, Rasna, we'll face any problem if and when it arises," Urmila replied firmly. "Don't forget, I am on your side."

"Thank you, Amma, that means a lot and you are right. It is important that I focus on Kirti now. Maybe when Dad sees the real Praana, he will realise how unreasonable and unjust he is being."

Urmila rose and patted the creases on her Sari.

"Well, I don't know about that, Rasna. Your father has a habit of closing his eyes and not seeing the obvious if he does not want to! Now I think you better finish your packing!"

After she had left the room, Rasna placed her legs under her chin and rocked to and fro, then rose and looked for her purse. She took out her mobile hoping she would be able to get through to Mark to tell him about the change of plans. However, as she feared, the mobile was switched off.

She sighed, went to the bathroom, splashed her face with cold water and changed into a fresh pair of jeans.

She came out of the bathroom, twisting her hair into a ponytail, wondering why most of the people she had met during her last visit to Colombo had been modern and why her father was so conventional.

By the time she had finished her packing and tried contacting Mark a few times, it was lunchtime. She went downstairs worried about encountering her father.

Her parents were already seated at the table when she entered the dining room, was given a reassuring smile by her mother.

"There you are, Rasna, I was just about to call you. I hope you are hungry; I have made your favourite dish."

"Oh, thanks, Mum! I am hungry," Rasna said taking a plate from Urmila.

As she ate, she kept her eyes on the plate.

Halfway during the meal, the phone rang and Rasna got up hurriedly.

"Sit down, Rasna," Puru said brusquely "I am expecting a business call."

As he left the room, Rasna turned to her mother angrily.

"Mum, I don't like the way he talks to me."

"All he meant was that you should finish your food. He meant well, Rasna."

"Yeh, right," Rasna replied sulking.

At that moment, Puru entered the room wiping his forehead.

"I don't understand it! Urmila, that was not the call I was expecting but Kirti on the phone. She wants to speak to Rasna, but I think Urmila you should speak to her to set your mind at ease."

Chapter 25

"No, I will speak to her, Dad," Rasna rose from her chair quickly, looking accusingly at her mother.

Before Puru could object, Urmila intervened. "Yes, Rasna, go ahead and speak to her, but don't take too long!"

Rasna ran to the phone and picked up the receiver eagerly.

"Kirti, I miss you and our chats. How are you? Is everything alright?"

"I miss you too Rasna! I had a premonition that you might not becoming, so just rang to confirm that I will see you soon, I need to talk to you!" she said with a sob.

"Kirti, please don't cry, of course I will be coming, it is not good to cry in your condition. Anyway, how is Praana, is he behaving himself now that he is going to be a father?"

"I wish, but no, his attitude remains the same, and I think he behaves so nastily because his mother encourages him to. All that aggro on top of being sick and overweight! I cannot wait for the baby to be born!"

"Kirti, don't worry. I do not understand their attitude. Praana should be over the moon at becoming a father and your mother-in-law at being a grandma! Anyway, we will be with you in time for the birth, in the meantime, just concentrate on the baby. Now, tell me, has Grandma been matchmaking for me? Dad mentioned someone called Annama?"

"That would be Praana's cousin, but other than that I do not know much about him, but I wouldn't be surprised. Grandma knows the only way she can please Dad is by getting us married. She has succeeded with me, but do not worry, you are well prepared and stronger to manage any crisis than I was, and I am on your side. By the way, how is Mark?"

"Oh Kirti! You are not going to believe this, but he has asked me to marry him! And Dad and Mum know about him too, I will tell you how that came about when I see you! I will really miss him, what with my being in Sri Lanka and him going to Thailand!"

"Whoaaa hold on, Rasna! Mum and Dad know about him? What was their reaction? Tell me now, I cannot wait till you come!"

Rasna gave a brief outline of the conversation she had had, cautious of the fact that her father might be overhearing their conversation

"I will tell you the rest when we meet, Kirti."

"Hey, Rasna, before you hang up can I make something clear, you are my sister and I love you very much, but you don't want to end up like me, do you? I would love to see you, but if you think it is the right thing to do, please don't come."

"Thanks, Kirti, you are the best., but we can deal with Annama or anyone like him together! Anyway, Mark will be in Thailand and I want to meet my niece/nephew! Bye for now and don't worry, we'll meet soon, that is after I have finished shopping for your stuff!"

"Shopping is not important, bye, Rasna give my love to Mum and Dad… I am soooo looking forward to meeting you."

"Will do!" Rasna replied cheerfully as she re-placed the receiver.

However, there was a doubtful and thoughtful expression on her face as she entered the dining room.

"How is Kirti, what did she want?" Urmila asked anxiously.

"She is fine, Mum. She sends her love and is looking forward to all of us being together once again."

"I am going out for a while, Urmila, do you need anything?" Puru asked.

"Puru! You told me not to go out and now you are doing the same! Anyway, should not we be leaving for the airport?"

"We leave at five, I will be back before then," Puru said over his shoulder. "Be ready by then."

"But…" But before Urmila could complete her sentence Puru had left, slamming the door behind him.

Puru got in the car, started the engine, and quickly drove away. He had no urgent errand, but felt he needed to be out of the house. Since the call from Kirti, he felt Urmila and Rasna where just waiting to tell him how unhappy Kirti was, all because of him… Well, he thought grimly, I am not going to give them the opportunity to throw that at my face again!

Chapter 26

He drove around for an hour, and at about four he turned back and parked the car outside his house.

"Urmila, Rasna are you ready?" he called as soon as he entered. "We leave in another half an hour."

"Puru, you are home at last! We were worried. That was not very wise, shopping on the day you are flying." Urmila came down the stairs carrying a suitcase. "We are ready."

"Urmila, why are you carrying the suitcase? You should have waited for me." He took the baggage from Urmila.

"Oh, don't worry there is another one upstairs, I got the lighter one!"

"Where is Rasna, what is she up to?" Although Urmila had convinced him she would be travelling with them, Puru had a feeling that something was sure to go wrong with his indecisive daughter.

"Puru, stop worrying, she is ready too and will be down any minute… Ah, there she is."

However, she saw with dismay that she had no luggage with her and had not changed.

"Rasna! Where is your luggage? I had asked you to be ready by the time I got back!" Puru glared at her angrily.

"Dad, I am not going."

"What! Urmila you said…?" He sputtered. "You are like a yo-yo! One minute you are coming the next you are not! We are not going round the corner you know!"

"Rasna, why have you changed your mind again? I thought we had agreed that you will come, at least for Kirti's sake."

"Of course, I will come, Mother. Just not with you. I will join you later."

"But Kirti is waiting for you, she is expecting, and you told me…"

"I spoke to her, Mother. I have a lot of assignments to catch up and it is only a matter of one week… Dad?"

"Young lady if you don't come now, I don't want to see you ever again! Urmila, you deal with her, we only have half an hour. She keeps changing her mind every hour! I cannot keep up with her!"

He stormed off as Rasna ran into her bedroom followed by her mother.

"Now, Rasna, tell me what has happened to make me change your mind, for I know you want to see Kirti, especially if she is in trouble," Urmila asked gently.

"It is Mark, he left a message… I spoke to him to clarify, his parents are now out of danger, which is a relief, for he is overly attached to them but I feel he needs me as his sister is too young."

"If it were upto me, you know I would not say no to anything, but it is your father."

"Why is he so stubborn and over-protective?" Rasna stamped her foot.

"Because he knows that you are staying back because of Mark, not your studies, as you claim. And do not be too harsh on him, Rasna, he has his reasons." She briefly told Rasna about Laxmi.

"Poor Laxmi Aunty! I wish I had known her." Rasna's eyes were shining. "Mother, I understand, and love him for it, for trying to protect us, but Mark is not like that. He would never harm me." She sighed. "All right, Mother, all things considered I will come with you. I had already packed so will be down in a jiffy. I will need to speak to Mark, and if I cannot get through, will leave a message explaining the change of plans. He will understand, that is why I love him."

"So why don't you give him our address in Colombo? You said he might come to Sri Lanka; he is welcome to stay with us. Now, are you convinced we have no ulterior motive in taking to taking you to Colombo?"

"Grandma wouldn't mind since we will be staying with her? He will be thrilled and oh… Mum I love you dearly!" She hugged her mother tightly

"All right, all right, Rasna, I can't breathe!" She patted her daughter on the head. "Now, quickly, go get your luggage. I can promise that you will love Sri Lanka, the greenery the beauty, the beaches, the palm trees the—"

"All right, all right Mother, you don't have to convince me. You know I was there last year!" Rasna laughed, her head thrown back, however, it was not long before her face became pensive. Although she loved her grandma, she knew her to be sly and manipulative and used to getting her own way.

Rasna went into her bedroom and dialled Mark's number, and it was not long before he answered breathlessly.

"Hello, princess, is everything okay?"

Rasna could picture him, the smile that would have lit his face, however, she also detected the sadness in his voice.

"Mark, hi, yes, it is, I tried calling you a couple of times, anyway, is everything all right? You sound a bit…"

"It is now, but it was worrying for a while, but my parents are fine now, thank God! We were all worried here, my aunt has come to look after them with my young sister so I can now go to Thailand without worrying about them. What about you?"

"I will be going with my parents after all, I now understand why my father is so overprotective, apparently something tragic happened to his sister. Anyway, I will give you my address and phone number in Colombo… will you be able to come from Thailand?"

"Hey, slow down. Hmm I suppose I could… can't stay away from you for that long!"

"Good, now I know you, please don't lose the phone number and address!"

"Princess, I will commit the phone number to memory so even if I lose the address…!"

"Mark, please don't joke about this. I will only feel comfortable and safe knowing that you will be coming to Sri Lanka, else I do not know how I will get through the days!"

"I don't think that will be a problem, you will be too busy chatting to Kirti and of course, getting married."

"Mark, shut up!"

She quickly gave him her grandmother's address in Colombo then hung up and joined her parents who were waiting for her, her mother patiently waiting whilst her father was shuffling his feet in impatience.

Chapter 27

"Ah, there you are, at last… I only hope we are not late," he murmured as he put the luggage in the car.

"No, we won't be late, we have enough time." Urmila put her hand on his arm. "It is a good thing we are parking the car at the airport; we won't have any trouble coming back."

Puru grunted and drove fast, overtaking cars on the motorway.

As they were behind schedule, there was not a long queue at the check in counter so after checking in their luggage, they walked down the terminal towards the plane.

As soon as Rasna had tied her seat belt, she turned towards her mother.

"Ma, do you think Kirti will be at the airport to receive us? I hope so," she sighed.

"I don't think so; it is not wise to leave the house in her condition."

"Then we will go directly to her house…"

"I don't think so, "Urmila smiled. "She is married now and lives with her in-laws, so there are certain formalities they will expect us to take into consideration. We will first go to your grandmother's house in Colombo, rest awhile and then leave for Matara which is two hours' drive from Colombo." She closed her eyes as Rasna looked out the window.

Rasna thought of Mark, and with a smile on her lips, she too gradually dozed off and was woken by the stewardess who was taking orders for dinner.

She rubbed her eyes, ordered for herself then turned towards her mother's seat, surprised to see it was empty, so ordered for her. She looked around her and found she was talking to a young woman who she assumed was travelling to Colombo.

"What a nice woman," Urmila remarked as she returned to her seat. "She is travelling to Colombo too, well escaping really."

"What do you mean, Amma, who is this new-found friend of yours?"

"Well, she said that she was married to an abusive man who she is escaping from to go back to her parents in Columbo. Poor thing, she is not sure of the reception she will receive from them either."

"Have I been asleep that long? You seem to have had a heart to heart." Rasna rubbed her eyes.

"Poor thing," Urmila repeated. "She needed someone to talk to. She had been married for ten years to a rich man but has only recently found the courage to leave her husband, I see you have ordered for me?"

"Yes, I did, I knew you are not fussy, and the food usually tastes good…"

"Whether the food tastes good is not important," Puru piped up from the seat at the back. "Urmila, you should not talk to any Tom, Dick or Harry, you never know, they might just strike up a friendship to put drugs in your luggage."

"Dad…! Rasna exclaimed.

"Rasna, ignore him… I am used to his remarks. Hmmm this looks nice," she commented as the stewardess placed a tray on the mini table attached to the seat in front of her. "I thought I was not hungry but… thank you."

Rasna finished her meal, returned the tray to the stewardess then stretched her legs.

"How long before we reach Colombo?" she asked impatiently.

"We will reach Bandaranaike airport at… and in the meantime, you have a choice of a movie you might like to watch." She rattled off a few names of which one was a movie that Rasna had been keen to see.

"Yes, I think I will, I have wanted to see this one, Amma. I think you might like it too."

"No thank you, Rasna. You watch it, I am going to sleep." Urmila yawned and closed her eyes.

As it was one of the movies that she and Mark had decided to see together, Rasna could not concentrate on it for long as her thoughts turned to Mark, his smile and his vivid green eyes. So engrossed was she in her thoughts, that in no time at all she heard an announcement announcing their arrival in Bandaranaike airport.

Sri Lanka (2004)

Chapter 28

The weather was warm and humid as they arrived but there was a gentle breeze that made the heat tolerable.

Rasna's thoughts were akin to different coloured threads, for she was thinking of Kirti, Mark, of the future and what it held for her? If she was forced into an arranged marriage, she would rather die like her aunt than live without Mark! She thought of Kirti, and if there was some kind of a tragedy in store for her, wondered if she could do anything to prevent it?

As soon as they had finished completing the arrival documentation and the officer had stamped their passports, Urmila turned towards her daughter as they walked out of the terminal.

"Now, Rasna, Kirti's husband is sure to be at the airport to receive us and I want you to treat him politely…!

"Mum! You know I am too well-mannered for that!"

Puru took a suitcase from Urmila's hand and remarked, "I agree with your mum, Rasna. We have bought you up to be a polite and well-mannered girl, but you have a very expressive face which usually shows exactly what you feel!"

"Appa! You don't know the kind of person he really is, so I do not think he deserves to be treated civilly!" Rasna replied indignantly, but when she saw her parents face hurriedly added, "Of course I will, Mum, but only for Kirti's sake!"

"That is better, Rasna! Now, will your mother come with Praana?" Urmila anxiously asked Puru for she did not like her overbearing mother in law.

"No, unfortunately, Amma cannot come but Kadamba will be coming, actually I am not sure about Praana either."

Rasna heaved a sigh of relief whilst Urmila smiled for Kadamba was Puru's brother and she liked him.

They passed through the 'nothing to declare' barrier where men in white uniforms were lounging around lazily. The arrival lounge was busy, and behind the barrier stood families, friends, businessmen taxi drivers and airport porters all waiting for the arrival of somebody.

"Puru, I don't see anyone." Urmila looked around her in panic.

"Don't worry, my dear, Kadamba said he would be here, and he is very dependable - he must have got held up in the traffic… ah there he is!" He waved frantically, and a tall man with a moustache came toward them smiling.

Kadamba had a tanned face with laughter wrinkles around his eyes, a smile that transformed his face, and every time he did, it seemed as if he was revealing a secret. Looking at his kind and sensitive face, Rasna felt that she could easily confide in him, should the need arise.

As usual, Kadamba looked groomed and handsome, as if he had just stepped out of a barber's shop. He was always well presented, and Rasna recalled the many stories her father had told her, of how he would spend a lot of time in their room organising his socks, shirts and trousers. Of how he would not wear his shoes unless they were immaculately polished; and the only arguments they had had was over tidiness - as tidiness had been her uncle's obsession and her father's weakness!

"Puru, Thangai, I am glad to see you and Urmila too."
He turned towards Rasna and smiled, the corners of his eyes
crinkling. "Hello there."

"Hello Chitappa," Rasna smiled, wishing her father were
more like his brother.

"And this, is Praana, who you all know." Kadamba
gestured to a young man standing beside him.

Praana looked uneasy and nervous, and Rasna wondered
if he had argued with Kirti, for she had told him that Praana
had not been pleased about their coming.

"Rasna, he a very weak man with no back-bone at all to
stand up to his mother!" Kirti had told her often.

Rasna had only met him briefly at Kirti's wedding and,
even then, had not liked either him nor his mother.

Praana straightened his slightly drooping shoulders, then
stretched his hand towards Puru, a slight smile on his sallow
face, his furtive eyes darting over his in-laws.

"Vaazhga, Maamanaar Vaazhga Maamiyar." Praana
smiled slightly.

"Vaazhga Praana Marumagan."

Kadamba saw the puzzled look on Rasna's face and smiled.
"Vaazhga is a welcome greeting in Tamil and I am sure you
know that Maamanaar and Maamiyar mean father-in-law and
mother-in-law."

"Yes, of course," Rasna murmured.

Puru, after a brief handshake with his son-in-law, turned
towards his brother.

"So, Anna, how are you and how is Amma?"

"She is fine, looking forward to meeting you, of course."
Kadamba smiled.

Whilst her parents were talking to Kadamba, Rasna
watched Praana from under half closed eyes.

He was shifting uneasily on his feet, and she intuitively felt he was an insecure man, one who was capable of venting out his frustrations on his wife, a man most likely to be associated with groups and gangs. What had her grandmother and parents seen in him? However, with an effort, she managed to control herself, remembering her father's remark about her expressive face and tried not displaying the revulsion she felt on it.

And Rasna was correct in her assessment, for Praana was indeed a weak man and a bully who was mean to those weaker than himself, but deferential to rich and powerful people. According to him, everyone had their place in the world, and nothing disturbed and infuriated him more than someone who had opinions, which, he thought to be above their station, however accurate they might be. But what was important to Praana was what people thought of him, and that they think he was the best. He liked to be the judge, jury, and in some cases maybe even an executioner?

Unfortunately, he could not control Kirti, and it infuriated him. In the early days of their marriage, she had been full of life; at the same time, he had thought her to be a meek and docile girl, one who would be easily intimidated, so was surprised when she had occasionally defied him. What irritated him the most was her refusal to admit that she had done anything wrong when he criticised her, which was often. This had angered him for she had dared to change her place in the role he had thought out for her.

Kirti, meanwhile, tried not to give him an opportunity that could result in any kind of confrontation, and when she noticed that his mother took pleasure in her son's attitude towards her, was not only hurt but disappointed at their animosity towards her.

"How is Kirti, Praana?" Rasna asked as she looked around the airport.

"Welcome to Colombo, dear sister. My wife is fine, she wanted to come but my mother thought it best that she stay at home, you know, in her condition." Although he smiled, Praana's eyes were cold and expressionless, his voice dry and unemotional.

They walked out of the airport and Rasna took a deep breath as she felt the magic of Sri Lanka in the air. The sunlight was so bright that Urmila screwed her eyes against the glare. She regretted not putting her shades in her purse, fearful that the travel and the glare would bring on one of her migraines.

"Here we are." Kadamba stopped outside a grey car and put the luggage in its trunk.

Chapter 29

They drove through Colombo's wide streets, and Rasna was delighted at the assorted colours, shades, and hues she noticed – for there were waves of crimson, orange and yellow leaves of trees that were gently swaying in the breeze. Was it her imagination, or could she smell spices, sandalwood and coconut mixed in the air?

Colombo was surrounded by trees and water and Rasna could smell the salty warm sea air. In the middle of the city was a lake from which branched small lakes that were surrounded by foliage – palms of every variety, masses of flowers and in the breeze, the swaying leaves of trees.

As Kadamba drove through the palm trees and wide avenues into the suburbs of Colombo, he looked at the rear window at Rasna.

"Rasna, it's your first time here, well, no second, but I don't count last year. That visit was hurried, so I don't think you had time for a proper tour of Sri Lanka."

"You are right, Chitappa, I did not." Rasna grinned as she looked at her uncle's reflection in the mirror.

"Well, so I shall explain as we drive, well, we are on the expressway, and it would take us twenty minutes to reach home. We will get onto the Galle Road which is 72 miles long and has palm trees on its fringes as well as beaches of the western coastline."

"Oh golly," Rasna remarked in awe as she looked at the lovely city of Colombo.

"So, as I am your guide today… I will introduce you to our lovely city, Sri Lanka, which is 'lapped' by the Indian Ocean, is surrounded by emerald green sea, has shimmering white sand and palm trees, and not only is it a charming city, but is a paradise on earth! We have landscapes of mountains, rainforests, paddy fields and waterfalls." Kadamba looked in the rear window and grinned. "The Beira Lake is a central part of Colombo and is connected to the harbour by canals."

"Chitappa, you sound like a tour guide! But please, not too detailed and Dad, how come you left such an exotic city to live in London with its awful weather?"

Puru just grunted and looked angrily at his brother.

"Colombo tries to preserve its old culture whilst trying to keep up with modern developments," Praana added. "Keep the old and bring in the new, so to speak."

Rasna jumped at what she considered to be an opportunity to express her views.

"Very wise, one should retain one's culture, but at the same time acknowledge and understand new and different faiths." She looked at her father who glared back at her unspoken insinuation.

"You are incredibly wise for one so young, for we have the same problem here, which is why there has been so much bloodshed! Anyway, let us get back to pleasant things. In Colombo, as you can see, there are broad avenues and modern buildings as well as narrow streets," Praana continued, missing the look that had passed between father and daughter.

"Everything does look so beautiful," Rasna remarked, as she looked at the purple bell-shaped flowers and other tropical plants. "We don't have anything like this back in London."

"We are now driving past Victoria Park, which, as you can see, is shaded by huge palm trees."

Rasna saw that there were people sitting on benches, enjoying the sunshine. Some were alone, others who were reading books or newspapers, and mothers who had brought their children to the park

"What about the climate here?" Rasna asked. "It's lovely now, but is it the same the entire year?"

"Well Sri Lanka is a tropical country with the usual two seasons – Yaha season which is from May to August and the Maha season from Oct to January. And we have just finished the rainy season."

The palm trees swayed for there was a gentle breeze which wafted through them. Rasna wrinkled her nose for the air was scented with roses, jasmine, and freshly sprinkled grass in warm lawns. The sun seemed to pour down an avalanche of sparkling light and she sensed an energy and exuberance emanating from the people on streets, pavements, and parks.

There was a lot of traffic which consisted of cars, buses and three wheeled trishaws (tuk tuks). The trishaws were a motorised version of man pulled rickshaws that were dangerously zigzagging their way through packed buses and cars.

"There must be so much pollution with all these cars that the carbon monoxide levels must be extremely high - so it cannot be very healthy, living in this smog."

She gave her father a meaningful glance, who scowled at her.

"Look, Mum back in London when the signal turns red, cars stop, people seldom use their horns and it is pedestrians and not beggars who are on the pavement, but here...!"

As they passed a residential area, Rasna saw colourful flowers blooming not only in pots and flowerbeds outside most houses, but spreading out over the balcony, whilst others colourfully entwined with the green shrubbery that was scrambling and clamouring onto the walls that added a tinge of colour to them.

"How beautiful!" Rasna quickly took a picture from her mobile.

Kadamba turned into a street that led up to a house that was situated away from the road and was barely visible because of the shrubs, bushes and trees surrounding it.

"Here we are, welcome home, Puru Anna."

"Ah, it is good to be home, Thambi!"

Rasna could not speak fluent Tamil, but it always seemed strange to Rasna that her father, who had lived in London for a prolonged period still liked to pepper his English with Tamil words and she knew that Thambi meant younger brother.

As soon as Kadamba had parked the car and was taking the luggage from the trunk of the car, an elderly woman walked towards them, smiling happily.

Chapter 30

"Amma." Puru saw his mother's beaming face, grinned then with his hand touched her feet as a gesture of respect.

"Puru Magan, it is so nice to see you." She took Puru's face in her hands and kissed him on the forehead. "Kadamba! Never mind the luggage, Ramu will see to it. Ramu, come here!"

Rasna thought her grandmother looked older and more fragile than the previous year and she had forgotten she spoke fluent English.

"Hello Rasna, how are you?"

"Hello Paati." Rasna folded her hands. "How are you?"

Her grandmother laughed with delight as she kissed her on both cheeks.

"So you know Tamil, do you?"

"Of course, Amma, she is my daughter!" Puru said with indignation, however he knew his mother was jesting.

"Yes, and I also know that we are the lion people." Rasna could not help showing off.

"Very good, Rasna. Puru, you should be proud of such a girl!"

His mother, Aadi, spoke in a clear, brusque tone and held herself with dignity. She was tall, thin and wore her silver hair in a bun. Rasna thought her to be about eighty years old, and the years were etched on her face, the skin of which was creasing finely. Rasna looked at her in admiration, for the light shone on her silver hair and she saw her to be a woman of steely strength and air of purpose.

Ramu had appeared quickly, taken their luggage and carried it into the house.

"Puru, why have you come after such a long time? Did you not want to meet your mother? You know, I am an old woman and don't have long to live!" There were tears in Aadi's eyes as she gently drew her son close and kissed him again on both cheeks.

"Amma." Urmila pressed her palms together and was acknowledged by her mother-in-law with a smile and slight nod of her head.

"Amma! Have you forgotten we were here last year for Kirti's wedding!" Puru exclaimed.

"Well, it is a year ago, too long for me. I don't know why you have to live in London, so far from me."

"Have you forgotten the cirmustances under which I had to leave? And if I remember correctly, it was you who urged me to leave!"

"Yes, yes," Aadi muttered as she led the way into the bungalow. "But that doesn't mean I like it," and as they reached the bungalow shouted, "Ramu, can you bring us some tea? Puru, Urmila would you like to freshen up whilst he gets it? Kadamba can you show them to their rooms?"

"No need for that, Amma, I know my way about, I have lived here, you know, it used to be my home!" Puru grinned. "At least that is if everything is the same?"

"It is the same old house, but we will be sharing a room, like the old days, whilst Urmila and Rasna can have your old room. Will that be okay?" Kadamba asked as he opened a door and led the way inside.

"Of course, it will, Kadamba. It is nice to be home."

Rasna and Urmila, meanwhile, had followed Ramu upstairs who had opened the door to a pleasantly sunlit bright room that opened onto a veranda. The décor of the room was white, with a white chest of drawers, white rug and pastel pink curtains, the light colours making the room seem spacious and cool.

After Ramu placed their luggage on the floor and left, Rasna ran to the balcony that overlooked a huge well-kept garden, then ran back excitedly into the room and sat on the bed.

"Wow!" she said, perching on the bed. "How can Dad leave this for London? I forgot the house was so huge with a garden to die for. Well okay that is too dramatic!"

"And you didn't want to come! Your dad had to leave the country for those were tough times, Rasna, but anyway, no time for that, hurry up and freshen up, everything here runs like clockwork!"

"Amma, from what you have told us, there has never been a dull moment in our family! First Atthai Lakshmi, then you joining the rebels to fight for a cause, and now you are saying there is something else I do not know? About Kadamba mamu maybe?"

Urmila nodded her head sadly, then went into the bathroom to splash her face with cold water, for the journey from London took 10 hours and she was beginning to feel the onset of a jet-lag. And, whenever she was tired or stressed, she was sure to have an attack of one of her migraines.

Rasna got the impression that her mother was in awe of her grandmother, an effect that was inevitable for her grandmother was indeed a formidable character. One who, Rasna thought, could shrivel a garden with the touch of her hand, turn warm water to cold and even turn children's games into punishments!

However, underneath the stony exterior she knew she meant well and loved them.

As soon as her mother emerged from the bathroom, Rasna went in to refresh herself. After some time, she came back into the room and sat in front of the dressing table, combing her hair.

"Mum, is Kadamba uncle married?" she enquired

"Rasna where are you going with this? May to see if there any family skeletons you can unearth?" Urmila smiled affectionately. "No, he is too good, your uncle, he was married but it did not last, for the girl he was married to was too clever and also because your grandmother meddled in their marriage."

"She couldn't have been a very nice woman, for I too think Mamu is a lovely person, he is so kind, and as for grandma meddling…"

She was silent as she brushed her hair, the only sound in the room was the rustle of the fabric of the sari Urmila was wrapping around her.

"Hey, Mum, how come you are wearing the sari in a different manner here." Rasna inquired.

"Yes, it is different to the usual way Rasna, in Sri Lanka, I wear the sari the Tamil way, that is, I will tie the Palu around the hip and then tuck it at the back. But you have seen me wear it like this back home sometimes!"

"Yes, but I thought that it was an informal way of dressing meant only for home!"

Urmila smiled as she finished tucking the Palu of the sari at the back.

"That looks nice, Mum, but how did Kadamba Chitappa's marriage break up? He is a such a nice and gentle person – and however clever and nasty his wife was, I am sure he could have won her over. She should have thought herself lucky, any girl would think herself lucky to marry him," Rasna exclaimed. "Mum! You are taking too long; I am ready, for you told me that grandma was very particular about being punctual."

"Yes, she is, Rasna, just give me a minute. You are right about your uncle, it was not Namisha's fault, but his mother's, she always interfered in their marriage and Kadamba was too good to stand up to her interference. Finally, Namisha got fed up and felt she had no choice but to leave Kadamba. And that is why your aunt Laxmi left home too, for your grandmother is a very forceful personality. I often think the only reason Puru and me are still together is because we live in another country!" Urmila deftly twisted her long hair into a bun.

"Yes, I noticed how she spoke to Kadamba mamu! Mum, come on, are you ready?

"Right, now I am ready!"

As they left the room, they were joined by Puru and Kadamba in the corridor.

Chapter 31

"My, I am hungry." Puru rubbed his hands. "I haven't had proper Sri Lankan food!"

"Dad! It is only tea-time and not dinner time!" Rasna exclaimed." And Amma often makes Sri Lankan food in London!"

"Ah, but you have not tasted the food here, it all tastes better, even the snacks!"

"I see you still have a healthy appetite, Puru." Kadamba smiled in his gentle way. "Amma knows it, and you are right, she will have made your favourite."

He led them to the dining room where the tea things were set out and Aadi was sitting on a chair, tapping her fingers on the table.

"And what took you so long?" she snapped as soon as she saw her sons. "The tea must be cold by now; I will have to ask Ramu to make us a fresh pot!"

Whilst she gave the order to Ramu, who had been standing nearby, the others sat around the table.

As her uncle had foreseen, there was an assortment of dishes on the table, only some of which Rasna was familiar with.

Aadi sat at the head of the table and passed an empty plate to Puru. "Whilst waiting for the tea, Puru, have some bhoodhi."

"Thank you, Amma, you remembered it is my favourite! Rasna, you must try this, it is delicious!"

He placed the deep-fried balls that were made from lentils, flour and spices on his plate.

"I would also recommend Bhado or Pola cutlets." Kadamba turned towards Rasna and Urmila. "I told you Amma would have prepared his favourite dishes!"

"Not for me at the moment, but I will have some godam bati – that is what they are called, aren't they?"

"Oh yes." Kadamba handed her the plate. "What about you, Urmila?"

"I will have a little of everything Kadamba Dada, I am hungry too!"

There were a variety of sambols to go with them and Rasna looked at them with a frown.

"Can't decide which one, huh?" Kadamba grinned. "Here, why don't you taste them all?"

Rasna returned his infectious smile and could not help but like him.

The servant came in with a fresh pot of Ceylonese tea.

"If you don't like tea, we have lime juice, Faludi or thambilli if you like," Addi asked.

"If it is Ceylonese tea, Amma, I would love that, thank you, Patti." Urmila looked at her in surprise. "You never drink tea, Rasna! You always have coffee."

"Ah Mum, but the tea here is world famous, and Grandma said that this tea is more special because it is from Praana's tea plantations."

"There you have it in a nutshell, young lady, everything here is different, fresh, and very, very tasty, not only the tea!" Puru said.

Aadi poured the tea from the pot and handed a cup to Urmila and Rasna.

"Thanks, Paati." Rasna took the cup gratefully for she was thirsty.

"Amma, can I have some Polla cutlets and Vaddai… with the pol sambol please?"

"Purushan, take it easy, please," Urmila remarked.

Aadi glanced at Urmila sharply. "Leave him be, Urmila, he is on holiday."

"Yes but…" However, the look on Aadi's face silenced her.

"How is Kirti, Amma?" Rasna asked.

Aadi looked flustered but hurriedly pulled herself together.

"I am sure she is fine, my dear, as Praana here will tell you."

"I can't wait to see my daughter, I, no we, have really missed her. You are lucky she lives close by.… I am sure you too are looking forward to coming with us. Especially at this auspicious time."

"About that, sorry son, I cannot come with you. I am not feeling very well," Aadi remarked nervously, patting her silver hair in place.

"Come on Amma, you seem to be fine, Kadamba will you come with us too?"

"Of course, I would love to meet Kirti again… when is her baby due?"

"Anytime, now, Amma." Praana looked up. "But maybe it is best you see Kirti later, especially as the others would only be able to stay for a day or two."

Rasna drew in her breath sharply for she sensed that Praana was insinuating they make their visit as brief as possible. She wanted to confide in her uncle, for he was so kind and sensitive, he would know what to do. She also suspected he too did not like Praana and again wondered as to why her parents and grandmother did not feel the same? She was confused, for sometimes she felt they were afraid of Praana, especially her father and grandmother, for they were being overly polite and genial. However, Rasna put it down to him being the son-in-law who, in their culture, should be worshipped like an idol!

"Mum, can you pass the sugar, please?"

Urmila looked at her daughter with a frown, for not only had she observed the outraged expression on her face at Praana's implication but had also noticed the nervous expression on her mother-in-law's face.

"Amma, will we have time for shopping?" she asked, tactfully changing the subject.

"Maybe not now, but you can when you return from Matara and stay with me. How long will you be staying with Kirti?"

"Well, at least couple of weeks after delivery, although I would have preferred that she had come to me in London for the delivery." She ignored Praana.

"Mum, why doesn't Kirti come back and stay with us for a couple of months?" Rasna asked.

"And there speaks a woman who has not had a baby. How do you propose Kirti would travel?"

"In England, a woman who has given birth is urged to move around normally after a day or two, why one of my friends was discharged the same day!"

"Well, we are not in London," Urmila snapped.

"But giving birth is natural, it the most natural thing in the world for a woman," Kadamba remarked, coming to Kirti's aid.

"Kadamba! Don't give your opinion on something you know nothing about, especially when it is regarding women!" Aadi fixed him with a piercing look. "Urmila, I am sure there will be no need to stay that long, and no need for Kirti to go back with you either! Praana's mother will look after her." She smiled at Praana who smiled back, grateful of her moral support.

Rasna became convinced that her grandmother knew all was not well with Kirti's marriage but was not acknowledging it, maybe because she felt responsible for it?

There was silence and the only sound was of the crushing of Pappadum which Rasna found frustrating. How could her parents be so calm, for it annoyed Rasna that her aunt had been through a similar experience that had ended in tragedy, yet here they were, eating and drinking, oblivious of impending tragedy. One would think they would have learnt from their mistakes…but no! Maybe it was this cold attitude that had driven her aunt to suicide?

After they had finished, Aadi got up from the table.

Chapter 32

"Puru, come with me, tell me what you have been up to. No, not you, Kadamba!" Aadi snapped. "You and Praana should make plans for travel to Matara tomorrow,whilst Urmila can take Rasna upstairs for a rest before dinner. You have had a long journey and the travel tomorrow too it is a long way."

"Amma, the journey only takes two hours!"

"Not if you have travelled previously on a 10-hour journey and are suffering with jet-lag!" Aadi retorted sharply.

Rasna, meanwhile had only heard the word 'dinner'

"Dinner!" Rasna exclaimed. "What dinner? We all have eaten so much that I am sure there is no need for dinner!"

"What nonsense! you have a lot to learn about our traditions; that was only snacks, dinner will be much later!" There was a hint of a smile on Aadi's lips.

"Okay, Amma, come with me Praana." Kadamba meekly said. "We will have some tea in the sitting room."

As Urmila and Rasna walked towards the sitting room, Rasna suddenly stopped.

"Rasna, what is the matter, are you feeling all right?" She placed her arm around her daughter's shoulder.

"I am fine, Mum, but why does Grandma want to talk to Dad in private? They are conspiring to arrange my marriage.

I knew it! Dad all along said…!" There were tears in Rasna's eyes.

"Now, now, don't jump to conclusions." Urmila opened the door to their room. "Maybe they just want to have a mother/son chat. You know, like we do sometimes. We mother's like that, you know!" Urmila smiled, hoping to distract Rasna. "You know, I would love a nap after the travel and the food!"

Rasna followed, now certain that her father and grandmother had planned it from the beginning. She should not have come, not only did she want to meet Kirt, but her mother had assured her that there was no ulterior motive - so did that mean her mother was a part of the scheme?

"Mother, did you know about this? I am sure that is what they have planned? You want me to get married like Kirti and be unhappy?"

Urmila rubbed her forehead wearily, first sat on the bed than lay back and closed her eyes.

"Rasna, you only told me about Kirti being unhappy yesterday – before we came here. I did mention it to your father, but he refuses to believe it. His mother arranged her marriage; therefore, it must be all right. Puru's mother, in his eyes, can do no wrong."

"And that was his explanation? Does he know that she has not once been to see Kirti or her mother-in-law? You heard Praana; he does not want anybody to stay at his house lest we find out the truth about them. Maybe that is what Grandma is talking to Dad about. Mum. Mum?"

But there was no answer as Urmila had dozed off, so Rasna walked over to the balcony admiring the magnificent lawn where the dusky faces of a variety of flowers were gently swaying in the breeze.

She returned to the room surprised to see her mother was wide awake and sitting up in bed.

"Mother, that was a short nap! You know, I feel so alone, as if all you are plotting against me."

Urmila sat up and patted the bed "Come sit with me, child."

As Rasna sat on the bed, Urmila hugged her, gently stroked her forehead then kissed her tear-filled face.

"Rasna, don't say that! I am with you and I promise no one will make you do anything against your will."

"But Father listens to Grandma and if she says…" Rasna hiccupped.

"If nothing, you are my daughter, and your happiness is important to me. I am only sorry I had not been strong enough and fought for Kirti and again, you are not alone, you have me, your uncle and of course Kirti."

"Thanks Mum, that means a lot, but I think we can take Uncle out the equation, he is too gentle and dominated by Grandma. And you too, Mum, you know at the end of the day you cannot oppose Dad and Grandma put together! They make a formidable team."

"I know you find it hard to believe, but I can withstand pressure from your dad. I think you are making a mountain out of a molehill! Now, before I go downstairs. I think I would like a bath then another cup of tea would be nice."

Rasna did not share her mother optimism, so while her mother was in the bathroom, took the opportunity of unpacking. She was halfway through when she realised it was a waste of time as they would be travelling again the following day.

She took out a pair of jeans and a clean T-shirt before putting the clothes back into the suitcase, then, with a sigh, rested her head on the pillow - not aware when her eyes closed in weariness. The next thing she was aware of was when her mother was shaking her gently.

"Wake up sleepy head! I thought you said were not tired?"

Rasna rubbed her eyes as she sat up. "I was not, am not, must be the food and the weather."

Urmila smiled, "Well, climate I cannot control but as to the food, there is more to come, your grandmother loves to feed her sons!"

By the time they finished dressing, it was early evening.

"Rasna, before we go down, I would like you to see the dusk of Sri Lanka blend into sunset. Its beauty will boost your morale, anyway you can see for yourself. ..." She took her daughter's hand and led her onto the balcony.

Rasna gasped as she looked at the sunset of red, gold and grey.

"Amma, you are right, its beauty and splendour have brushed away the problems of the morrow!" She affectionately hugged her mother.

"Mum, maybe I am suspicious of everyone, sorry. Anyway, I am surprised that even after the sumptuous tea, I am famished and looking forward to the delights of dinner! I am also curious to see and taste for myself the famous traditional Sri Lankan food!"

"I am sure you will be delighted with it Rasna, and whilst discovering the cuisine, you can forget your worries: you have already had a taste during teatime, and I can assure you that what is to come will be even better!"

As they went towards the dining room, Urmila, even though she had tried to put on a brave face for her daughter's sake, knew in her heart that Rasna's doubts were justified, for Aadi was conniving and manipulative, and she did not trust her either.

But although Rasna was young, she was wise, for she had pinpointed Kadamba's weakness, mainly that it was his mother who dominated him for he was not strong enough to oppose her; if he was, maybe he would still be happily married?

"Ah there you are, my two girls." Puru smiled.

"Hello Puru." Urmila smiled but looked at her husband warily. "How was the tete-a-tete with your mother?"

"Rasna, my dear, you look lovely." Kadamba smiled at his niece.

Rasna had changed into her favourite black outfit: black jeans with a blue shirt that was open at the collar. Her gleaming black hair and black brows were in sharp contrast to her olive skin, whilst her big almond-shaped eyes were tinged with black lashes that fluttered like wings on her cheeks.

Her black hair, which she usually wore lose down her waist, was tied in a knot at the top of her head, and she moved with a catlike grace as she crossed the room.

"Thank you, Uncle."

"You have a lovely daughter, Puru Magan. There will be no difficulty in getting her married, not at all. Maybe you should get her married whilst you are here?" Aadi chuckled.

"I don't want to get married!" Rasna looked with desperation at her mother, who tried to reassure her with a slight shake of her head.

"Let us eat first, I do not know about all of you, but I am starving. I believe dinner is ready, Amma?" Kadamba sensed the underlying tension in the room,

"Yes, it is," Aadi replied, but not before she had winked at Puru. "I have had your favourite dishes made, sour fish curry that is cooked with sour fruit. You love that, son."

"I do, Amma, but I am full. Well okay, not for that dish, I love it!"

Chapter 33

As they walked into the dining room for the second time that day, Rasna noticed that the setting of the room was the same as before, a servant stood close at hand whilst the cutlery that was displayed on the table glittered and shone. She wished they had such facilities back home, for her mother's sake, who ended up doing the house chores alone for her father, who missed the Sri Lankan cuisine.

As soon as they were seated, the servants bought in steaming bowls of fresh boiled rice, mutton curry, Kang Kung, spinach with chilli and of course her father's favourite, sour fish curry.

"That looks delicious! Sorry everyone, I cannot wait, I am starting," Puru put some plain rice on his plate and filled the little bowls with the different curries.

After forming a round ball of rice dipped in curry, he steered it towards his mouth, taking care the curry did not trickle past his knuckles.

Rasna watched, fascinated, as her father, uncle, grandmother and mother deftly ate with their hands.

As soon as Rasna picked up her spoon, her grandmother glared at her.

"Rasna, you are not in England. When you are here in Sri Lanka, you do things our way. We eat with our hands, the food tastes better."

"She is right, Rasna, it does! Kambada, can you pass me some salt?" Puru added rice on his plate.

As Kadamba passed the salt, Puru thanked him and turned his attention to his food.

Rasna ate a little bit and as soon as she had finished, got up abruptly "Will you excuse me, Grandma, I cannot have any more, I think I will go up to bed."

"But you have hardly eaten anything. Are you feeling all right?" Urmila asked with a frown.

"I am fine, Mum. I have eaten a little, though I would have loved to have had more, the food looks delicious. And Dad, you are right, Sri Lankan food is great and tastes better here. But it has been a long day and tomorrow we will be travelling again… Uncle, what time will we be leaving?"

Before Kadamba could reply her grandmother interrupted.

"Early, well after breakfast of course, but Puru Urmila, why don't you spend Christmas with me? Rasna can leave tomorrow with Kadamba and Praana. I am sure the sisters will have a lot to talk about!"

"Well, we could go later, I suppose…"Puru said

"No!" Urmila interrupted. "The baby is due any time this week, and having come so far, I don't want to miss the happy occasion. Unless, Puru, you want to stay back?"

Urmila usually indulged Puru's every whim and it was she who managed the running of the household. Puru realised this and was grateful and devoted to his wife. Whereas he would have been influenced by her in London, in Sri Lanka it was different; here it was his mother who dominated him, however, he knew his wife was right in this matter.

"Very well, Urmila, we will go together tomorrow, and we will stay with you on our way back, Amma."

Twilight had given way to a dark and moonlit night, and the crescent of the moon looked like a finely sharpened finger beside the evening star.

Rasna left the room whilst they made plans for the morrow, and as soon as she entered their room, quickly changed, and threw herself on the bed. But although her eyelids felt heavy, she could not sleep.

She yawned then went out into the balcony and sat on a chair, admiring the intricate embroidered tablecloth that over the round table. She sat in silence, looking up at the galaxy of stars and listening to the night sounds.

The stillness of the night was seductive and Rasna wearily brushed her hair from her forehead when she heard her mother enter the room.

"Mum, I am out here in the balcony."

"What are you doing there? I thought you would be asleep by now. Are you feeling all right?"

"I am fine, Mum, just having a little think. And you know when I am too tired, I cannot sleep."

"That is what you said earlier, but when I came from the bathroom you were fast asleep! In fact, if I had not woken you, I am sure you would have slept through the night!"

"Maybe that is the reason why I do not feel tired." Rasna remarked

"Anyway, I don't feel like sleeping either, so why don't we just sit outside for a bit and enjoy the tropical weather?"

They sat in silence, the only sound in the stillness being the whirr of the fan from inside the room that was blowing a gentle breeze onto the balcony.

"You missed your favourite pudding." Urmila broke the silence. "Aadi had made Kirti Halva and there was Wattgluppam as well."

"Yummy I would have enjoyed that, but was the feast made only for today, or do people here think of food a lot? I saw stalls of coconuts and…"

"No, today is an exception, but as long as your father is here, your grandma will go out of her way to make your dad's favourite dishes, but in general, yes, there are three meals a day to be organised, plus snacks in between! Oh, I am hot! I going to change into something cooler."

Urmila went into the bathroom after collecting her clothes and Rasna followed her into the room continuing her train of thought.

"Well, it is nice of Grandma and I appreciate her hospitality, but I ate too much at teatime, plus, I did not want to be in the same room as Praana! I know he is my brother-in-law, and I must respect him and all, but my god, he seems to be everything Kirti described, and then some!"

"Don't you think you might be being too harsh on him? Some people are reserved, you know," Urmila shouted from the bathroom.

"I don't understand you and father!" Rasna stamped her foot in exasperation as Urmila entered the room wearing a sarong.

"Whew! That is better, this sarong is cool," She said wiping her forehead "I have lived here all my life but, after staying in London where the weather is much cooler, I cannot get used to the heat!"

"I agree, I need to wash my face with cold water too." Rasna said, but, before she went into the bathroom, she took out the pins from the knot in her hair and her gleaming black hair tumbled down her shoulders to her waist.

"Rasna, you are reading too much into what Kirti told you." Urmila was stretched out on the bed when Rasna remerged from the bathroom.

"No, Mother, I am not," Rasna said as she sat on the bed. "In fact, I think Kirti has not confided everything to me and there is much more to it." She lay on her side, wondering how people slept in this heat.

"Go to sleep now, child, everything will be clearer tomorrow. And, whatever the circumstances, we will support her."

As Rasna's lashes gradually came to rest on her cheeks, she drifted off to sleep, happy in the knowledge that she would be meeting her sister soon.

Chapter 34

The following morning, Rasna opened her eyes slowly, excited at the prospect of meeting Kirti, but when she turned excitedly towards her mother, noticed with surprise she was still fast asleep.

Must be the jet lag, she thought as she shook her gently.

"Amma, Amma are you all right? She shook her gently.

"What? What is the matter?" Urmila got up and hurriedly then looked at her wristwatch. "Oh my God! We are going to be late, why didn't you wake me earlier?"

"No, Mum, we are not late, but you haven't changed the time on your watch!"

"Whew, thank god for that, your grandmother is very particular about mealtimes and I don't want to be in her bad books! Oh, thanks for pointing out about changing time, I clean forgot about it but will it later!"

At that moment there was a knock on the door, and as soon as Rasna said 'come in' a servant came carrying a tray with two steaming cups of tea, placed it on the side table and withdrew.

"How thoughtful of Grandmother. I would love a hot cup of tea."

As soon as she handed her a cup, Puru knocked, opened the bedroom door and entered.

"Puru, you are already dressed! How come?" Urmila poured a cup of tea from the pot. "Would you like a cup?"

"Yes, thank you. Kadamba and I were up early, so, went for a walk, but why are you still in bed? You know how punctual Amma is."

"I am on holiday, you know. Something your mother pointed out."

"I know, I know," however he looked at Rasna quizzically

"Anyway, you better hurry up and get ready, for Praana is impatient to leave after breakfast."

As Urmila went to change, Rasna turned towards her father.

"Dad, what do you think of Praana?"

"Rasna, what a strange question to ask. He is Kirti's husband and seems a genuinely nice young man. Amma guarantees that."

"Dad, he is not a nice person, he is only using his charm to impress you."

"Enough of that, young lady! You have an over- active imagination! Your mum told me that Kirti is unhappy and having problems in the marriage. Well, for your information, I spoke to Amma this morning and she assures me that everything is fine, and that Praana is a good family man with a sense of responsibility. What else would I want, other than that my son-in-law looks after my daughter?"

"Dad, that is just it, he is not looking after her, nor is he making her happy! How can you make light of Kirti's problems just on Grandma's say so? Of course, she will not admit it, she arranged the wedding! And how does she know everything is all right with Kirti? She only went to visit her once and has not spoken to her…"

Urmila entered, heard the end of the conversation and quickly changed the subject for she saw Puru's face had reddened.

"Rasna that is enough, your dad is right!"

"Mum, you are taking his side, I knew it! He never even asked me what the problem was. Come to think of it, you did not either!"

Puru glared at her and had just opened his mouth to speak when Urmila interrupted.

"We discussed this yesterday, Rasna, nothing can be said till we meet Kirti and hear the full story… till then there is no point in making false accusations!"

Rasna stamped her foot in desperation and before running to the bathroom sobbed, "I am just trying to prepare you."

"Urmila, how can you allow your daughter to speak so rudely to me and about my mother? As if we would have anything but the best interest for our daughter! And mother went out of the way to arrange a match she thought was suitable for Kirti."

"I know she does, but it is true that she only visited Kirti once, that too for a brief time. She could have at least phoned her and kept in touch, and that is why Kirti felt isolated from her family, she was in a strange country trying to adapt to strange people," Urmila said angrily.

"I am sure she had her reasons. Anyway, I am going downstairs, make sure you come soon!" Puru stomped out of the room.

As soon as Urmila was dressed and had tied her hair into a bun at the nape of her neck, Rasna walked in from the bathroom wiping her damp hair with a towel.

"Rasna, you better hurry, else we will be late!"

"Won't be long, sorry about earlier. I don't understand you though; I thought you were on my side."

"I am but I cannot let him see that I side with you. He does not see that your frustration only stems from your concern."

Rasna had changed into brown jeans with a white shirt and was plaiting her hair when she asked.

"Mum, did you ask him if he and Grandma have the same thing planned for me? I keep thinking and worrying about it and want to enjoy my holiday."

"Rasna! Be quiet! This is becoming tedious for you keep repeating your concerns and I keep reassuring you! And I would like to inform you, once and for all, that the reason why I agree with your father is so that, when the time comes, he tells me what he and his mother are planning, that is, if they have a scheme, which I doubt. And, by the way, why are you plaiting your hair while it is still damp? You will get a headache…"

"Nooo Mum." Rasna's laughter echoed in the room and lit up her eyes. "It is a quick perm for the hair. When I open the plait after some time, it will be frizzy and permed, hopefully."

"Oh, okay, sounds like a promising idea, saves a trip to the salon. Hurry up Rasna!"

"Mum, don't worry! After all, what can Grandma do if we are late?"

"I refuse to think about that, but I am not afraid of her, just that your father will have a heart attack if I don't follow the rules of the house!" "Oh okay, shall I bring the suitcases down with me?"

"No need for that, Ramu will take care of it."

"Oh, I forgot about that, how I wish we had that sort of help back in London. You know, Mum, I think I will skip breakfast, I really am not very hungry."

"Might be due to the jet lag and change of weather."

"No, it is not only that, just that I wish we would leave immediately instead of wasting time over breakfast, which, I know will be a lengthy affair, for as usual Paat will make have made a feast for her beloved son."

"That Aadi will do, but don't forget, your father has met his family after a long time, so he wants to spend quality time with them. It is not only the food but the love…"

"It was not too long ago, Mother! He met them at Kirti's wedding last year!"

"Rasna, you always have an answer for everything! You have chosen the right profession to get into, you will not lose a case!" "Urmila chuckled "Anyway, you know your father. He believes one should not travel on an empty stomach, oh, and have you remembered to pack all the presents for Kirti?"

"Yes, I have, but, mum, we don't have many for her, shall we give Grandma hers before we leave?"

"We can't, not if they are all still packed; we should have remembered to pack them separately so now, her presents will have to wait."

"Mum, is there a shopping centre here?"

"Yes, of course, why?"

"I did not pack clothes for this weather, so would like to see the market here. On the other hand, I don't want to waste time for I can't wait to get to Matara."

"You could stop at the bazaar, but that would depend on Praana, for he is already impatient to be on the way, that is, after breakfast.. Anyway, you can borrow Kirti's clothes, you should be used to that!"

"Yes, but I have a feeling her taste in clothes has changed, she sent me her snap a couple of weeks ago and all I can say is…Yukk! She told me that Praana and his mother chose her clothes and they were very gaudy and loud, not her type at all, but, if push comes to shove, I suppose I could."

Kadamba was in the sitting room wearing white shorts, red T-shirt with white loafers, and soon as he saw them, rose from his seat.

"Good morning, Urmila, Rasna."

"Good-morning, Kadamba. I believe you have been out jogging with Puru?"

"Not really, more like a walk in the fresh air."

"Wasn't it cold? I could see the morning mist on the green grass."

"No, the weather was exactly right, should we go in for breakfast? I am famished, must be the fresh air!"

Puru, Aadi and Praana were already seated at the table, and as Urmila had predicted, there was a feast laid out on the table.

"Ah there you are!" Praana looked at them impatiently. "We have to hurry, you know."

Rasna looked at him in distaste whilst Urmila looked at her in alarm.

Chapter 35

"Hello Praana Marmagan, why, Aadi, you have gone to so much trouble again!" she said tactfully. "You are spoiling Puru."

On the table was the traditional Sri Lankan breakfast of hoppers, (appam) which were bowl-shaped pancakes and Rasna's favourite Kala Kanda, which was porridge of rice, coconut gran, vegetables and herbs.

Rasna helped herself to Kala Kanda, having forgotten her earlier remark about not being hungry.

"Praana, how far is to Matara?" She turned politely towards Praana.

"Like I said earlier, it will take us about two hours!" Praana answered impatiently. "If we leave immediately after breakfast, we should be there late morning."

"About that, Urmila, I have been talking to Amma and there has been a change of plans," Puru said.

"What change of plans, Puru? You know that I want to be with Kirti as soon as possible for she is due any day, and yesterday you agreed we should leave today."

"I know I did, but, don't worry, it will be fine. I spoke to Praana's mother, and she confirmed that there has been some confusion about the delivery dates, the baby is due end of December and you know how the first baby is always late in arriving!

"Anyway, Urmila, we thought that Rasna and Praana should leave for Matara as originally planned whilst we spend Christmas with mother and Kadamba. I would hate to leave her alone at this time, for I do not know when we will get a chance to spend Christmas together. Most importantly, Kirti and Rasna can spend some time together before we get there.!"

"Mother, I am not going anywhere without you," Rasna exclaimed, horrified at having to spend two hours alone in a car with Praana. "It is already the 24nd today and the baby can come early too so I think you should come with us."

"You know, Rasna, I think they should spend Christmas with Mother, instead I will come with you and Praana. I have not seen Kirti for some time and this seems a good opportunity to do so." Kadamba offered.

He had sensed Rasna was anxious and that the tension was in some way connected to Praana, whom he did not like either. He had recently heard unsavoury things about him and wanted to ensure that his niece was safe.

Urmila knew she would not be able to change Puru's mind for she was sure that if there ever was a choice to be made between his mother and herself, she would surely lose.

"But if Kadamba leaves today, who would take us? Why doesn't he stay back, and I go with Praana? We don't know how to travel to Matara or how to get there."

"Urmila, we have lived here our whole lives! Anyway, we decided it would be the best thing, Urmila, and do not worry how to get to Matara, we will travel on the Samudra Devi." Seeing Urmila's puzzled expression, explained, "Samudra Devi is a train that will take us directly to Matara and Kadamba can pick us up from the station. In fact, whilst we were jogging in the morning, Kadamba booked our tickets for twenty-sixth December."

Although it was December, as the morning had progressed, Rasna was beginning to feel the heat.

"But that is Boxing Day, the day after Christmas! Puru, how could you do this without consulting me? To top it all, you gave no indication of the change of plans this morning, instead, leaving me, no us, with the impression that you will be travelling with us!" Urmila's eyes flashed angrily.

"Mum, don't worry, Dad is right, I will be with Kirti, and it will give us a chance to catch up." Rasna tried reassured her, relieved her Mamu would travel with them. "We will call you as soon as we reach Matara, if it is okay with you, Praana?""

"Of course, it is." Praana answered happily. "you just rest spend some time with Amma, rediscover Colombo and we will see you on the 26th."

"I wanted to spend Christmas with my daughters, but I suppose I can do some shopping for the baby instead," Urmila muttered.

"Yes, you can travel on the Samudra Devi, and in the meantime, like Praana said, I can show you how much Colombo has changed."

"Amma, you seem to have forgotten that I was here last year for Kirti's wedding!" Urmila reminded Aadi.

"Yes, but you were so busy with the wedding, I don't think you had time to notice it."

"True, everything was arranged in a hurry, in fact so hastily that there was no time to perform all the rituals." Urmila sighed.

"Urmila, what is done is done, Amma, may I have some appam please?" Puru asked.

"Yes, of course," Aadi replied as she passed the plate of appam to her son. "Rasna, what would you like?"

"Noting, thank you, Grandma… no, actually I think I will have some fresh fruit."

There was a bowl laden with it at the centre of the table, names of some she knew, and others she had heard about but not tasted.

"I don't think you have this one in London, why don't you try the 'Jak' it is a different kind of guava and very sweet," Kadamba suggested.

"Oh, that does sound nice, but I think I will stick to a pineapple please, Mamu."

Kadamba passed the pineapple and Rasna was enjoying the cool fruit when Aadi said brusquely, "That is settled then, Kadamba, you go with Praana and Rasna whilst Puru and Urmila will spend Christmas with me."

"Dad, I thought you were keen to attend 'Unduvap paya' a tradition that celebrates the arrival of the Bo tree sapling, and that it was the main reason you agreed to come in December, to pay homage to the tree?"

"You are right, Rasna, that is one of the main reasons I came and also why I am staying back in Colombo." Puru glared at her, his face flushed.

"That cannot be true for the tree is in Anuradhapura!""I know that Rasna, are you just showing off your knowledge about our traditions?" Puru glowered at. Rasna who was taken aback so quickly finished her fruit and turned to Praana.

"Right, shall we leave now?"

"Yes, yes, of course," Praana answered, flustered at Puru's sudden outburst.

"Uncle, are you sure you would not like to stay back and celebrate Christmas with your brother and mother?"

"No, he will go with you," Aadi said sharply. "He is here every year whereas your dad…"

"Don't worry, Rasna, Mother is right." Kadamba rose from the table. "Praana, I know you are in a hurry, but I have to take care of some urgent errands, which will only take fifteen minutes. Can you delay our departure please?

"Of course, Kadamba, Actually I was thinking we would stop in Galle and have lunch with my cousin Annama who lives there. And if we leave a little later, we will reach Galle just in time for lunch. It will also give Rasna a chance to see as much as possible of our beautiful island." Although he smiled, his eyes still looked cold and distant.

"I would like that very much, Praana, that is very thoughtful of you." However, she cringed at the mention of his cousin Annama and saw that the stage was being set. Had she made a mistake in trusting her parents?

Whilst they waited for Kadamba, Rasna helped herself to a mango.

"Dad, apparently I don't know much our traditions, tell me about this festival you are so eager to attend?"

"I thought you knew it all! Anyway, Undavap Paya commerates Sangamtha, who accompanied her brother Mahiotra to Sri Lanka to get a cutting from the sacred Buddha tree."

"Is that the famous tree which is in Anapardha? And how and when do you plan to go to Anapardha?"

Puru glared at her however, when he replied, his tone was encouraging. "That is very impressive, Rasna, I did not know you knew so much about Sri Lanka."

"Well it is all due to Mother. She has ensured that we do not forget our roots by always telling us legends and stories." Rasna reluctantly dipped and scraped her spoon into the last mango slice.

"Rasna, if you are ready, we will wait in the sitting room for Kadamba. Is your luggage ready?" Praana asked.

Rasna nodded, and as they went into the sitting room, Aadi called to the servant to take Rasna's luggage to Praana's car.

"Would you like some tea or 'Thomboli' whilst you are waiting Puru, Urmila?"

"I'll have tea please…" Puru piped up, sitting on the sofa and crossing his legs.

"Tea for me too, Amma, my migraine is getting worse!" Urmila brushed her hand across her forehead.

"Not for me, Grandma." Rasna strolled over to the side table which was full of photographs. "Dad, is this you?" She pointed to a photograph and bought it over to Puru.

Chapter 36

"Yes, it is Rasna."

Puru's eyes grew misty as he looked at the smiling girl looking up at him in the photograph.

When Rasna saw the sadness on her father's face, assumed the girl to be his sister Lakshmi, so hurriedly placed the photo back on the side-table.

"Rasna, if you want to see your dad when he was young, I have an album here you can have a look at while you wait for Kadamba. I do not know what is taking him so long! "she snapped "Oh, and I have an album of your parents' wedding too."

"Oh, that one I would definitely like to see for there are only a few photos in the album we have in London."

"That is because Puru wanted to take this with him, but I didn't let him!" Aadi grinned impishly.

"Rasna, you can see them some other time." Urmila interrupted "I don't think you will have time to go to the market now, if you tell me what you need, I will bring them later."

"Ok, well, not much, just a few dresses, and something nice for the baby. I could not find anything nice in London… Jewellery I think would be great too. Oh, and Grandma, can I take the albums with me? Kadamba Chitappa can explain, and I am sure Kirti would like to see them as well. I know how much they matter to you, so I will bring them back."

"All right, Rasna, as long as you take care of them, they are of great sentimental value to me!"

"And I will find something for you too, don't worry. Amma, as far as I remember, Pettah is the best place for shopping, isn't it?" Urmila asked.

"Yes, it still is, and if you remember, it is situated in an old district of Colombo. Do you want me to come with you?"

"Thanks, Amma, but I have just remembered the horrible smell of bloody meat and rotting fruit and vegetables! So Rasna, nothing for you I am afraid, you will have to explain to Kirti, who, I am sure will not mind lending you her clothes/"

"Don't worry about it Mum," Rasna tried to assure her.

However, Puru looked puzzled.

"Urmila, you must have gone at the wrong time and spot for Pettah market is huge and not at all smelly! I would like to take you there, for I loved going to Pettah when I was young, in fact it was one of my favourite haunts."

"That it was, I remember it well!" Aadi confirmed "I had a tough time in persuading him to come home!"

Aadi's smile lit up her face, but although Urmila could not picture her as ever being a young woman, she was sure she must have been beautiful. She reckoned she had only become hard and cynical after her husband's death, for she had not only became a widow at an early age but had the responsibility of bringing up three children alone. Urmila found it strange that Puru's father was never mentioned in conversation, nor was there a photograph of him in Aadi's house, which made her suspect there was more to his death than met the eye.

She had broached the subject to Puru once tentatively, and he had finally shared his pent-up emotions about his father.

He had finally disclosed to her that his father had been one of the few Tamils in the Sinhala government who had been an informer, passing on Tamil info to the Singhalese government. It was on his inaccurate information that there had been rioting and killing, and many innocent people had been killed on July 1983, a day that was thereafter called Black Friday. Many people knew of Puru's father's involvement, so Aadi, fearing a reprisal against the family, had persuaded Puru to leave Sri Lanka, whilst Kadamba, who had believed in justice for the tigers, had joined the LLTE.

Urmila had told Rasna about it because she too was curious to learn about her grandfather. However, this information had made Rasna wonder if her mother was aware of the underlying reason of their marriage? Mainly, that Aadi had only urged her son to marry Urmila because she was a ex-Tamil tiger, a union, she felt, that would somehow atone for her husband's half-truth information given to the intelligence, information that had had many innocents people killed.

Puru's father had been extremely fond of Laxmi, and his death had hit her hard, so soon afterwards, when she met Sarvash, a married man of her father's age, she had turned to him, needing him to fulfil the void in her life, a need that Aadi, despite her forceful personality, could not meet, for her nature was not warm and affectionate.

Rasna looked at her grandmother's austere face and wondered if she missed Laxmi, or at the very least, felt remorse that had she managed the matter differently, and that had she shown her the love that her daughter so desperately sought, her daughter would still be alive?

Rasna was impatient to be on her way, whilst Praana sat quietly, his hands lying motionless on his lap. However, his attitude appeared to be deceptively like that of a leopard, who although appeared to be sleepy and drowsy, was only waiting to pounce on his prey.

Kadamba entered the room, rubbing his hands "Thank God that is over and done with! Now we can leave. Praana, have you decided on the route?"

"Of course, I have! Remember we discussed it over breakfast? However, I will go through it again." Praana quickly outlined the trip to Matara and Galle in a few quick sentences, emphasising his words with gestures of his long-fingered hands.

"Sorry, Praana, you are right, I forgot, we had discussed it - it sounds perfect, so we can leave anytime"

"Kadamba, why don't you wait till Praana and Rasna finish their tea?" Aadi snapped.

Rasna glared at her for she was beginning to dislike her.

"It's all right, Paat, I am in a hurry to leave anyway," Rasna snapped, but when she saw her father glaring at her angrily, continued politely, "We are planning to stopover at Galle anyway."

"Rasna, now that your route has been decided on, and after you leave, Puru, I suggest that once Urmila has had a rest, you have tea at the Galle Face Hotel and watch the sunset from there. You have always loved that place. And Puru, whilst Urmila is resting, we can take a walk."

Rasna could not help but notice how her grandmother had organised everybody's timetable according to her convenience.

"Why from the Galle Face Hotel, what is so special about that place?" Rasna asked

"Rasna, you have forgotten!" Urmila exclaimed "I have told you that story so many times! I used to watch the sunset from the Galle Face Hotel with your dad, it is such a beautiful place that I can't wait to visit it again."

"Why particularly the Galle Face Hotel?" Rasna repeated, looking puzzled. "I am sure there are other places too, and Amma, I thought yours was an arranged wedding?"

"It is an ideal view from that spot; it overlooks the sea and has a giant size chessboard. And Rasna, ours was an arranged marriage, we just met once or twice before the wedding." She winked at her husband as she rose from her chair. "Your grandmother is right, I need to rest so am going to lie down to nurse my migraine, as I want to enjoy the sunset at the Galle Hotel! Be sure to give lots of love and hugs to Kirti and we will see you all on the 26th!"

"Puru, will you wake me in an hour's time?" Urmila asked as she too rose.

"Yes, I will, Urmila, can I get you something that might help?" Puru looked concerned for Urmila looked pale. "Aspirin or something?"

"Puru, we have to go!" Aadi interrupted. "We'll only be gone for an hour."

"Amma, I don't want to leave Urmila…"

"Puru, don't fuss! If she needs something there are servants in the house."

"Yes, yes don't mind me, you must not miss your exercise or whatever else you will be doing." Urmila said sarcastically and with a quick 'excuse me' went to her room.

She took the eau de cologne she carried with her for just such an emergency, drew the curtains, dipped her handkerchief in the cologne, closed her eyes and placed it over her eyes.

Puru walked with Praana and Kadamba to the car.

"Goodbye for now, Kadamba and Praana. Look after my daughters and we will see you on the 26th."

"Bye, Dad." Rasna hugged her father, opened the car door, and slid into the back seat.

Chapter 37

As soon as they had left, Puru and his mother left for a walk, and as soon as they had returned, Puru went straight to Urmila's room.

He took the handkerchief from her forehead. "Urmila, are you awake? How are you feeling now?"

He put the palm of his hand on her forehead to make sure she was not running a temperature, which thankfully she was not.

Urmila sat up with a smile. "I am much better, Puru. You know the only way to treat these migraines is to dab eau de cologne on my forehead and an hour's sleep! And hey presto, it is but a distant memory, till next time, that is. Anyway, how was your walk and talk with Amma? And have Rasna and Praana left?"

"It was not really a walk and talk, as you put it, Mother just needed to run an errand and yes, Rasna Kadamba and Praana have left. Now, we have the afternoon to ourselves, so what say we go to Pettah market and from there to the Galle Face Hotel as Amma suggested? Are you up for it?"

"Oh yes," Urmila exclaimed, getting up from the bed and patting the pleats of her sari in place. "I will first need to freshen up and a cup of tea would be lovely."

"I will have Ramu bring us some..... "

"Perfect," Urmila said over her shoulder as she disappeared into the bathroom.

As soon as she re-entered the room, feeling and looking rejuvenated, she saw that Ramu had already brought them tea and Puru had poured himself a cup. He poured one for her and handed it to Urmila.

"Whew! After that headache, I really needed this," Urmila said, taking a sip. "Now, how are we going and are you sure Amma will not mind us leaving her alone?"

"No, I don't think so, she suggested it, remember? And as I recall, you said the market only smelt of rotten fruit and vegetables! I take it you did not mean it?" Puru chuckled. "We will have the driver take us to the market first."

"Oh, I did, and it did smell!!" Urmila exclaimed, wondering as to the motive behind her mother-in-law's suggestion, for normally she liked her son to stay close to her.

The driver dropped them at Pettah market and Urmila was surprised at the crowds.

"Puru, I remember the last time I was here… it was awful!" She wrinkled her nose.

"Last time you went to the wrong end of the market. Here, follow me."

As he led the way, Urmila saw that the shop windows were crammed with precious and semi-precious stones. There were a variety of them, some with cat's eyes and a hundred others that were strange.

A man hurried after her trying to sell his product whilst a woman gestured at a basket lying at her feet, a basket that was crammed with ebony elephants and carved ivory. She was admiring the ebony elephants and other products in the basket when she was pushed by a woman carrying a basket of fruit on her head.

There were shopkeepers who were laying out their foods on their stalls, whilst fishmongers called out their wares and little boys and girls crawled through the crowds, gathering crumbs of food.

"Oh Puru, how sad!" Urmila remarked when she saw the children scrambling for food. "This makes one realise just how lucky we are."

After having spent an hour at the market, Urmila wiped her forehead.

"Puru, I think we better go to Galle Face Green, it is too hot and crowded here and I would love a cool drink of coconut water."

"I second that." Puru stopped an auto rickshaw, and as soon as he had told him the destination and having agreed upon a fare, they climbed into it.

As it drove down the promenade leading to the Green, Urmila noticed there were not only carts but stalls selling all manners of soft drinks.

"You know, Puru, each time I come here is seems like the first!"

"Maybe because it does not change, and also due to the atmosphere of the place," Puru remarked than added, "I wonder if they still sell spicy prawn bites and bags of sliced pineapple that are soaked with pepper and oil?"

"Puru! You are always thinking of food!" exclaimed Urmila.

"Of course, what else is there?" Puru grinned.

The Tuk Tuk dropped them at Green, which was magnificent, it had the backdrop of the Indian ocean on one side and high-rise developments on the other.

They strolled down to the hotel and passed families with children who were either flying colourful kites, playing cricket, football or having a picnic on the Green. And on the southern side of the green was the famous majestic Galle Face Hotel, the oldest hotel in Sri Lanka.

When Puru saw courting couples strolling along the promenade looking into each other's eyes, he turned to his wife.

"Urmila, do you remember we met here whilst our marriage proposal was being discussed? I was expecting an interrogation by you, for my mother had told me that you had been in the women's rebel army. I had expected you to be strong and dominating, in fact, I had come prepared to reject you, but you were not at all what I expected, you were very beautiful and uhh ..feminine!""

"I remember that time too, Puru" Urmila looked affectionately at her husband. "But I don't know whether to take that as a compliment or not! You were not what I expected either, and I was also going to reject the marriage proposal. What a time that was! I was telling Rasna that this place has a great deal of sentiment and memories associated to it, for me at least."

"Yes, it has, hasn't it?" Puru put his arm around Urmila. and with a twinkle in his eye asked." But tell me, what was there about me that changed your mind? Was I so dashing and handsome that you could not refuse?"

"Puru, I am getting tired, "Urmila smiled shyly, tactfully changing the subject" I think we should head back; it has been a long day." Urmila wearily brushed her hand across her forehead.

"I hope it is not your headache again?"

"No, no headache, thank God. I meant we should leave soon; you know that the restaurants will be opening soon and there will be an aroma of fresh smell of spices!"

"Urmila are you suggesting, in your sweet way, that I will be tempted by them?" He looked sheepish, but then grinned ruefully. "Okay, Urmila, you are right, it would be tempting, but, honestly, I would much rather have Amma's home cooked food, for she knows exactly what I like and even how I like it!"

"Okay, Puru, but not before I have had one of those!" She pointed to a stall which was selling green coconuts that were opened at the top and overflowing with rich coconut milk.

"Sorry, I forgot you wanted to have coconut water… actually I wouldn't mind one of those too!"

He quickly bought two, handed one to Urmila than stood drinking the cool coconut milk whilst looking out at the blue sea.

After they had finished, Urmila tugged at Puru's sleeve.

"I see a vacant Auto rickshaw, Puru, let's grab it while we can!"

When they arrived at the Villa, Aadi was waiting outside, and as soon as she saw them waved to them.

"About time you were here! Tea is ready, I hope you have not eaten anything. Urmila, did you buy anything for the baby?"

"No, Amma we have not eaten - how could I miss your cooking?" He grinned.

"And we didn't have time to look around in the market, so no nothing was brought for either the baby or Rasna."

Chapter 38

Praana drove out of Aadi's bungalow which was situated in one of Colombo's best residential areas. Cinnamon road had long gone, but the whole area, with its crossroads and crescents, stately homes and gardens, was still Colombo's posh residential area.

They passed Cinnamon Gardens whose main charm were the large trees that lined the road. A gentle breeze wafted through the palm trees causing their leaves to sway and the brightness of the sun outlined every leaf, branch and blade with clarity. There were flowering shrubs of infinite variety and Rasna admired the creepers that scrambled abundantly not only on roofs but on the pillars of some houses.

They passed the waterfront, the streets and the great buildings and the never-ending ebb and flow of people.

"You worked out the route?" Kadamba asked, before he realised that Praana had done just that before leaving.

"Of course, I have! I told you earlier, twice!" Praana answered impatiently. "We will be travelling on the Galle Road."

"Oh Chitappa, is that the one that is supposed to be long?"

"Yes, Rasna, that is the largest road we have here, and it extends to all destinations! And as I stated yesterday, I will explain about the countryside and its surroundings as we go along."

"I would like that, Chitappa, thank you, everything here is so beautiful, green and exotic I don't want to miss anything!"

"But if you get bored or sleepy, let me know!" Kadamba grinned into the face mirror where he could see Rasna's reflection. "We are now passing a temple, in which there are a lot of statues of gods, some bronze of wild spirits with green faces."

"That sounds interesting, but Chitappa, do we have to go to Galle?" Rasna asked impatiently and when Praana nodded, continued, "Oh all right, Praana, but tell me about Matara."

"With pleasure, now, Matara is a small place, which has, over time, been occupied by the Dutch, Portuguese and English so has been influenced by all three. But, one of the main things to see is the Parey Dewa Rock."

"A rock!" exclaimed Rasna. "What could there be anything to see there?"

"Well, it is not ordinary rock, but a rock that is in water that is a Buddhist temple now."

"Oh right," Rasna said looking out of the window.

Praana ignored her look of boredom, for he loved Matara and just needed an opportunity to brag about its historic features.

"There is Weragamipta, this also is a Buddhist temple and is the site of the sacred big tree, as well as the Matara Bodhiya – a Dutch reformed church."

"Are there shopping malls?" Rasna asked, smiling slightly, for Mark always teased her that her hobby and favourite pastime was shopping.

Praana smiled slightly as he slowed the car.

"There is the Nupe market, but I don't think it would be of any interest to you, one part sells fruit and vegetable, and the other meat and fish. Though I think there is a small portion that sell textiles and household items. I am not keen on that sort of stuff myself but can always take you there after Christmas."

"Thank you" Praana," Rasna replied "but I don't think that would be possible, for it will be very difficult for Kirti, but as we will be collecting Mum and Dad from the station, we won't have time, anyway, the market does not sound interesting."

"Don't worry, we will think of something interesting to do! Oh, and we won't be collecting your parents from the station, they will be getting off at Galle to meet my cousin, Annama, who after lunch, will bring them to Matara."

"Oh, I did not know about the change, but no worries, I will ask Kirti about the sightseeing spots worth visiting in Matara, so you won't have to worry about me. She will tell me everything there is to know and make it seem interesting too!"

"Ah, Kirti won't be of any help there I am afraid., she has not seen Matara at all."

"I find that hard to believe., Praana, Kirti is an adventurous kind of girl who loves to explore a new city."

"I asked her many times that we should go out, but she always refused, said she would rather stay home."

"Kirti refused to explore a new place?" Rasna exclaimed. "That is a surprise, maybe marriage has changed her and to be honest, I would rather spend time with my sister at home rather than go sightseeing. Maybe we will walk to nearby places and…"

"Any kind of physical effort is difficult for her, so she won't be able to travel to nearby places either," Praana mocked. "She is too fat and can barely walk!"

Both Rasna and Kadamba were shocked at his tone and snide remarks and looked at each other in disbelief.

"Praana! She is expecting your child and must take extra care of herself at the moment. But surely she must have gone out with you when she first came to Matara after your honeymoon?"

"We did not have a honeymoon, Kadamba," Praana said quietly "Amma was not well so we had to cancel it to look after her. This might sound strange to you I know, but even after my mother's recovery, Kirti did not bother to visit the few tourist spots in Matara,"

"Praana, wasn't it your duty to show your new bride around?" Kadamba laughed. "A young bride new to the place? Did you expect her to go out on her own?"

Praana looked disconcerted, thinking how offensive and disrespectful his remarks must have sounded. He cursed himself for letting his guard down for he was trying desperately to appear noble and decent.

He was not the marrying kind and had only agreed to it when he heard who her father was. There were two important motives behind his approval, one of them being that Kirti's grandfather had deviated from the beliefs and values of the Tamil and become an informant for the Singhalese government. Not only had he digressed from Tamil's way of life, but he had played a key role in their massacre, and the second concerned her father,

In addition to the above, Kirti was a very gentle and timid girl, and being a bully by nature, it was important to Praana that she be vulnerable and defenceless, someone he could control and manipulate.

Chapter 39

Kadamba saw a momentary look of loathing on Rasna's face as she heard the nastiness in Praana's voice and was suddenly afraid for Kirti. He remembered her as being a sweet girl and regretted he had not been to see her.

However, he had suggested it to his mother, but, as usual, his suggestion was met with indifference.

"She is not a child, she should be left alone to adjust to her new family, and if there any problems, I am sure she will be able to deal with them!"

"But Amma, she is in a new country with people she does not know. She must be feeling lonely, and her family should stand by her. We promised Puru we would look after her!"

"Kadamba, what has come over you? Praana is a good boy and I know her mother, they are a good family."

That is the only time Kadamba had spoken to his mother about Kirti and having sensed his mother's unsympathetic attitude, had not broached the subject again.

However, listening to Praana, the unkind tone of his voice and stony expression on his face, he recalled a conversation with one of his friends when he had casually mentioned Praana.

"Your niece is married to that man! Be careful, he is not a nice man."

But when he had asked for details as to why he thought so, his friend had refused to give a plausible reason. Kadamba, therefore, had ignored him and concluded it was only a piece of useless rumour that was most probably instigated by jealousy.

Kadamba was sure now that there had been something his friend was not telling him about Praana, followed by an uneasy thought of how much, or how little, his mother really knew about them? He had not known his mother to have many friends, and had they been close, as his mother had led everyone to believe, he would surely have met them.

Rasna meanwhile, closed her eyes and thought of Mark. She had tried to phone him, but he was not available, so had left a voicemail detailing her plans. All being well, he too would have left for Thailand by now.

As she was still suffering from jet lag she had dozed off when Praana's voice boomed in the car.

"Rasna, wake up, you have been sleeping and missed all the scenery."

"Er… sorry are we there?"

"Well, we have reached Galle, Rasna. We will stop here for lunch," Praana said as he drove into an impressive looking hotel. "My cousin will meet us for lunch here and Matara is only 45 kilometres from here," he said getting out of the car. "Anyway, like I said earlier, this will give you an opportunity to see as much of Sri Lanka as you can."

"That is very considerate of you Praana, but as it is only 45 kilometres we could have driven straight on and had lunch with Kirti."

"Rasna, Praana is right, and we should be thinking of him for he must be tired and stressed, driving in this heat is no joke and we still have an hour to go! Anyway, you always say you are not hungry and then enjoy the food!" There was a twinkle in Kadamba's eyes.

"Sorry Chittapa, I am being inconsiderate, and you are right, I always enjoy the food here!" She got out of the car and blinked for the sunlight was glaring. She rummaged in her bag and took out her shades.

"Whew! It is hot!" she remarked as she put them on.

"Breaking the journey here will give you a chance to stretch your feet and have some cool thambilli. I know I could do with some!"

"Kadamba Chitappa, I think you were spot-on, the idea of lunch and a cool drink does sound tempting." Rasna remarked as she followed her uncle and Praana into the hotel, for she had begun to feel the pangs of hunger.

As soon as they were seated at the table, the waiter handed them a menu list, and as soon as they had ordered, Rasna decided to phone her mother.

"Uncle, she was not feeling very well, can I use the mobile here?"

"Your mobile will not work here, but you are welcome to use mine, I have the home number stored under speed-dial."

To her surprise, her dad answered. "Dad! I thought you had gone out with Grandma. How is Mother?"

"We only went out for about half an hour, but have you already reached Matara? How is Kirti, can I speak to her?"

"No, Dad, we are not in Matara but stopped for lunch in Galle, so whilst waiting thought I would find out how Amma was feeling, she had a headache when we left.".

"She is still sleeping and later, if she feels up to it, we might go to Pettah market and Hotel Galle, did you want to speak to her?"

"No, Dad, I just wanted to find out how she was and to tell her that there is no need for her to shop for me. Praana just told me that there is a bazaar in Matara on the 26th..if and if you are not too tired we can go the market after we pick you from the station?" She was going to end the conversation when she recalled the change of plans. "I have just remembered, Dad, there has been a change of plans, yet again! Praana told us has that you will drive down with his cousin from Galle so we will go the market later? Kirti would love that I am sure, anyway, give my love to Mum and I will call again when we reach Kirti's house."

"Rasna, you know I don't like your kind of shopping, especially after travelling, and don't you go dragging your sister around!" Puru snapped.

"Okay Dad, love you too!" Rasna tried desperately trying to change the subject.

"I don't know much about these things but remember that Kirti is expecting... your mum will definitely want to stay with her... at home!"

"Okay okay, Dad, chill, we can sort that out once you get here. Kirti can stay home or mum and myself can go... anyway, either way it is not important."

She gave a sigh of relief as she switched off the mobile as the waiter came with fish curry for Praana and a meat dish for Kadamba and herself with the usual side dishes of a variety of sambols.

"Praana, this looks delicious!" Rasna helped herself to a Papadum and crumbled it in her plate.

"I am glad you like our food, do you have Sri Lankan food in London?"

"Of course! Father would have nothing else, but somehow the food does not taste the same there. And now I see why he loves coming to Sri Lanka, for not only is the food delicious here, Grandma pampers him by making his favourite dishes!"

Praana took the bowl of plain rice and dished out a few spoons on his plate. He then took the various sambols and put them in the bowls provided.

"Maybe it is the climate, together with the fact you are on holiday and relaxed."

Praana was busy eating, and watching him Rasna was fascinated, for he was eating food by applying the same technique her father had used earlier. Praana first separated the boiled rice on his plate than gradually added the sambol. He formed a round ball then put it in his mouth, careful not let the curry slip through his fingers. Her father did not eat in this manner in London, so Rasna assumed that this was his way of blending in with the Sri Lankan society?

"I thought your cousin was joining us for lunch?" Rasna enquired as she helped herself to some boiled rice and sambol.

"I am afraid he will not be able to make it, some work emergency. Anyway, you can meet him on the twenty-sixth, for he will be coming down with my aunt and your parents."

"Oh, so the trip to Galle was wasted! I could have been with Kirti by now!" Rasna exclaimed angrily.

Kadamba saw that his niece was upset so quickly intervened.

"Rasna, calm down, we spoke about this earlier. Stopping in Galle was not only about meeting Annama, Praana too needed a break from driving. I am sure he meant well and did not realise how impatient you were to be with Kirti. The other reason being that by choosing this route, he wanted you to visit Galle, be it as a detour, for believe me, after Colombo, tourists come down to see Galle. Am I right, Praana?"

"Yes, you are!"

"Sorry, Chitappa, I did not mean to sound ungrateful, but I haven't really seen much, I mean we have to explore the city to appreciate its many splendours."

"It is not only the city that is magnificent, but the countryside too, and that you are not aware of its beauty because you had dozed off and missed it all – the beautiful beaches and the exotic beauty of the countryside, anyway, apart from all that, it is best to give the person who is driving a rest, especially in this heat, which I am sure you must be feeling intensely."

"Maybe" Rasna nodded her head then glared at Praana's smug face.

As soon as they had finished their lunch, a waiter came up with a bowl of clean, scented water for them to dip/clean their fingers.

They paid their bill and walked down to the car in quietly, listening to the noise of the traffic, and as there was a slight breeze, Rasna could see the leaves swaying on the trees.

As they drove, Rasna asked impatiently, "How far is it?"

"Not far now, Rasna," Praana replied. "Oh, the beach we are passing is known as the Polhena beach. It is one the quietest and cleanest around here and, since you enjoy shopping, one of Matara's specialities is Batik."

"Oh, I love Batik, but am surprised Kirti did not mention this for she loves Batik too." Surely it must be because she was not aware of it, and how could she be if Praana did not permit her to leave the house?

"Not only Batik, there are a variety of brass and metal, but you will find that out for yourself."

"I am already looking forward to it, but of course only if Kirti is up to it." Rasna looked out of the window at the beautiful beach with the sea waves gently licking the shore of the white sand.

"Don't worry, Rasna, we will come here again later." Kadamba smiled as he saw the wistful look on her face.

"Yes, of course we will. Oh, over there is Dilwala bridge." With one hand on the wheel, he waved with the other at a bridge.

"We must see the 25-foot Buddha statue at Veharana temple. I have lived in Sri Lanka for so long, but still haven't got round to seeing it!"

"Well, now's your chance. We'll make a plan for the twenty-seventh or twenty-eighth to see these places."

Praana was being so thoughtful and considerate that Rasna was finding his consideration disturbing, for it was unlike him to be so kind. Was he preparing the ground, and if so, what for?

Chapter 40

"So tell me, Chitipa, everything is so lavish here, the weather no nice, why did my father leave it all for London?" Although her mother had told her, she wanted to hear from her uncle.

"Didn't he tell you?" Kadamba looked at her in surprise. "You know there has always been trouble with the Singhalese Govt and the Tamil Tigers?"

"What has that got to do with Father? But come to think of it, Mother did mention that something major had happened in July of 1983? She was actively involved for some time I believe, and 1983 was around the time Father came to London?"

"Yes, that was a terrible day, and is now known as Black July. That day a lot of innocent Tamils were killed, and motorists were dragged from cars and beaten. Mobs of youngsters ran through the streets, ransacking homes shops and offices of ethnic minorities, well, of Tamils mainly then they set them on fire."

"These particular atrocities you are mentioning were happening before that day too, but that that particular day was the worst," Praana added.

"Didn't the army do anything to stop it?" Rasna asked, shocked.

"No, they did not, some people said they even encouraged it!"

"That sounds awful! Tell me more about it, Chitipa. When I ask Mum, she avoids the subject, as does Father, but as Mother was in the liberation army, she must have felt strongly about the cause."

"Well, there were riots between the Tamils and Singhalese, but it actually started, as Praana pointed out, long before that day when cars and buses were burnt, but that is not the reason why Puru left."

"No?" Rasna asked, feeling confused.

"No, at that time the LTTE recruited young boys to fight for them, actually one child, sometimes two, from each family so Amma thought it best Puru left the country."

"OMG!" Rasna exclaimed. "So how did you manage to escape recruitment?"

"My dear girl, I did not escape, I was enlisted by them." Kadamba looked at gently. "I had already been recruited and was a member, and if one child is, they target the younger child too. But Amma foresaw that, so, before they had a chance to enforce their rule arranged your father to leave for London."

"But Uncle, you are so kind and gentle, I cannot imagine you undertaking anything violent, or even thinking about it!"

"It is nice of you to say so, and you are right, I don't like violence. Luckily, I did not get a chance to be so for I was discharged soon after, would you believe it, just because I broke my leg!""

Praana had been listening silently fidgeting in his seat and Rasna turned towards him.

"How did you manage to escape being drafted?" She asked Praana "Err I was very young and…" Praana replied gruffly.

Why was Praana evading her question? She felt she understood her father better, first having to deal with Lakshmi's tragedy then the political issues in the country. Maybe those were the reasons that made him over-protective and suspicious?

"Uncle, I am surprised that a country as beautiful as Sri Lanka could harbour such violence in their country. So far, I have only met nice people, but having said that, I have only been here for a day! Well, nice people, with exceptions of course," she muttered under her breath, looking at Praana.

However, she smiled and asked "So, Praana, Kirti said you were with the police?"

"No, not anymore," Praana mumbled. "I have my plantation business."

"Oh yes, of course, Paat did mention it."

Praana did not want to tell them that during those terrible years, he had been a student. That was a time when he was coming to term with the sudden death of his father, a time when idealism was high amongst the students, especially the senior ones. Although Praana had been a junior at that time, the senior students had somehow persuaded him and his friends to go on strike, an act which displayed defiance and one which the government had not taken kindly to.

Somehow, they had unearthed his address, and one day they had turned up at his house. They dragged him to a jeep, taken him to an isolated house then shoved him into an empty room with only a chair in it.

"Why did you go on strike? Who told you to do so? Tell us their names?"

He had no information to give them so he was beaten so badly for two days that his skin had split, he was spat on, and just when he thought things could not get any worse, he was hose-piped on his back, chest and thighs. And after some time, the split skin on his back dried and became crusts, and for food he was sometimes thrown scraps of bread.

And all the time they shouted at him "Confess! Confess you know who was behind the strikes!"

What could he say? He cowered against the walls, denying everything, and the truth was he really did not know, and even if he had, he would not want to grass on them.

His uncle, his mother's brother-in-law, too had not escaped their cruelty. He remembered the tragic night with amazing clarity, for that night the street had been echoing with gunfire. This had been followed by the faint sound of scuttling feet which had grown louder till they reached their house - after which he had heard a scuffle and the echo of heavy breathing and wondered what had happened?

Instead of going to bed, he had gone to his bedroom window curiously and seen a policeman first chasing his uncle, then catching him just as he was trying to jump over a fence. After they had dragged him down, they had first kicked then smashed their boots in his face, thinking he was a rebel, which he was not.

These men wanted to terrorise and control the rebels, some of these men, he later found out, were gang members whilst others, to his surprise, were from the police!

His had seen his uncle, whom he loved as a father, first helpless and broken at their hands then die slowly of his injuries soon after. His aunt's grief at his torture and subsequent death had made her, together with his mother, vow revenge on the culprits.

How could she forget that it was Puru's father who had been one of informants for the police and government? They were sure that it was because of him that his father, uncle, and many others had been killed.

Aadi had wanted Puru to leave Colombo because she was afraid that some group or gang member of the rebels, or even a family member of the many innocent families he had had killed, would want to seek revenge.

And she was right, for Praana, his mother, and his cousin Annama had been weaving their web for a while, but, unbeknown to most, it was not only for that reason alone.

His mind recreated the death of his uncle, father, and of many other fathers and brothers who had been dragged out of their houses and burnt, of the innocent women who had been raped and killed.

After that trauma, Praana and Annama had not only came to hate Singhalese authority, but everything they had once respected – which was a just and fair law and orders system. His relative's death, and those of his many friends, had adversely affected him and his behaviour had changed dramatically.

So much so that his mother, Ruvini was worried, but when she spoke to the other mothers whose sons had gone through the same situation, their advice had been the same. That under these circumstances, all Ruvini could do was to help him put his life together again, but to do that he first needed to regain his confidence in their justice system but how was that possible?

When Ruvini had found out that it was Puru's father who was responsible for the torture and deaths of many, she had vowed that she would avenge the deaths of her husband, brother-in-law, and many others. This thirst for revenge she had instilled in Praana and Annama, and she did so by continuously reminding them of the arrests, beating, abuse and torture of their relatives and friends and the person responsible for it.

Ever since Ruvini found about Puru, she had closely monitored and subtly manipulated the incidents in Aadi's life, the tragedy with Lakshmi and Puru's marriage. She respected Urmila and Kadamba, but felt nothing but contempt for Puru for fleeing his country.

Finally, her family had come up with a plan – they would create a set of circumstances, by way of which Praana could easily access Aadi's house, in short become a mole. She knew Puru had daughters of marriageable age and her own son and nephew were of marriageable age too; what better way was there other than get them married and once Puru's daughter was her daughter in law…!

"Looking forward to being a dad, Praana?" Rasna smiled disarmingly, unaware of the web they had been caught in

She looked out of the window at the fields of wildflowers, with streaks of yellow, crimson and orange. They were vivid colours and looked as if they had been woven into the grass.

However, she did not like the politics of the country - for she did not think of herself as being either Tamil or Singhalese, only Sri Lankan. Although her mother had told her about the situation numerous times, the different beliefs and traditions of each one had seemed trivial, yet it seemed that in Sri Lanka it was important, and she said so to her uncle.

"Yes, it is unfortunate there are still some extreme people, but we are hoping to come to some kind of reconciliation soon."

"That is a relief, so Praana, living amidst it all, you would know first-hand?"

"Let us talk of something pleasant Rasna, how long are you planning on staying with us?" Praana tried to change the subject.

"Not for long, I have to get back to sit for my university, in fact I was not sure I would join Mum and Dad on this vacation, anyway, coming back to the so called 'situation of the country'…"

Praana interrupted, "I do not want to frighten you, but actually I am afraid for your dad. Most people know your grandfather worked for the Government so some might think of that as a betrayal and want vengeance!"

"Praana, stop worrying the poor girl! I hope you have not said anything like this to Kirti, she should not worry at this time. And Rasna, there is no cause for concern," he looked angrily at Praana. "I have lived here without any intimidation from anyone."

"Uncle, I think you're right, for he came last year and nothing untoward occurred." Rasna glowered at her brother-in-law.

"You know my uncle was killed, and my father too," Praana said, placing his foot on the brake.

Rasna had always wondered about Praana's father and this was the first time he had been mentioned him, however briefly.

"Oh, I am sorry to hear that, Praana, and here I was talking casually about it, had I known how closely it had affected you I would not have… " Kadamba said hastily. "I think we have all lost someone close to us in some way or another."

"Ah here we are, at last."

Chapter 41

They pulled into a street and Rasna gasped as she saw a house that was so beautiful it surpassed her grandmother's house in its splendour.

Amongst the manicured lawn and flowerbeds, there stood a white bungalow, but what was striking was the ivy climbing up the walls of the house. There were flower buds on the ivy, some pale pink others yellow.

Standing in the veranda were Kirti, waiting eagerly and looking heavily pregnant, and Praana's mother, for Praana had telephoned them of their arrival as soon as they turned into their street.

Rasna gave a shriek of delight and opened the car door before Praana had parked the car.

"Hey, steady on, Rasna." Kadamba looked alarmed but Rasna was out of the car and running towards Kirti, her eyes glistening with tears as she looked at her sister.

Kirti was wearing a bright pink sari which surprised Rasna, for she had always dressed elegantly in pastel colours, Her hair was pulled back from her forehead into a bun that had a flower garland around it, and the style emphasised the smooth lines of her neck, the curve of her cheek and the depth of her eyes, which looked sad.

She had kohl in her eyes and the gold Mukkuthi in her nose enhanced the darkness of her skin, and at first Rasna thought she looked radiant. However, when Rasna looked closely, she saw that she looked pale and exhausted.

Kirti had the same soft, big innocent eyes, yet, somehow, she looked different to Rasna. It was more than a change in her choice of clothes, was it perhaps in her demeanour?

Kirti's mind had always been a haven of peace which nothing or nobody could penetrate. She had had an endless reserve of good humour, but since her marriage, she had first felt confused and trapped, then angry at the hopelessness of her situation. However, she was strong and could withstand a great deal of pain, hurt and disappointment that she kept concealed from everyone. But to those who had met Kirti before marriage and the Kirti today, the difference, together with the aura of unhappiness, was obvious.

"Rasna, at last! I was beginning to think you would not make it!" Kirti smiled.

"Kirti, I want to hug you but am too scared to touch you!"

"I won't break, you know, just be careful." She put her arms around Rasna, then asked in alarm. "But where are Mum and Dad, have they not come with you?"

"Oh, Grandma insisted they spend Christmas with her, but they will be here on the 26. In the meantime, Kadamba Chittapa is here, and of course, moi, is here!"

"Hello Uncle, it is nice to see you again." Kirti smiled gently. How kind and gentle he was, not at all like his overbearing mother, she thought. "Uncle I am so glad to see you, and this is Maamiyar Ruvini, Praana's mother."

"Madhiya vanakkam(Good afternoon)." Kadamba greeted Kirti's mother-in-law politely then towards his niece. "Hello Kirti, how are you?" he asked anxiously, noticing the dark circles under her eyes.

Kirti's face looked pinched making her eyes look bigger; the sadness in them was so marked that he felt mortified at not having come to see her sooner.

Praana's mother, Ruvini, was as grim faced and sharp nosed as her son. She was about seventy-five years old and wore thick rimmed glasses on her wrinkled face. Her thin white hair was pulled back tightly, making her forehead seem broad. Her complexion was a sickly white and her teeth were yellow, especially when she smiled, which, Rasna guessed, was not often - to top it all she looked to be arthritic. All in all, not a very pleasing sight, Rasna thought to herself.

Ruvini took her into her arms and brushed her cheek with thin lips her before turning her attention to Praana.

"Praana, you look thin!" she scolded. "Have you not been eating properly?"

Kirti had long since realised that for her husband, the only important relationship was one with his mother, leaving room for no other.

"I have only been away for two days, Amma!" Praana exclaimed, ignoring Kirti, an attitude that spoke volumes.

"Ah, Kadamba, I am glad you could come."

However, there was a brief expression of contempt on Ruvini's face and tone that had been noticed by both Rasna and Kadamba, who felt snubbed by her attitude.

She shuffled on her feet and turned to enter her house. Rasna had always wondered about Praana's father, but the conversation in the car had clarified matters.

"Kirti, how do you like Sri Lanka?" Kadamba asked kindly, his eyes twinkling.

Kadamba noticed how Praana's face hardened when Kirti answered in her soft voice.

Being reunited with her beloved sister had transformed Kirti's face and she looked radiant as she led them into the house clutching Rasna's hand tightly.

As they entered, Kirti slid her hand through Rasna's arm. "Rasna, why don't you come up to my room? I am sure you will want to rest, but if you are just as excited as I am, we can catch up? I'll get somebody to get us something to drink…"

"What are you talking about, woman?" Praana snapped angrily. "Amma would like to talk to her and you need your rest."

Praana had a shifty expression on his face which he could cover, at will, with a look of angelic innocence.

"Praana, I have not seen my sister for a year and want to talk to her?" There were tears of humiliation in Kirti's eyes and there was a hint of temper in her voice. "Please?"

Praana pierced her with a diamond hard glare.

Rasna was annoyed at Praana's attitude but tried not to show it.

"It's all right, Kirti, there is no hurry we have loads of time for catching up, I am not going anywhere! And Praana is right, you do need to rest as much as possible. You know how it is, once we start talking, we find it difficult to stop! Especially now that there is so much catching up to do!" Rasna said.

"Kirti, you don't need to worry about her, we look after her." Praana said rudely

"I am sorry, Rasna," Kirti whispered, ashamed of her husband's behaviour.

Rasna gave her a reassuring look.

"Truth to tell, I am thirsty and tired too, and am beginning to feel the jet-lag."

Although she spoke lightly, the tension in the atmosphere confirmed her suspicions about Kirti's unhappiness. She did not like Kirti's mother-in-law, Ruvini, who she felt was too possessive of her son and who, she was sure would not only support, but even encourage his egoistic behaviour. She was sure Kirti was being tyrannised by both, and in the brief time that she had been in her sister's house, resented the disrespectful way Kirti was being treated.

Kirti tightly grabbed Rasna's hand and said stubbornly,

"I don't need to rest, Praana. My sister has come all this way to meet me and you want me to take a nap?"

"Praana, I know I said earlier that she should rest but I would like to be with her too, never mind my jet-lag! And I promise I will not tire her and will do all the talking! Anyway, I know she won't be able to relax, knowing I am downstairs."

"Or better still, she can sit with us for some time?" Kadamba tactfully suggested. "It would be comforting for her to be with her sister, and she can rest her feet,"

Ruvini rudely ignored him.

"Come along, Rasna, Kirti has told me a lot about you," Ruvini said curtly. "Although we met last year at the wedding, it was only for a very short time."

Kirti, meanwhile looked from Praana to her mother-in-law, terrified that any decision she took might provoke a confrontation which she wanted to avoid, especially in the presence of her uncle and sister.

Yet again, Rasna felt angry at her parents for putting Kirti in this intolerable situation. She was also upset with her uncle, in fact more so, for she had believed him to be a thoughtful and kind man. Kadamba sensed Rasna felt let down by him, for he should have looked after Kirti and seen to it that she was happy in her new home.

He looked uncomfortable, but his voice was firmer when he repeated. "Kirti will join us, Praana."

"Actually, she was resting when you called so it should be okay…" Ruvini interrupted brusquely.

So why the unnecessary fuss, Rasna thought, was it because they wanted to keep the sisters apart for as long as possible, and if so, why?

They went into the lounge which was decorated in bright colours, which, Rasna was sure, Kirti did not have a hand in because... one, Kirti would never have chosen such garish colours and, secondly, well, her mother-in-law would not have allowed her to make any household decisions. Why, she was not even allowed to leave the house!

Chapter 42

"Don't worry about it, Kirti, we will finish tea then go up to your room on some pretext," Rasna whispered as she squeezed her hand before they were taken to a lounge with sofas.

As soon as they had been served tea with back hopper Pappadum and other various snacks, Kadamba turned towards Kirti.

"Kirti, I am sorry I have not been to come up and see you, I planned to many times, but something always came up." He looked apologetic.

Praana glowered silently as he looked at Kirti with narrowed eyes but tried to soften the edge that crept into his voice.

"Now, I want to get to know my sister-in-law too!" Although Praana's face held no trace of irony, it also lacked humour. "She has only had a fleeting glimpse of Matara, although I have told her a lot about it. I am sure she will be keen to see the rest, not that there is much to see here."

Kirti felt that her breathing space was being violated yet again, for Praana was making it clear to her that she should spend as little time as possible with her sister. Maybe he was afraid of what she had to tell her?

"Praana, thank you, but sightseeing is not important; I would rather stay with Kirti. Nothing else is important … unless she comes with us."

"That will be out of the question." Ruvini's voice was harsh and brusque. "She needs to stay at home."

"That will be no problem, whatever is best for her, but I will stay with her. And, that will work out fine for we have loads to talk about." Her voice was firm as she glared at first Praana then his mother.

They looked surprised, for nobody had ever defied them, Kirti was too kind and gentle and could be easily bullied, and today was the first time she had resisted Praana's suggestion.

"When are Kirti's parents coming and how long will they be staying with us?" Ruvini asked Kadamba.

"They will be here on the 26… I don't know for long though."

Rasna sat impatiently, tapping her foot, for Kirti was sitting at the end of the sofa, making it impossible to talk to her. It was not in her nature to take an instant dislike to anyone as she had to Ruvini. Her withered yellow face and shifty eyes made her skin crawl, and once again, she felt sorry for her sister.

"Praana, I would like to freshen up… Kirti, could you show me the bathroom?"

"Yes of course." Kirti got up slowly, supporting her back with one hand.

Rasna and Kadamba did not miss the look of disapproval on Praana and his mother's face.

Kirti had long ago ceased to expect any kind of affection from either of them; and the expression on their faces filled her with disgust.

She had only accepted the marriage proposal to Praana to satisfy her parents, but, now, wondered if her unhappiness and daily sacrifices were worth it? On the one hand, when she thought of her innocent unborn baby, the only joyful result of their union, she smiled tenderly, and on the hand, she couldn't help but feel abandoned yet again by her parents; for although they were in Sri Lanka, they had not come directly to Matara, but stayed back in Colombo, and she needed her mother at this time of her pregnancy.

She was also deeply concerned and anxious for Rasna, for Praana had told her that his mother and Puru's mother, between them, had arranged to get Rasna married, to none other than Praana's cousin, Annama, to whom, although she had only met him once, had taken an instant dislike to.

Although she would have loved to have Rasna live close to her, she realised that that would cause Rasna unhappiness. She knew her sister well, and not only was she deeply in love with Mark, she was by no means a submissive girl who would adapt to strangers and reside in unfamiliar surroundings. Therefore, Kirti felt she had to warn Rasna as soon as possible, but Praana was aware of this, so was trying his best to keep them apart, but for how long could he be successful in achieving that?

Kirti took Rasna to her room, which was large with a balcony overlooking the garden.

"Sorry about the mess, Rasna, I was arranging baby clothes to see that I have not forgotten anything." She pointed to the room that was strewn with baby clothes.

"Don't worry about it, Kirti, looks like you have been busy, I hope Praana helps you?" When Kirti shook her head, continued "Not even his mother? For her first grandchild?"

Kirti shook her head and had tears in her eyes. Rasna felt she would burst out crying, so quickly ran into the bathroom to splash her face with cold water, for she wanted to be strong for her sister.

By the time she emerged, Kirti had put on a brave face as had Rasna. With a smile she suggested they sit out in the balcony, not only because of the cool weather, but because it was the only place where she could sit comfortably.

Before they had come up, she had asked Murugan, their home help, to get them a glass of thambli and as soon as they were seated, he came to the balcony with a tray, placed it on small table and withdrew.

"Wow, It is cool out here... Kirti this country is beautiful, and the home help, we don't have anything like this back home."

Rasna helped herself to a cold glass of thambli which she quickly gulped, then wiped her mouth with her handkerchief.

"Kirti, you have a lovely house, at least that means Praana is doing well in his business?"

"Yes, he runs the family business of tea... they have tea plantations."

"Oh yes, that was mentioned at grandma's house, I keep forgetting that, but, I am surprised he can do anything alone, he is so much under his mother's thumb... you did not tell me he is a 'mama's boy!"

"You are so right, Rasna, those two have a strong bond. Praana needs nobody in his life but his mother, so much so that I, his wife, feel like a stranger in my own home!"

Rasna's hair fell onto her shoulders like thick black silk and, as was her habit, she absent-mindedly looped one strand over her ear.

"I noticed that too Kirti, I don't know how you can tolerate the way in which they treat you! Anyway, I thought I would never be alone with you, Kirti. Now, tell me, how are you? I mean really." Rasna got up from the chair to hug her. "Kirti, it breaks my heart to see you so unhappy! All this aggro with the baby coming! And what exactly do they do to make you feel like a stranger?"

Kirti shifted in the chair then put her feet on a nearby stool.

"In short everything! I feel I am stepping on stones, having to mind my p's and q's in my own house, always being scolded and insulted by Amma. Kirti, go see if the washer man has got our clothes, Kirti, go tell the cook to cut mangoes. Kirti, you have spilt your tea and ruined your clothes, Kirti why are you wearing that suit, the colour does not suit you! Shall I go on? All this she says in front of Praana, who ignores them, so, of course, that attitude just goads her to carry on criticising!"

"If mother and son are so content in each other's company, why on earth did Praana marry?" Rasna exclaimed, horrified.

"Maybe because custom demand a man marries? And, I am sure that in some way, Praana feels that because I am from London, I raise his status in society?" Kirti sighed as she shifted her position again, but try as she might, she could not stay comfortable for long.

"I don't know how you put up with them," Rasna exclaimed again

"What choice do I have?" Kirti replied miserably "But never mind about me, Rasna, you have to get away from here as soon as possible."

"Kirti, what do you mean? I have just arrived..." She looked at her sister in alarm.

Chapter 43

The sun was reddening in the west in preparation of the sunset. Through the sky an occasional beam of yellow ray would peep through the trees on the lawn. Although it was cool, there was no breeze and the trees were still, as if drawing together in sleep.

"Kirti, what do you mean?" she repeated. " Is everything okay?"

"I would have warned you sooner if I could, but Grandma and Dad have arranged your wedding" Kirti wiped the sweat from her forehead with her handkerchief. "Since Praana's mum found out I had an unmarried sister, she has been showing me photos of men who were all either bald, fat, old or with greasy hair! Yuk." She shuddered.

"No, no that cannot be true," Rasna cried "I thought so at first, but I don't think so now. But come to think of it, ever since we arrived, Dad and Grandma have locked themselves in a room at every chance they got, and you know what that means… closed doors mean secrets! I asked Mum and she assured me that nothing was in the pipeline, and I believe her for she sounded sincere. Though back in London, Dad did hint at it and mention the name Annama. And when I asked Mum about it, she assured me it was not true, and was only said in jest, else he would have told her."

"That should have warned you, Rasna, when has Dad ever said anything as a joke? And yes, the man in question is Annama, Praana's cousin, and since when has Dad consulted Mother? He only listens to Grandma, who he thinks can do no wrong."

"Why is that all the men in our family are too weak to stand up to their mothers? First Dad, then Mum, told me how Grandma broke up Mamu's marriage with her meddling and Chitappa not being strong enough to oppose her, and now I find that Praana also is under Ruvini's thumb! Maybe because they are too dominating? No correction, only because their mothers are overbearing!" Rasna exclaimed

She felt confused and trapped, for although she wanted to help Kirti who she was sure was being ill-treated, she felt she also needed to protect herself. She gave a start as she heard Kirti's voice.

"Rasna, why did you come, I told you not to in the last conversation we had?"

"Yes, you had, but you sounded so unhappy; Dad was pressurising me, mother was blackmailing me emotionally, and I was genuinely worried about you. I decided it was best to come and see for myself if I can help you in some way? Last, but not least I wanted to be here to welcome my niece or nephew! But if you had hinted how serious the matter was…."

"Believe me I wanted to, but one, I was not sure, and secondly, every time I spoke to you, either Praana or his mother would watch me like a hawk, ensuring I persuade you to come."

"Kirti, on another matter, has Praana or his mother been physically abusive toward you?"

"Yes, but that is not important now, I want you to leave Matara as soon as possible."

"And how would you suggest I do that? And anyway, Mum and Dad are coming on the 26… I am sure Father will sort Praana out, you know Grandma has connections and as for me, Mother is on my side and Father cannot force me to do anything against my will."

"Rasna, it is not like you to be so naïve! They did not force me either!" Kirti cried tears in her eyes.

"That is different, Kirti, you are good, and kind therefore Mum and Dad knew you would not disobey them."

"I don't think you are taking it as seriously as you should, Rasna! They won't openly pressure you, but they will create circumstances which will make it impossible to oppose them."

"Kirti, now you are scaring me." Rasna looked at her in alarm.

At that moment Praana walked into the bedroom, and when he saw them sitting out on the balcony, walked across,

"And what are you two talking about?" he asked, his voice throbbing with unspoken criticism.

As soon as she heard Praana's voice, Kirti trembled and looked out into the lawn, trying to control her the inner turmoil she felt from showing on her face. She had been denied the right of choosing her partner, but had believed that love, or at the very least, friendship would develop and grow after marriage. How wrong she had been!

The leaves on the trees trembled in the evening gentle breeze.

Praana scowled at Kirti and the tension showed in his gaze. He was afraid; worried that Kirti would tell her sister about their scheme. At first, Praana had not disclosed their plans to Kirti, but he suspected she had heard them discussing it. And later when she had asked him, he had blatantly confirmed it, and now was regretting it.

The fear and tension revealed itself in the twitch in his face.

Kirti tightened her lips and looked away, knowing that if she did or say anything that either Praana or his mother did not approve of - would only result in terrible consequences for her.

She had thought that the news of a baby would soften them, on the contrary, when she had first told him, Praana had flown into one of his rages, and, if possible, had become meaner and more vicious. Kirti had expected a kinder reaction from his mother, a woman, but it had been the same, if not worse.

Rasna sensed the tension and tried to lighten the tone of her voice.

"Kirti, in the car we were making plans for the 26… we could go to the shopping bazaar?"

"I thought Mum and Dad were coming on that day?"

"Don't you realise that Kirti should not leave the house in her condition!" Praana said rudely.

Rasna winced, taken aback at the vehemence in her brother-in-law's tone.

"Praana, don't you dare speak to my sister in that tone!" Kirti's face was flushed, and her eyes flashed in anger.

Praana was taken aback for Kirti had defied him twice in one day, something he had not thought possible.

He raised his eyebrows, finding it difficult to contain his anger. He paced the balcony, unclasping and clasping his hands behind his back. Sometimes he would stop and run his fingers through his hair, then finally, he turned towards Kirti.

"Kirti, how dare you talk back to me! I knew the moment you had your family around you would forget that a good wife does not contradict her husband."

"I don't care what you think; now please leave us alone, I would like to talk to my sister!" Kirti's voice was firm.

Praana was taken aback and Kirti, too, was surprised at her outburst, for she normally did not do so, but the thought of her sister losing Mark, her imminent unhappiness and her parent's betrayal and abandonment had given her the strength to express her displeasure strongly.

Praana heard the determination in Kirti's voice with surprise, but the fact that she had done or said nothing improper infuriated him, however, he controlled himself.

"Of course, Kirti I am sorry to have interrupted you." Praana said mildly

But although he smiled, the look in his eyes was so cold and impenetrable that Rasna shivered. He stormed out, eyes glaring and muttering under his breath – his face grim for his authority had been challenged, that too in front of his sister in law.

After he left, Rasna put her fingers over her mouth to suppress her giggles. "You go, girl! You should do that more often, that showed him!"

"It is only because you are here that I had the courage to do so; usually mother and son encourage each other as to who can be the nastiest to me!"

"That is horrible Kirti, I am so sorry." Rasna got up and hugged Kirti. "You have changed so much, the way you dress – you did not like wearing a sari, the way you speak, even your laughter! Overall, you have changed your personality to suit and please them," Rasna whispered sadly. " I feel I have lost my sister."

"No you have not, I am still the same and love you very much, but I had no alternative but adapt to their lifestyle, a way of life that is very different to ours, different customs that included unfamiliar foods, Uppama in the morning, Rava ladu in the evening etc. Although mum did cook that at home sometimes, at least, we had the choice not to eat it and were never forced. The odd thing is that Praana and Ruvini both realise I have sacrificed so much to try and blend in with them, yet they resent me. At first it hurt, then I felt that maybe I was to blame to warrant such cruel behaviour? But I have now come to accept their cruel attitude, but I have no confidence in them, so much so that even a compliment or positive comment by them sounds belittling to me!"

Early in the marriage, she was sparkling and vivacious, she always had something to say, some opinion to give. But she found that each time she did, it was met with Praana's and his mother's disapproval, so had soon learnt to hold her tongue.

"Poor Kirti, I am so sorry you have been left to fend for yourself."

"Thanks, Rasna, I appreciate that, but I realise now that Dad felt it was his duty to get me married, and, that loss of hope is not the same as despair. It is accepting life as it is and not what it could have been. In short, I now have nothing to look forward to but the birth of my child."

"Oh Kirti don't say that! I am sure Dad will find a way to help you out of your unhappiness once he knows what kind of person Praana is and how miserable you are. Now, tell me exactly what Praana and his mother have in store for me so I can find a solution, if I can." She added. However, the look on Kirti's face worried her. "Kirti, what is the matter? Is it the baby? Should I call Praana's mum?"

"Huh! Fat use she would be! No, I am fine, no need to worry, Rasna, you don't know how devious Praana, and his coming here earlier was a warning for me."

"Warn you? Kirti, I don't understand, what can they do now that we are here?"

"I don't know, but he is capable of anything, and I am afraid for my child. Rasna, not only have they arranged Annama as your husband, they have arranged the wedding date too! It is to be on the twenty-seventh, and that is why Praana is making sure that everybody will be here by then."

"Nooo…" Rasna cried then calmed herself. "They can't force me, and Mother won't let them! Anyway, are you sure about the date set for the so-called marriage?"

"At first, I overheard them talking, but couldn't believe they would go to that extent- just so they could arrange Praana's cousin marriage to you! So, later I asked Praana- I expected him to be angry for daring to question him, but he calmly confirmed the whole thing, smug in the knowledge their conspiracy would succeed! I know you believe that Mother is unaware of it, but she is actually aware of the conspiracy, and I think is even in favour of it." Kirti shifted her body as the baby kicked. "Why do you think you were sent here earlier?"

"I still do not think so, Kirti, we were all coming together, but it was Dad and Paat who changed the plan at the last minute! And when Dad told her they would travel to Matara on 26th December on the Samudra Devi, she looked genuinely shocked!"

Chapter 44

Kirti tilted her head and looked at Rasna with thoughtful eyes.

"Hmmmmm…..I am sure the switch was made at Father's suggestion, wasn't it? Proposed by none other than our grandmother, who supposedly has our good will at heart!"

Rasna nodded her head miserably.

The warm breeze was pleasant and Rasna swept her hair from her forehead with a long slender hand, and Kirti noticed that her long pointed nails had been painted a delicate shade of pink.

"Maybe you are right, Kirti, but don't worry about it." She reached out and stroked her hand. "I am worried about you though, what are you so scared of? What does Praana do to you when you said your actions have terrible consequences?"

"Look, don't worry about me, yes, they do occasionally knock me about, but that they consider only disciplining.! They say they do it out of love and a desire for me to see the wrong I have done! Anyway, back to your problem, please treat this seriously, and that least try and save yourself from a situation like mine. Praana's cousin will be coming tomorrow, and I have seen his photo! And believe you me, you would not like him!"

"What cousin? Oh, you mean Annama, we were supposed to meet him in Galle, but he got held up. No, he is not coming tomorrow, he will come on Boxing Day because Dad and Mum are first going to Galle and they will come down together. Oh my God! Why, what is he like?" she asked curiously. "Anyway, even if he was handsome, you know there is none other than Mark for me."

"Oh, so now he is coming on the 26th of December? They were originally coming for Christmas, but yes, Rasna, that is who I mean; he is short stocky with specs, horrible personality …and do you want me to go on?"

"Yuk!" Rasna wrinkled her nose as she looked at the photo Kirti had handed her. "Right, then I just have to make sure I am not here! We will have to quickly come up with a plan. In the meantime, I will phone Mark for he was planning to come to Colombo from Phuket. Except, whatever action we think of, has to be acted upon quickly, for it is already the 24th and only have a couple of days! And Kirti, Mark warned me that something like this might happen. He also told me not to worry, for the only marriage that would take place would be to him!" Rasna was speaking fast.

"Hold on, Rasna, when is he planning to come? The reason everything is being done in a hurry is because they know you will not be able to get away."

"How clever of them! But I only wish Mark would answer his mobile. I have tried a couple of times, but it has been switched off." Rasna said exasperatedly. "Maybe he is on the plane?"

"Wise man, more than you I can say of you! You knew what happened with me and still you…! Anyway, keep trying and in the meantime, we will pretend to know nothing, come up with a plan, and, hopefully, they will not suspect anything out of the ordinary."

"I think we may to omit Mark, for he too was supposed to leave for Phuket on the 23rd and be there by Christmas Eve, and even if I talk to him today, he won't be able to make it in time, today is Christmas Eve and everything will be shut on the 25th,! I am going to run away, like Laxmi aunty and, like her, commit suicide!"

"Don't be so dramatic, Rasna…" .

"Wait, we do have another option, actually, the only one, I think. If I explain the dilemma to Uncle Kadamba, who is a kind man, hopefully he can help us, he has got a car and…"

"Whew, Rasna, you might have something there." Kirti smiled. "And knowing Chitappa, he will definitely help."

"Kirti, do you know this is the first time I have seen you smile? I was beginning to feel unwelcome and that you wanted me to leave as soon as possible!" she said lightly. "But since you are so unhappy why don't you come with me?"

"Ha ha, very funny. Rasna, you know I want you to meet your niece/nephew in a house or hospital, not in a car or on the road!"

Kirti was to remember her remark later.

"Now who is being dramatic?" Rasna smiled tenderly at her sister.

They sat in the twilight evening, the sky still, dark, and mysterious – so like our lives, Rasna thought.

"You know, you always told me you were unhappy, but not how much, and I always thought, and hoped, that Praana might possess a little bit of goodness or decency. But having met him, and your mother-in-law, I can see that they are plain nasty and the cause of your unhappiness! I still think you should have told me.!"

"Rasna, I did not want to confide in you because I did not want to worry you. But I have kept quiet in for so long…

I thought I knew Praana, but not that he had such a vengeful and spiteful streak in him."

"Now who is being naïve? Kirti, how can you be so calm and brave? I would have divorced him by now! You are a kind girl, but instead of appreciating that quality, they take advantage of it! But surely you have made some friends out here, somewhere you can escape to from these two?"

"No, I haven't, because they don't allow me to! I am not permitted to have any hobbies; I would have love to do something like join a drawing class or flower arrangement. Most ladies go to the cinema, spend an afternoon in the beach, go to the salon, have their nails done, have massages, but no, whatever I do, or don't do, has to be approved or decided by Praana or his mother! Even to the extent of what I should wear and what programmes I should watch!"

Rasna had tears in her eyes. "They have made you a captive, but whilst driving down, Praana told me that it was you who did not want to leave the house, but I didn't believe him for I know you are an adventurous girl."

Kirti's face flushed. "Is that what he told you? See how clever he is, before I could complain or explain the situation, he has tried to justify his action! He can be so charming, which is how he duped Father and mother to think that he is the best son-in-law!"

Rasna saw her eyes shining so hastily interrupted.

"Yes, he can and did, but I was not fooled, and I am so sorry for bringing it up! Please do not cry, it is not good for the baby. Let us talk of something else. Is it dinnertime?"

Although it broke her heart to see Kirti so unhappy, she tried to keep her voice light and carefree.

The sun that had been preparing to set, finally did so, leaving hues of copper and orange on the leaves of the trees and in the sky. The evening had given way to twilight, which in turn had disappeared with the onset of darkness. Gradually the moon rose and flooded Matara with its pale light.

"I think we better go down; you are right it is dinner time. I am surprised Praana has not been up to order me to do so!"

They had been sitting in the darkness with only the faint light from the bedroom.

Kirti got up slowly, supporting her back with her hand, as it was getting more and more difficult for her to move about. She went to the bathroom to rinse her swollen eyes with cold water.

Rasna sat on the bed waiting for her, again shocked at the change in her sister. Kirti was affectionate and kind, she had had a great sense of humour and a lovely smile. But the Kirti she saw now was a shadow of that girl, a girl who was unhappy and afraid and oh, so so sad, afraid that anything she might do or say might have reprisals.

Kirti came out of the bathroom, wiping her face with her towel.

"Whew! I feel better now, I do wish the baby would hurry up and come. I am forever tired."

Rasna sat watching her sister silently as she combed and plaited her hair.

"Rasna, don't you want to change?"

"No, I am fine, anyway, a bath does not cool me for long, in no time at all I feel just as hot! Now what are we doing tomorrow?" Rasna grinned and held her sister's hand.

As they walked towards the drawing room, Kirti stopped breathlessly and turned towards Rasna.

"Honestly Rasna, I know you have said you do, but I do not think you realise the gravity of the situation here. Praana's cousin will be coming… You must speak to Mark. I know you said you have phoned him, but do keep trying, leave a message or something, but please do something."

"Oh, I forgot to tell you that I did phone him whilst you were in the bathroom. He is in Thailand now and said he will be here as soon as possible… within the week that is."

"And you were going to tell me this… when?" Kirti asked crossly. "did you tell him that a week will be too late?"

"I did and but that is the earliest he can make it. Somehow we will have to stall them."

"Any suggestions?" Kirti asked sarcastically. "Actually, I liked the one which includes Chitappa. But you have also managed to talk to Mark and that is a relief, I am sure he will not allow anything to happen to you." She smiled and the smile transformed her face.

She squeezed Rasna's hand, and they walked into the sitting room.

Chapter 45

"My dears, you both look refreshed and happy, no doubt after your long chat."

Ruvini was sitting on the sofa with an expression of tight-lipped disapproval. There was a crease of discontentment between her eyebrows, and she looked nervous even though an Ayah was squatting on the floor, massaging her feet.

"We are, thank you, very happy," Kirti said, craving to have her feet massaged, for they were swollen and painful.

She had suggested it to her mother-in-law once, but she had been met with such a stony silence that Kirti had not mentioned it again. But after that incident, both mother and son began to use a stony silence as a weapon to silence her.

However, as soon as they entered the room, Rasna noticed a change in Kirti. The smile that had so transformed her face was replaced by an expression of wariness.

Praana's mother looked at them with her sharp shrewd eyes.

"Has Kirti told you that Praana's cousin, Annama, will be spending the holidays with us?"

"Yes, she did, have you met him, Chitappa?" Rasna asked

"No, Rasna, I have not, though I have heard a lot about him. He lives in Galle and is a partner in a firm of architects?

Is he the one you are talking about?" He looked at Rasna and Kirti with raised eyebrows, sensing the underlying tension.

"Yes, he is the one and no, he has not met my cousin!" Praana confirmed and almost spat out the words.

His tone sounded venomous, and Rasna wondered at the underlying reason. If he disliked his cousin, why was he so anxious to get Rasna married to him?

Since they had entered the lounge, Praana had looked at them suspiciously. He was certain Kirti would have told her sister about Annama- and expected an outburst or disapproval by them. Therefore, he was surprised when he saw them sauntering into the room casually. Even after his mother had mentioned the arrival of Annama the following day they had seemed unperturbed. Was it possible that either Kirti had not told Rasna, or that she consented to the proposal? Maybe they were delighted about it, because that would mean Rasna would live in Galle, near Kirti. and, that idea Praana did not like and one he had not thought through; for under no circumstances did he want her to be happy.

Kirti, meanwhile, smiled gently as she felt a stirring in her stomach, and closing her eyes, rubbed her stomach gently, feeling the movement of the baby in her womb. The baby's gentle kick filled her with maternal warmness, and she felt she would do anything to protect her baby. This was followed by blind panic, which she tried to contain, but knew that as long as she was with Praana, the panic attacks would surface continually.

She glanced at Praana's grim face and Ruvini's shrewd wizened face, and suddenly realised that they were ruthless people; she wanted to protect her unborn child, for she intuitively felt there was violence and dishonesty in Praana's family.

What kind of kind nurturing and love would the baby get from this selfish family? She put her arms across her stomach possessively and glared at Praana. Maybe Rasna was right and that she should leave, with her, but as that was not possible, she decided that soon after the baby was born, she would ask her uncle to help her return to London.

Rasna could see the varying expressions on Kirti's face and was almost tempted to agree to the arranged marriage just so she could be close to her sister to protect her from harm.

Chapter 46

Although Praana liked his aunt Mega, his mother's sister, and had, as a child, spent a lot of happy times at their house in Galle, he did not like his cousin Annama. When they were children, Annama had fabricated tales about him to Ruvini, his mother, who had not believed them anyway, so high was her opinion of her son.

Annama's behaviour had grown worse all through his teen years, and was now at its peak, because he had been recently appointed as a partner in a reputed firm of architects, with his own air-conditioned office and a secretary. Ruvini too, felt that with her son's success, Mega, her sister, had become patronising and arrogant, whereas, previously, they had been close, for she had been warm and affectionate.

Annama bragged about his success at every chance he got, and Praana could not stomach his voice, which was high and shrill. His face too, repulsed him, with his thin-lipped smile and black rimmed glasses. Even his attire annoyed him, for he always wore black trousers with bright coloured shirts. His jokes, which Annama thought were funny, were always directed at others under the cover of geniality, and the only thing the cousins had in common was that they wanted to avenge their fathers.

The subject of Annama's marriage had begun a week earlier when Mega had visited them and seen a photo of Kirti and Rasna.

"Who is this beautiful girl?" she had asked Kirti.

"That is Rasna, my sister; she lives in London with my parents," Kirti had remarked proudly. "They might be coming for a holiday in time for the birth of the baby."

Mega had turned to Praana. "Is she married by any chance?"

"No, she is not but…"

"You know I am looking for a girl for Annama… and she seems to be ideal!" she said with a wink.

"I think you are right Aththai, leave it to us," Praana smirked. "I am sure my in laws will be looking for a boy for my sister-in-law, and who better than my cousin?"

Soon afterwards, Praana's mother had spoken to Kirti's grandmother, and before Kirti could warn Rasna, her marriage to Annama had been finalised and a web was weaved to ensnare Rasna.

Inwardly, Kirti wanted Rasna to get married and live in Galle, for then she would have somebody to laugh and talk to, somebody who could share her worries; in short, someone who would make her present life tolerable. On the other hand, her sister loved Mark, she did not like Annama and most of all she wanted to protect her sister from a life of misery.

If only she had been more assertive, she mused, if only she had not agreed to her marriage to Praana if only she had not been pregnant… if only…!

Praana looked at Rasna and asked, "Rasna what are your plans for tomorrow?"

"You mean before or after she meets my grandson?" Praana's mother looked at her son, cackled and winked.

"Amma, it could be a girl you know, and tomorrow is Christmas, and oh, I forgot to tell you about the slight change of plans!"

"What are you talking about?" Ruvini looked worried.

"Tomorrow is Christmas, and everybody was planning to be here for Christmas lunch, but since Kirti's parents will be coming on the Samudra Devi, we thought it best Annama meet them in Galle for lunch and come together on the 26th. But I don't not know whether Aunt Mega will come down tomorrow as originally planned or with Annama on the 26th."

"Oh, and when were you planning to tell me?" Ruvini looked angrily at Praana. "Never mind, as long as he reaches here by the 26th, I will telephone Mega and find out, for I was quite looking forward to our Christmas lunch together."

"Praana, instead of shopping on the 26th why don't we go tomorrow?" Rasna suggested. "I don't like to leave Kirti, but would like to see what little Matara has to offer, I have heard there are some beautiful things here, precious semi-precious stones, ivory etc and Praana you said it excels in Batik?"

"Hey, steady on, Rasna, what are you going to do with all those jewels?" Kirti's gentle smile lit up her face. "And I did not know Matara excels in Batik!"

"Kirti, don't interrupt!" Praana said rudely. "I think she was joking, for she said earlier she was not interested in sightseeing! You always interrupt me, let me finish! I thought I would take Rasna around and show her a little of our well-known sights first and, then to the market."

"Hey, what about me? Rasna, you are not planning to leave me here all alone, are you? You have come from London and I would like to spend some time with you, and you want to spend Christmas day shopping? Better still, I will come with you.!

"No, Kirti, you are not to leave the house!" Praana said firmly.

"I think he is right, my dear," Kadamba said gently.

"I only agreed because I want you to rest, Kirti, it is especially important for you and of course for the baby. Anyway, what else is there to see in Matara?" Rasna asked. "Sorry, I was half asleep when you were explaining in the car."

"No problem, my dear. Well, there is the Matara Bodhiya which is a fort, there are a few temples and there is Old Nupe market."

"There you are, Kirti, that should not take us long, I will stay with you in the morning, and we will leave in the afternoon, after lunch, after which you can rest."

"And be back in time for Annama!" Kirti's mother-in-law finished.

"No, Amma, Annama is coming on the 26th."

"Oh yes, I forgot, never mind."

"So Kirti, we will have the whole morning to talk, followed by Christmas lunch.

"But…" Kirti glared at Rasna.

At that moment, Murugan came into the room to announced that dinner was ready. When everyone got up to leave the room. Rasna stayed back to help Kirti, who was finding it difficult to get up from the chair and Praana had thoughtlessly walked off with his mother.

"Here, let me help." She gently helped Kirti to her feet, looking angrily at Praana and his mother as they left the room. "How rude are they?"

"Rasna, what are you up to?" she asked breathlessly, one hand supporting her back whilst with the other she held on to her sister's hand.

"Shhh, I will tell you later but for now, please don't say anything."

Kadamba had turned back and come up to them.

"Rasna, Kirti, are you all right?" he asked gently though his eyes looked worried.

Rasna looked at Kirti then decided she would confide in her uncle.

"No, Chitappa, nothing is fine. I cannot talk now, but can I see you after dinner? I must talk to you, and please nothing of this to anyone!"

Kadamba looked worried but assured her he would not.

"I presume it has something to do with Annama's visit?" he whispered.

Rasna nodded her head and when Praana shouted from the dining room, answered "We are coming Praana, Kirti here is having a slight problem in getting up from the chair."

Chapter 47

When Rasna and Kirti entered with Kadamba, Praana and his mother had already started eating.

"Ah, there you are at last," Praana said between mouthfuls, pointing to the empty chairs.

"Thank you." Rasna pulled up a chair then remembered that Kirti would need help, so gently ushered her into a chair.

Rasna was feeling hungry so helped herself to a steaming bowl of pickled fish and hot vegetables that were covered with a reddish gravy.

"Here, Kirti, do you want me to serve you?"

Kirti pulled a face and turned away. "I am not hungry, thank you,"

"Hey, but you must eat, at least for the baby…!" Rasna implored. "Otherwise, I will not eat either."

"Don't be silly, Rasna, she doesn't need to eat!" Praana retorted. "More room for the baby, huh?" he sniggered as Rasna and Kadamba both glared at him.

"Sorry, I did not mean that" he muttered when he saw his mother glaring at him.

"Here, have something," Rasna coaxed as she handed a plate with a little rice and vegetables. "Eat as much as you want."

"Thank you, Rasna." Kirti nibbled at her food, grateful for her sister's and uncle's moral support.

As soon as they had finished, a bowl of water was given to each so they could dip and clean their fingers, and as soon as everybody was finished, they left the dining room.

"Although I am very tired, I don't think I can sleep in this heat, what about you, Kirti?" Rasna wiped her forehead.

"Oh, me too, but it has been a lovely day, thank you, Rasna and Chttappa." She stood on tiptoe to kiss her uncle on the cheek and hugged Rasna. "Rasna, I thought you could sleep with me whilst Praana can share with Uncle?"

"No way is that going to happen Kirti!" Praana glared. "You know there will be no rest for you with you two chattering away! No, it is better you let the sleeping arrangements stay the same. I will show Rasna to her room."

"Kirti Akka, I hate to say this but he's right And. Praana, no need to show me my room, I will find it. Is it the one next to Kirti's room? She actually showed me the room and I believe Murugan has already taken up my luggage."

"Oh, that is settled then, what about you?" Praana turned towards Kadamba, his voice dry and unemotional.

Rasna noted angrily again how rude he was. It was one thing to be rude to them, but he showed no respect to Kadamba Chitappa, who was not only older than him, but was too kind and decent a man to either notice or be upset about it.

"Oh, don't worry about me, I know where my room is too, but if you don't mind, Praana, I would like a cup of tea before I retire?"

"That sounds like a good idea, Uncle! I think I will join you," Rasna said. "I cannot sleep in this heat so if it is okay with everybody we would like to stay back for a bit?"

"Of course, it is, I will see to it that Murugan gets tea for you."

"Whew!" Rasna sighed with relief as Praana followed Kirti and his mother out of the room.

Murugan entered the room and placed a tray of tea on the coffee table, and Kadamba waited till he had gone before turning to Rasna.

"Now, Rasna, what is this all about and what are you so worried about?"

"Well, I don't know where to start!" Rasna's eyes flashed angrily.

"Well, you said earlier that it had something to do with Annama's visit?"

"Yes, it does, Chitappa! Your mum, my parents and Praana's mum have only gone and arranged my wedding to him and…"

"Whoa, hold on, Rasna, that cannot be possible, for neither my mother nor your parents have been told about this! What makes you think that Annama is coming here with that intention?"

"It is true, Uncle, Kirti has told me that Mum, Dad and Paat have arranged my marriage to him, proposed and organised by Praana and his mother, of course."

"I find that hard to believe, but if it is true, nothing should have been arranged without your consent, on the other hand I am sure they have your best interests at heart…" Kadamba remarked, adding sugar to his tea then stirring it with the teaspoon provided.

"Just as Grandma organised Kirti's marriage who, Uncle, you must have noticed, is very unhappy? Praana is not a nice person, and neither is his mother, they snub her at every chance and are rude and disrespectful to her. If they behave in this manner in front of us, can you imagine what the poor girl goes through when she is alone with them? But what really surprised me was when Kirti told me your mother is not even a good friend of her mother-in-law, as she led us to believe."

"Well, I suspected it too, but as for being unhappy, maybe it is just teething problems? I have heard there are always hitches at the start of the marriage and that it takes time for both to adjust; maybe after the baby...?" Kadamba looked distressed. "But I agree with you, these are not teething problems, for Praana, I know for a fact, is not a nice man, I have heard unpleasant things said about him, nothing concrete, mind you, but worrying nonetheless."

"That does not surprise me at all, he seems the kind of man to get involved with unsavoury people. But I, too, had thought that after the baby was born, things would get better. But that will not happen, for Kirti told me that Praana was horrified at having a baby, and as for his mother, she feels the same! I mean, you saw her behaviour today. It is Kirti who should be having her feet massaged, but she did not even suggest it once! Apparently, that kind of cold behaviour towards Kirti is typical in this household."

"Yes, I noticed that too and sensed the tension in the family, but I thought it was due to Kirti's pregnancy. Coming back to your problem, I still do not understand why you are worried about yourself, Rasna. All you must do is to refuse! Nobody will force you to do anything you do not want to, I am sure."

"Just as Kirti had a choice? Uncle, my wedding is set for the 27th!"

Chapter 48

"Rasna, what do you mean?" Kadamba expostulated. "How can they arrange such an important occasion in such a brief time, and without your consent?"

"I could not believe it either, Chitappa, when Kirti told me, but it is true. So, it gives me little or no time to do or plan an escape route, and as for Kirti, she told me that she is in a difficult position. And what is hurtful is that we all thought Grandma would look after her, but she has only visited her once! And Chitappa, you not at all!" Rasna's eyes filled with tears.

"I am so sorry, I feel terrible about it, Rasna, I should have come to see she is okay. That sort of behaviour is inexcusable, and I apologise on behalf of my mother and myself. I am fond of Kirti, she is such a kind and affectionate girl, she should not have been left alone in a strange country with unfamiliar people. But honestly, I thought Amma met her regularly, why, she even told me that Kirti had adapted herself in her new home and was happy!"

"She told the same thing to my father, and I don't know how she assumed that, considering she only came to see her once. Maybe she said it to distract us from the real problem, which, I am sure, she knew existed. Anyway, what are we going to do now? Can you help, Chitappa?"

"I would love to help, Rasna, if for nothing else but to make up for the fact that I ignored my niece's problems! But I do not see how I can, for in the brief time you have you been here, you must have noticed that I am mostly ignored…"

"Chitappa, I did not have a verbal intervention in mind, for that would create confrontation, and only make things difficult for Kirti. And, because everybody in our family is too stubborn, and I mean your mother and brother! I had something else in mind, you have a car, I thought if you could give me a lift back to Columbo, I could take a flight to London from there, but only if you are up for it."

"And how do you propose to do that? You have agreed to go sightseeing with Praana. And what with Kirti expecting any day and your parents coming on the 26th?"

"I have thought about that…and Kirti agrees there is no other way. If you think it is okay, I was thinking we could leave on the 26th without telling anyone of course. That way I can spend Christmas with Kirti and do some sightseeing with Praana, for he insists he wants to show me around Matara. That will not raise any suspicion about my scheme. I am sure Kirti can help in distracting them somehow on the 26th, although I do not want to leave her behind. God knows what they will do to her once they find out that I have escaped. Oh, sorry Chitappa, look at me rambling on but it all depends on whether you want to help."

"Of course, Rasna, I will do whatever I can, but don't forget your parents are coming on the 26th and would take the appropriate action, for I am sure they will not wish any harm to come to their daughters."

"One would think, but Kirti said that Mum and Dad have approved of it, and what if they refuse to see reason? It will be too late by then."

"There is that of course." Kadamba looked at his watch and exclaimed, "Rasna it is very late, I suggest we go to bed and talk in the morning!"

"We have to be careful that Praana does not get a whiff of this so we will text and make sure to delete it soon after. But do you think the plan is viable?" she asked as she got up from the sofa.

"Yes, it seems fine to me," Kadamba replied. "And don't worry, Rasna, everything will work out for the best."

As Rasna went to her bedroom, she felt relieved that they had formulated an escape plan, for time was short. And as soon as she got a chance, she would ask Mark to meet her in Columbo and they would return to London together, but what a botch up of two individual perfect holidays! Well, they would have been if her grandmother had not taken it upon herself to organise her life!

However, now, her main worry was how to get Kirti alone to tell her their plan, for Praana was making it extremely difficult for them to be alone. Maybe she should not tell her at all, for that way she would not be blamed for being party to it? On the other hand, if she did not tell her, Kirti would unnecessarily worry.

She sighed, turned on her back and went to sleep.

Chapter 49

The following morning was Christmas Day and Rasna got up in the morning feeling rejuvenated and excited. As soon as she had had a bath and changed into jeans, there was a knock on the door. She was expecting Murugan to bring her a cup of tea, but Kirti opened the door slightly and peeped in.

"Kirti, since when do you have to knock?" Rasna exclaimed happily, rushing to give her sister a hug. "Oh, and Merry Christmas!"

"Whoa, hold on, Rasna. Merry Christmas." Kirti smiled, hugged her tightly and waddled into the room. "But as you will notice, we don't really celebrate Christmas here, not in the way we did in London." "Yes, I noticed, but did you sleep well?"

"Yes, I did, how are you, did you sleep well? Do you think the baby will come today?"

"In answer to your questions, I am feeling bloated and horrible, I did not sleep well, and I do not think the baby will come today for till now there has been no indication of anything happening! I hope I am wrong, and it does happen, but mainly I have been worrying as to how you will get out of your dilemma in so short a time. And underlying all the problems is the fact that I cannot either lie or sit in one position at a stretch!"

Rasna smiled, glad to see that the old Kirti was back and hoped her good humour would last the day.

"Kirti, Rasna, breakfast is ready," Praana shouted from below.

"Now, Kirti, Praana is not going to let us be together, so I will say this quickly. I had a talk with Chitappa, and he has agreed to take me back to Columbo on the 26th. that is tomorrow.

"But why the tomorrow, why not today?"

"Because of two reasons; no, three actually. I want to spend some time with you because I do not know when we will meet again; Mum and Dad will be here on the twenty-sixth and because we need to behave normally. I do not Praana or his mother suspect anything, for they will only blame you for it later. I will need your help though, can you distract them somehow tomorrow morning, so all attention is focused on you, we were planning to leave early?"

"Of course, I will Rasna, anything I can do to help, thank God you have found a way to get out of here! What about Mark, does he know?"

"I spoke to him and he will meet me in Colombo, that is if he can make it in time, but, if not, back in London. What a waste of a holiday for both of them because he will be cutting his holiday short because of me. And Kirti, I am not overly happy that we have outwitted them, because that means I will be leaving you behind and I hate that! I will be worried as to what impact this will have on you! But I promise I will talk to Dad and we will bring you and the baby back to London where you will be treated with the love and respect you deserve." She hugged Kirti.

Both the sisters had tears in their eyes as they walked hand in hand and saw Praana coming out of the dining room excited, full of energy and wearing his summer coat.

"Praana, don't tell me you are going out today, it is Christmas Day! You were going to take Rasna to see Matara?" Alarmed, Kirti asked.

"Oh, woman, you ask too many questions! We were going in the afternoon, but now I have to go to the plantation for a couple of hours. I will be back by this afternoon, in time to take you around, which won't take long, Rasna, for there is not much to see here."

Kirti bit her lip, accustomed to his offensive manner towards her, but embarrassed at his behaviour in the presence of her sister. She hoped his behaviour would not be so rude in front of her parents, then almost wished it would – maybe that would prove the type of person he really was?

She had adapted herself to Praana's mental abuse, his consistent criticisms and bouts of shouting. His temper would have intimidated most women, but Kirti had an inner strength, and although she was scared of him, gave no indication of how she really felt - for she had learned to guard herself against the physical abuse that would inevitably follow if she did.

Rasna glared at him and opened her mouth to voice a scathing retort, but he had already turned his back on them, opened the door and slammed it after him.

Kirti sighed as she took Rasna's arm and led her to the dining room.

"Don't let him bother you, it is not worth it, at least I am not going to let it come between us and the little time we have together. In fact, I am surprised that he is not worried that we will be alone during the morning!" Kirti's eyes twinkled as she smiled.

"Huh!" Rasna snorted. "What is he up to, I wonder? I too thought it was going to be difficult to talk to you, but hey, surprise, surprise. But I do not trust him, I am sure he must have told his mum to do that for him!"

"Shhh." Kirti put her lips to her mouth as they entered the dining room where Ruvini and Kadamba were seated, and as soon as he saw them, Kadamba rose and pulled out a chair for Kirti then gently helped her into it.

"Thank you, Chitappa." With her hand holding her back, Kirti sat down gingerly.

On the table was the traditional Sri Lankan breakfast of Hoppers (bread dipped in curry) Pittu (mixture of rice flour and coconut steamed in bamboo mould. And of course, there was the special tea from Praana's plantation, and in the centre of the table, in a cut glass gleaming bowl, were fresh fruits, mangoes, rambutans, papayas, bananas, pineapples coconut etc.

Although Rasna had thought she would only have a cup of tea, which she always thoroughly enjoyed, she found, with surprise, that she was hungry, Back in London, she had never had breakfast, only a cup of coffee in the morning, much to the distress of her parents.

She poured some tea into a cup and looked with confusion at the variety of food on the table.

"Rasna, would you like your hopper with yoghurt and honey or with eggs? In which case, I will tell Murugan to make some fresh eggs," Ruvini asked.

"No, thank you, Paat, honey and yoghurt will be fine," Rasna said, glad the decision had been made for her, for she enjoyed the hoppers, which were small bowl-shaped pancakes served with either yoghurt and honey or eggs.

After they had finished, Kadamba helped himself to some pineapple, and strangely, sprinkled some salt on it before proceeding to eat it.

"Hey, Chitappa, you have made a mistake, that is not sugar but salt!" Rasna pointed out in alarm.

Kadamba grinned. "No, I have not, Rasna! Here in Sri Lanka, we sprinkle pineapple with salt and sometimes even a dusting of chilli powder. And would you believe it, it is delicious. Here, try some."

"No, thank you, Uncle but really, how original."

As Rasna had foreseen, as soon as they had finished breakfast, Ruvini turned to Rasna.

"Praana has left for the plantations and will be back in time for lunch."

"Yes, we met him just as he was leaving," Rasna said.

"Anyway, he has left strict instructions that Kirti is to rest after breakfast and…"

"Oh yes, I realise that, Amma, I will see to it that she does rest in the afternoon. There is so much we still have to talk about."

"And do you think she can rest whilst you are in the room? No!" Ruvini said vehemently, then as she saw the shocked look on the faces of both Kadamba and Rasna, added in a gentler tone, "My dear, I mean, Praana told me that Kirti could not sleep at night, so thinks it best she try to catch up on it in the morning."

"But Amma, Rasna has come all this way just to meet me, anyway, I can only relax if she is with me. Please?" Kirti implored, and it broke Rasna's heart as she thought that her sister had to ask for permission in her own house!

"Kirti, don't argue, go to your room." Ruvini said firmly. "I have told Ayah to wait for you there. She will massage your feet, that should relax you."

"She is right, Rasna, Kirti needs to rest, let us go to the lounge and we can plan our day," Kadamba said, giving Rasna a meaningful look

"Sorry, Chitappa, I am being selfish, of course you must rest, Kirti and that massage sounds wonderful and will help! Don't worry, we will have plenty of time to talk later."

However, Rasna was glad she had outlined their escape plan earlier, for Ruvini was determined to keep them apart, which, she was sure, was done at her son's behest!

"Okay, Amma, I do feel tired and a massage sounds heavenly." Kirti smiled weakly and left the room.

"Hey, Kirti, do you need help in getting to your room?" Rasna called after her/

"No, she will be all right," Ruvini said curtly. "Come, let us go to the lounge. I will show you an album with photographs of Annama's house in Galle."

Chapter 50

The sight and behaviour of Ruvini had begun to repulse Rasna, and she again felt terrible that she had to leave Kirti behind alone with her, especially with a baby to care for, but how could she help her? She tried to reassure herself with the thought that it would only be a couple of months before she would bring Kirti to London, but, even so, she was distressed at the prospect of leaving her, with a baby, alone with Praana and his mother.

Ruvini sat on the sofa, took an album lying nearby and patted the seat empty beside her.

"Why are Sri Lankan's so fond of keeping albums?" Rasna asked, "Amma has one in London, as has Paat in Colombo."

"We like to store our memories. These days you youngsters do so on your mobiles, but come, my dear, let me show you Annama's house in Galle. As you will see it is huge and beautiful."

She opened the album and pointed to a photograph of a house that had a huge garden. Outside the house stood a woman with grey hair tied back in a bun and was wearing thin rimmed spectacles. She was wearing a long pink skirt with a matching top and beside her stood a man.

"And this is my sister Mega with her son Annama," Ruvini said "They will be coming with your parents on the twenty-sixth."

Rasna looked at the photograph and shuddered slightly, for it was a copy of the one Kirti she had shown earlier, and one both had disliked.

Annama was short, and the little hair he had left on his scalp looked greasy. He wore specs and was dressed in a bright printed shirt with black cotton flared shorts.

He was smiling confidently into the camera, and Rasna instinctively felt that it was his success and arrogance that had shaped Praana's resentment. And it seemed to her that Ruvini's remarks too had an underlying tone of envy which spoke volumes.

At about 11 a.m., just when Rasna was beginning to get bored at looking at the photographs, Kirti waddled in, one hand supporting her back, and sat on the armchair gingerly.

"Hi Kirti, how was the massage? Did it help you to sleep, at least for a while?" Rasna rose to hug Kirti.

"Kirti, how are you feeling?" Ruvini echoed.

"I am fine thanks, maamiyar. I could not sleep but Ayah's massage helped a lot, thanks for organising that for me. I did not know a massage could be so relaxing! Whew! For a few hours everything was tolerable!"

"You say that as if it is the first time you have had one, Kirti. I am sure that cannot be true for Ayah lives here, which means you can have a massage at any time!" Rasna cried.

Ruvini glared at Kirti who looked uncomfortable and bit her lip.

"There is no need for her to have massages! She is young and strong. Why, when I was pregnant, having a massage was unheard of!"

"If that is the case, why was ayah massaging your feet earlier?"

"Young lady, I see you have not been taught that not to talk back especially to your elders! I am much older, and my bones need it!" Ruvini's cold eyes looked her up and down.

Kadamba inhaled deeply and in his gentle manner tried to diffuse the situation.

"Rasna, I am sure Ruvini has Kirti's health at heart, after all, it is her first grandchild."

Ruvini seemed flustered, so turned her attention to the album. By the time she had finished showing the whole album, and along with it singing her nephews praise, which, to Rasna, had not sounded sincere at all, it was lunchtime and Praana had returned.

"Amma, is Aunt coming today or will she be coming tomorrow?"

"I rang Mega and she says she will come with Annama tomorrow."

Although it was Christmas, they had a quiet lunch and soon after, Kirti went up to her room to rest.

"Chitappa, why don't you come sightseeing with us? I would have gladly stayed back, but Kirti does look tired."

Kadamba nodded so Praana took them to see the beach and fort of Matara. And as there was not much to see, they were back in time for tea, after which Rasna went to Kirti's room, but seeing her pale face, lightly kissed her, and left without their usual chitchat.

"Bye for now, Kirti." Rasna kissed her gently. "Look after yourself, and don't worry, I will see you back in London! If Praana asks, I will not be down for dinner. I am still getting over Christmas lunch!"

"Bye Rasna, thank you so much for coming, you don't how much strength that has given me. I feel now I can cope with any kind of pain and misery, but you take care, and do not forget to call Mark again to confirm your plans. I love you Rasna."

"I love you too Kirti, and look after yourself also. Just keep in mind, when things get tough, that you will be back in London with us soon."

She blew her a kiss, turned, and opened the door, but before she left, turned to take a last look at Kirti, crying softly and wishing she was leaving under happier circumstances. Wiping her eyes with the back of her hand, she closed the room gently and went to her room where she called Mark. But as she could not get through, left a brief message confirming her grandmother's phone number and address in Columbo.

But before going to bed, she packed her suitcase for the morrow, wiping the tears from her cheeks as she did so.

Tsunami

Matara 26th December 7:45 a.m.

Chapter 51

Kadamba had decided it would be best if they left early in the morning of the 26th,,, since Rasna's parents were arriving later on the same day.

It was early in the morning and dawn was nudging an opening in the sky, and as soon as it had succeeded, a faint rose pink light gradually flowed out and spread across the sky.

However, although it was still early, the city was wide awake with the noise of the rickshaws, blaring of horns, and along with them, there were lot of different sounds that bespoke of an exotic Sri Lanka

As they walked towards the car, Rasna wrinkled her nose in pleasure as the whiff of the various scents from the flowers in the garden reached her nostrils.

She looked around her anxiously, but apart from the usual sounds of Sri Lanka, the normal morning routine of the household had not yet begun.

"Did you tell Kirti that we were leaving today?" Kadamba asked.

"Yes, I did, but not the time, I will send her a text so she does not worry, which I will tell her to delete as soon as she has read it. Uncle, as it is still early, can we stop at the beach for a while? I just had a brief glimpse of it yesterday and have not had a chance to savour the exotic atmosphere; I don't know when I will get a chance to come here again."

"Of course, Rasna, it will only take us a few minutes, and actually, it is a good idea, for the beach will not be so crowded at this time of day."

As he turned the car, he remarked, "It is so strange, that even though we live here, we do not appreciate the beauty of our country as we should. Now, you have just come here and are appreciating its beauty, and in the process, reminding me of it too!"

Rasna smiled. "I think that is the case with everybody. I have not seen most of the major spots in London, just because I know I can go and see them anytime!"

As they drove, Rasna noticed that there were flowers at the verge of the pavement of the road leading up the beach and their scent was drifting in the wind. As they neared the beach the gentle breeze from the sea filled the air.

The shops were beginning to open their shutters, men wearing sarongs were sitting on their heels whilst street sellers and beggars stood together.

"Oh, how beautiful," Rasna gasped as she saw the blue sea. "Can I walk on the beach for a while, Chitappa, do we have time?"

"Yes, we do, but not much, so you go on whilst I find a parking place." Kadamba smiled at the look of excitement on Rasna's face as she asked." Shall I wait here for you?"

"No, don't worry, I'll come and find you."

"Okay, Uncle. I cannot wait to feel the cool sand under my feet!" Rasna got out of the car quickly, turned and waved to her uncle before walking down to the seaside.

She stood motionless as she saw the sea, its waves arching their back and catching the light of the sun as they shimmered as the sky lightened.

As she strolled towards the beach, she sent a text to Kirti and then asked her to delete it after reading it.

Although it was early in the morning and her uncle had said the beach would be partially empty, there were a lot of people trying to make the most of the sun. There were a few sunbathers on the beach, students and children who were either playing Frisbee or volleyball, whilst some families were paddling in the water. There were a few people who were attempting the sea waves on a Kayaks that were on the undulating waves.

She picked her way across the beach, avoiding the garbage lying on the white sand.

Why can't people be considerate? she thought angrily as she stepped over a tin of beer.

She looked at her watch impatiently as there was no sign of her Uncle and found it was 7.59 am. They were still time, so she found a spot on the sand and seated herself. As she relaxed, she forgot her troubles, soothed by the warm sand and the light breeze that was drifting in from the ocean.

There were shops that catered for all, there were stalls on the beach selling beach balls, toys, sweets, fruit and Thamboli, cafés that sold drinks, snacks and ice cream, whilst there were some shops that sold souvenirs for the tourists.

Suddenly, the weather changed, the breeze picked up and the previously calm water began vibrating and rocking. Rasna looked above and saw that dark clouds had suddenly covered the sky whilst the birds began to take flight, squawking and screeching.

Suddenly, and quite unexpectedly, there was a great boom that echoed across the island. Rasna was startled and waited for it to abate. She looked around for its origin, but apart from the fact that the clouds had suddenly darkened, there was nothing that suggested a major storm.

But, abruptly, the situation on the beach changed drastically and she saw the ocean water receding back into the sea. Everybody looked puzzled at the strange scenario unfolding before them, so whilst some people quickly collected their belongings and headed back to their hotel, others stayed looking towards the sea in fascination.

'Oh, where is Chitappa? I don't know what is happening here, whatever it is, it looks terribly frightening, I wish he would hurry up and park his car!'

She got up from the sand and walked to a log nearby where she waited for her uncle, when she heard a rumble that sounded like a stampede of elephants.

Alarmed, she stepped back looked down and saw that the sea water had come up to her ankles, covering her shoes. In the distance, she saw a frothy white line arise from the sea and thunder towards the beach; at the same time, it seemed as if the beach was growing bigger. But how could that be? She closed her eyes, and when she opened them, it seemed that the beach had extended 100 yards from ocean to beach and was startled when she heard another sound.

The noise was faint at first, then became an image that took Rasna a minute to comprehend, for a churning mass of water raged towards her, uprooting every tree in its path. The view was terrifying, for the water rose until it completely obscured the tallest tree. The wall of water smashed into the palm trees close to the beach and first engulfed them than yanked them out of the ground.

The roar was deafening as the water reach the beach and she watched in fascination as the wave drove into a building and smashed its structure.

The water had gradually reached up to her neck and she floundered in it, struggling and flailing, water pouring from mouth and hair. The water closed quickly and tightly around her, the current clasping and dragging her with it. In the water beside her was a man who was also trying to stay afloat. They saw a piece of wood and grabbed the strong piece plank of wood that was adrift. In amazement they saw clothes, furniture and bodies drifting in the water.

Just as suddenly the seawater poured back into the sea revealing the fish that were flagging around on the now uncovered beach. There were screams and mass panic as people began to rush in all directions, some back towards the island, others caught by the incoming wave before they reached the trees.

"Here, hold my hand, we should find a high piece of land as soon as possible, where hopefully we will be safe, at least for a while."

Rasna grabbed on tightly on to his arm. "What is happening, my god, everything was perfect! Where is my uncle, I must wait for him, he said he will find me!"

"My dear, there is no time for that, I hope for your sake he is safe, but this looks like a tsunami and there will be a second wave, higher than the last. I will explain later but first we must find a place that is high!"

Rasna, along with a few others ran towards a hill, where they cowered, terrified as they saw a wave boil and bubble in front of them then, getting bigger and heading right in their direction. The wave first crashed along the shore, then headed inshore, towards buildings and uprooting anything that stood in its way for it was like a diagonal wall rising out of the sea.

Chapter 52

Rasna was confused and terrified, for everything had happened within three or four seconds. The noise by now was chilling, for she heard, what she presumed to be metal screeching on metal, tree trunks snapping and splintering and the wind shrieking. What a contrast to the paradise earlier, and the sky too looked different.

From the top of the hill, where some of them had collected, she wondered what had happened, even though the man beside her had explained briefly that it was a tsunami. She did not know anything about it and wondered why the streets had begun to flow like canals that were full of debris? Had the sea done it, she wondered and, if so, why was the sun still out, surely it should be raining if there was a freak thunderstorm? And where had all the trees gone too, she could not see any palm trees that she loved.

Rasna looked around her and saw that the people were in various degrees of shock. As the waters began to roll back out to sea, the chaos and confusion among the people subsided, as they thought they were now safe, however, there were a few who were crying for help and Rasna saw some children, who were alone, crying for their parents.

She thought of Kirti and wished she had not deserted her, for the disaster must have struck at her house too and she would need someone to help her in her condition. She hoped she was safe for she could not help herself, and neither Praana nor her mother-in-law were going to assist her in any way. Why, Praana could not even help her to her chair!

A couple of people had joined them, and the entire group suddenly realised the severity of the situation.

"My god, what is happening?" one of the ladies cried. "One minute my children are playing Frisbee and the next they were in the water! I have to find them." She looked around her frantically.

The man who had helped Rasna tried to first calm her, then introduced himself.

"Hello everyone, my name is Steven, and I am a scientist. What we are looking at is a tsunami, but I think we should not panic, I know that is not easy but…"

"And how dangerous is this tsunami? When is everything going back to normal?"

"I am afraid the tsunami is extremely dangerous. I think we are lucky to have survived so far, but there are many others who have not and who have been swept back into the sea… Is anybody missing a relative?"

"Yes, my uncle," Rasna whispered. "He went to park the car and was going to meet me at the beach, and I have not seen him since. My sister also lives here and, oh my God!"

"I know how you feel, my wife and daughter were with me on the beach and my daughter was looking forward to having her ears pierced later on," He smiled tenderly.

"My daughter went with her friend to a shopping mall, do you think they will be safe there?" a young woman implored.

Rasna saw the water retreating "Hey, look I can see the tide ebbing! Does that mean we are out of danger?" She asked hopefully.

"I can see it too, and the force of the wave seems to be receding too; everything will be all right now." A lady with frizzy hair heaved a sigh of relief.

"I am afraid not; the tide waning is a sign that a second, bigger wave is coming, actually there is a strong possibility of more than two waves. The one we have seen, the first, was not large, yet we have seen the destruction it caused. The biggest wave I have heard, could be over 200 feet in height, so it is best we make our way inland as soon as possible."

"Oh my God! We are going to die, and we had only come here for a holiday!" another woman in the group cried.

"Please do not panic, madam, maybe I should not have been so blunt, but it is better you know the truth. We should make haste and go inland before the next waves hits us. Has anybody got a radio or mobile?"

There was a young boy amongst them. "Yes, sir, I have."

"Well, I suggest we switch it on, for I am sure the authorities will be trying to evacuate the people."

And sure enough, as soon as he switched on the radio, they were newsflashes that a tsunami had not only hit Sri Lanka, but Thailand and other countries.

"Oh no, Mark!" Rasna cried. "Oh, Mark, stay safe for me," she whispered.

She looked across the beach and saw that the road they had travelled down was now jammed with cars. The cars were moving very slowly, but a few were still emerging from hotels and houses, trying to get on to the road, but only succeeding in blocking the slow progress the cars that were already on the road had made.

There were only a few people remaining on the beach, for most of them had gone back to their hotel. However, the individual, or groups that had stayed back, looked out at the sea, either oblivious to the mass panic and its cause or chose to ignore it. Didn't they realise the danger they were in?

Rasna looked at the few hotels and saw people standing on balconies watching in fascination. Once again Rasna thought, didn't they realise the danger they were in? And if not, was it not up to the evacuation authorities to warn them?

Maybe they had no way of knowing that another wave was approaching and what if the wave was 200 feet high which was a possibility?

Rasna prayed that Kirti was in one of the cars, but suspected that Praana and Ruvini would abandon her - she also hoped that her uncle had found some means of shelter from this horrific wave of water.

The police were trying to direct the cars towards safety, a task that was impossible due to the sheer volume of the vehicles.

She looked around her for a tall building that could provide shelter, at the same time searching for a sign of her uncle or Kirti amongst the tourists from different countries, all who had come to this exotic place for a holiday.

Steve saw Rasna's face and said gently, "I know you are worried about your relatives, but can we just concentrate on finding somewhere that would be safe from the second wave?" He put the radio to his ear for the latest updates.

"Repeat, this is a Tsunami which is very dangerous, and you are recommended to stay as far away from the beach as possible!"

They had started walking inland and Rasna could not help noticing how disasters brought out the worst in people. People who took advantage of the situation, for she saw that two young lads had smashed a glass window and grabbed a few items from a store.

A policeman who had been trying in vain to guide the traffic ran after them shouting.

"Maybe we could get a lift in a car?" Rasna turned to Steven.

"Only a handful of people are helpful at a time like this, it is a question of survival, and, anyway, the cars are moving so slowly it would be quicker to find a tall building on foot."

"Do you have any other suggestions to get us out of here?" Rasna asked in desperation. "I need to find my uncle and sister. She is pregnant and needs help!"

"No, I haven't, my dear, let us just concentrate on ourselves, shall we?"

They noticed that most drivers, in frustration, were now abandoning their cars. leaving the road blocked with unattended vehicles. So now there were cars amongst the other debris that the first wave had consumed in its intensity and power.

However, amid the panic, she saw a ray of hope, for she saw UN trucks and various rescue teams that had responded quickly to the disaster, as well as helicopters, flying overhead to rescue people.

"What about buses? Is there a bus service we can use? I am sure the evacuation authorities must have set something up?" Rasna asked.

The policeman had given up chasing the lads that had looted the shop window and happened to be passing when he overheard Rasna.

"Yes, ma'am, there is a bus service going to Colombo, but the last bus left a few minutes ago, and from what I heard, the driver and passengers had to push other cars out of the way, which wasted a lot of time."

"Is there be another route I can take? I need to get to Colombo as soon as possible!"

"I don't think anyone can go anywhere now," Steven said. "Don't forget, there is another wave on its way."

Rasna turned to Steve and asked anxiously. "How big is the next wave going to be and what will happen when it comes?"

"It could be up to 80 feet, or even 200 feet high, and as to what will happen, we will be lucky if we survive that one. All I know is we should find someplace safe, someplace high, and that will not happen if we walk slowly! We need to walk faster!"

The path was littered with objects people had thrown on the streets in their rush to escape. Rasna kicked a ball aside and could see beach towels, several types of clothing, sunglasses pool chairs, everything that one would take for a holiday on an exotic island.

People were scrambling on foot, not even slowing to avoid anyone. They were screaming, running, or only plain flustered as to their next course of action. Rasna found there was no pattern or discipline in their manner, and most were calling out names of the relatives they had been separated from.

Rasna searched the crowds for a sign of her uncle and felt bad that he was only caught in this disaster because he had been kind enough to help her escape. She sighed and once again, wondered how Kirti was managing in this calamity? In her last stage of pregnancy, Kirti could barely walk, so hoped that Praana had eluded the disaster and escaped with Kirti in his car.

With a sinking heart, she realised that most of them would not live to see the end of day, but she took comfort in the fact that her parents were safe in Columbo. Then she suddenly remembered they were not in Colombo but would be travelling on the Samudra Devi today.

The few cars that were on the road had come to a standstill and were filled with people desperate to be on the move.

She saw a family of three in a car packed with suitcases, a couple in a car, a hippie loitering near in what was left of a shop whilst one of the drivers of a van was shouting into his radio handset.

A clap of thunder ripped the air along with the sound of the rumbling crescendo of the tsunami.

"What was that?" Rasna cried in alarm.

"That was the sound of the second wave of the tsunami. It begins quietly, then its intensity builds to a crescendo, which we heard. It usually fades and disappears, giving a false sense of security, but assembles again in a second wave."

The sound had shaken the glass windows of buildings and was so loud that people halted and looked up, trying to figure out where the sound came from.

The sound continued for a good ten seconds before it subsided and Stephen explained "That is the sound of a shock wave of the tsunami, which means that the second wave cannot be far behind the sonic sound. We don't have much time; I have known buildings bigger than five stories being washed away.".

"I only came to meet my sister; she is pregnant and due at any time. I don't know how she will escape this disaster!" Rasna kept repeating, shocked, at how, in so short a time, there was so much destruction, loss of lives, and buildings in ruins.

Chapter 53

Although they were walking fast, Rasna turned her head to look back at the beach. Some of the people on the beach had finally grasped the danger they were in and begun frantically seeking any kind of shelter.

With the water still flowing out, an even more ominous sign approached, the sun reflected off a line of water stretching from the sky. The line came towards them at an impossible speed, but seemed to slow down, however, as it did it grew in height! It was a wave of water!

Steve looked at the advancing wave with awe.

"Just to make sure that you know how dangerous the tsunami is, it is not only the force of the water and drowning that is dangerous, buildings collapse too, and there is a danger from that also, but I am sure that inland is definitely a safer place to be in at this time. Also, evacuation has begun, for I can see rescue helicopter flying above."

Fascinated and frightened at the same time, Rasna saw a frothy white mass of water churning towards them in horrifying splendour, rising higher and higher than collapsing as it reached the island. Instead of a vertical wall of water, the ocean rose like the world's biggest rising tide.

At first, the sound sounded like the crashing of water on beach, but the difference was that it did not subside. Instead, it kept growing louder, reminding Rasna of a plane getting ready to take off.

They stood there, transfixed, feeling they were watching a washing machine through its glass window as the water tossed and churned, the only difference being that instead of clothes, they were watching bits of debris in it..

Steve shook her by the shoulder and said impatiently

"Look here, we don't have time. I see there is a tall building, come on, hurry up! Hopefully, once on top, a helicopter will evacuate us."

The sound was so loud that Rasna could barely hear him as he grasped her by the hand and pulled her forward, the rest of the group following.

They ran towards the hotel, the sound of tsunami behind them and sprinted upstairs.

"We have to get higher," Steve yelled to them and they scrambled up to the 10th floor as fast as they could.

They had barely reached the top when the tsunami crashed its wave into the beach, smashing everything in its path.

Many of the guests had crowded up the window to see the wave, but most of them ran back in fear. Screams and yells filled the hotel whilst Rasna stood, fascinated, by the window.

As the water rumbled towards the hotel, it shook as if a minor earthquake had jolted it and the glass vibrated with the motion.

Rasna hoped to catch a glimpse of her sister or uncle, but instead saw that the palm trees that had stood so firmly were being bent easily like toothpicks as they could not resist the force of the water. Rasna saw empty surfboards and Kayaks bouncing on the churning water, their owners nowhere to be seen.

They heard again a chilling sound over the roar of the water, and then there was the sound of glass splintering and fragmenting. In quick succession, the wave smashed the windows on one floor after another.

The building lurched, throwing Rasna off balance, and she gripped the railing, hoping to survive this wave, but all one could do now was watch and hope for the best.

"Look, I do not feel comfortable waiting here, the wave could be higher, and this building has twenty-seven floors. I suggest we get to the top."

"You are right Steven and thank you for directing us to safety, if I had been on my own, I would not have taken this seriously, and most probably would have drowned in the sea." She impetuously stood on her toes and kissed Steven on the cheek.

"Thank you, that is sweet of you, but this is no time for expressing appreciation, that can come later. If we live through this, that is." However, Steven smiled tenderly.

Most people in the group wanted to stay back, because not only did they feel safe at this height but were elderly and unable to climb further.

As they climbed the stairs, Steve turned to her and said "We are in the same boat, you are worried about your sister; me about my daughter and wife, yet we are powerless to help them and only hope for the best.."

"Oh Steve, please don't worry," Rasna had tears in her eyes for despites being anxious about his family, Steve had managed to sustain the morale of not only her, but of the whole group "I am sure, like us, they found some shelter from the tsunami."

"I hope that is true for your relatives, but sadly, that is not true in my case, for I know they are dead, I only wish it were not so. We got separated during the first wave, - my daughter was paddling near the seaside whilst my wife kept an eye on her. I am only alive because I left them to fetch my wife a cup of coffee. How I wish I had stayed back; I don't want to live without them." His eyes were shining, and he wiped his forehead. "It was me who suggested this place at this time of year, it will be a holiday to remember, I said!"

"Same here, it was I who insisted we come at this time to be here for the birth of my niece/nephew. On top of having to deal with the tsunami, my sister does not have a good husband nor a good mother-in-law. They will put themselves first, oh I wish I had stayed back with her. As for my uncle, he is the kindest man alive, but just so he could help me, we decided to leave Matara on the morning of the 26th, and as if that was not bad enough, he, at my suggestion, stopped at the beach! We would have been halfway up-country by now…!"

They were silent till they reached the top floor, both enveloped in shame and guilt.

In the meantime, the tsunami kept up its pressure and was rising higher and higher. As she looked down, Rasna saw a lot of debris in the water, cars, boats, pieces of building, trees - and shuddered when she sat there were even bodies floating in the wreckage! The water had come up to seven floors of their hotel and flooded the streets.

Suddenly they heard a voice on a speaker.

"If you have evacuated to the upper floor of a building, you are not safe. Repeat, you are not safe. Please leave this building immediately and go to another higher building or hill.; Please do not panic, if you leave now you will have time to reach high ground and the authorities will assist in your evacuation. Good luck."

"What are we going to do now?" she asked in desperation

"I don't think we have many options, even if we go out when the water retreats, there will be no time till the next wave. I see there might be some air evacuation. I suppose we can go downstairs as the water ebbs, and then we have ten minutes before the next wave to find a higher building." Many of the guests had crowded at the window to see wave come in and were screaming and yelling.

"We can't get far in that time?" Rasna exclaimed. "I am exhausted and there will be debris and objects on the roads, making it difficult to move fast."

"I know, but we have no other alternative, with waves this size, the water would travel a mile inland, so I suggest we go to a building nearby which is higher, and then on to the next till we reach a safe distance. Plus, there is flight evacuation in place, and they need to see us!"

Rasna saw a man with a beard, cell phone in his hand, his flowered shirt blowing in the wind, his face showing a look of desperation.

As the water rumbled towards them, the building shook and the glass vibrated.

"Look at the size of that wave!" one man standing nearby exclaimed. "Some of the people who trying to flee the water are being swallowed by it!"

The smell of seawater was strong, much stronger than it should have been at this height, Rasna thought.

"Are we all agreed that we should go down? I guess the others were right, the water has receded, so we only have about ten minutes before the next wave," Steve said.

Some of them agreed whilst the others opted to stay back.

After having decided on the next course of action, the ones who had decided it best to go downstairs as quickly as possible, began their descent down the stairs.

They stepped gingerly on the rungs and the surface, for the floor beneath them was dripping with water. There were pieces of trash caught on the railing wrapped around the pillars that were holding the staircase, and they noticed with surprise and horror that included in the debris and trash were floating dead bodies.

"Yukk!" Rasna wrinkled her nose as a pungent smell surrounded them.

The bodies had not begun to decay yet, but the tsunami had mixed sewage, gasoline, garbage and assorted chemicals into an odour that none had experienced before.

They quickly ran out of the building and within five minutes, had entered another taller building where they were joined by a group of tourists,

As they climbed the stairwell of the building, one of them remarked, "Isn't it strange how quickly one reacts in danger situations? Who would have thought that we could walk here in less than ten minutes? And anyway, I don't think coming to a higher building is any safer for they are all collapsing like cardboard boxes!"

"I agree that people react differently to dangerous situations -some people panic whilst others take advantage of the situation." Rasna recalled the youngsters trying to loot a shop. "And as for a taller building being safer, you are right, there is no guarantee, but at least we will safe there, even if it is only temporary, for we will have to find another taller building!"

"Let us try and be optimistic please" Steve tried to calm everyone. "Now, everybody who has a phone, please try and ring the police, fire department or anybody for help! Earlier on somebody queried about rescue buses being set in place, and, just to let you know, they have been. We will have to try all venues to safety."

"Yes, we will." Some of them took out their mobile phones. "But we have been trying since the tsunami began, and the phone lines are either jammed or there is no signal!"

In desperation, they tried calling repeatedly, but, even when they finally did manage to get through, were encountered by voicemail. and even though they left messages, had no way of knowing if they were heard.

Chapter 54

Kirti go up on the morning of the 26th after a restless night and saw that there was a text from Rasna.

'Kirti, delete this text as soon as you have read it, this is just to let you know so you don't worry. By the time you read this I will have left for Colombo with Chitappa, where Mark will join me on the 28th. If Praana asks about me, tell him you know nothing. Will talk to you later when everything has calmed down and do not worry, Mum and Dad will be coming later today. Lots of love and look after yourself. Don't give up hope, you will be London soon, with my beautiful niece or nephew!'

Kirti smiled, for although she would miss Rasna, she was glad that she had left. She deserved better and Mark was a decent guy.

After she had had a wash, she went downstairs, wishing Murugan would bring a cup of tea for her too, as he did for Praana and Ruvini. She sighed and entered the lounge where, to her surprise, Praana had not left for the plantations, but was listening to the TV with Ruvini

"Praana, how come you are watching TV so early in the morning?"

"Shhhh, Kirti." Praana glared at her. "Don't say another word!"

'A tsunami has hit the islands of Sri Lanka, /Thailand and India and many thousands of people are feared dead. Another wave of a bigger size is expected, and all people are warned that they should either move to a taller building or look out for evacuation planes.'

"Oh my god," Kirti exclaimed her hand on her mouth, fearing for Rasna. Where was she?

"We should leave as soon as possible," Praana cried. "Amma, you can come with me and Kirti, you can come with your uncle and your sister."

"No, I will have to come with you for Rasna and Chitappa have left! I just got a text from Rasna!"

"What!" both Praana and Ruvini cried in unison. "How selfish are they? They knew about the tsunami and have left you? And here you are all the time telling us how much your family love you!"

"No, Praana, they left long before the tsunami hit us! They would not have known about it."

"Why are you arguing with her, Praana, we have to leave as soon as possible."

"Yes, Amma." Praana turned away from Kirti and turned to look at the television where there were scenes of complete chaos as women and children were running around, looking for any type of shelter that would protect them from the wave. "I will get the car."

"Come on, I am ready, let's leave!" Ruvini cried impatiently.

"I am ready too." Kirti clutched her stomach as she felt a searing pain. "Praana, I think I am in labour. I need to go to hospital."

"No, you are not coming with us," Praana said nastily as he opened the front door.

Kirti felt another spasm and had a strong premonition of half understood fears and dread of what was in store for her. But surely Praana would not be so cruel as to leave her?

"He is right, Kirti. Murugan is here, he will look after you." Ruvini looked at her with a calculating look in her narrow eyes.

"But, Praana, Amma you cannot leave me here! Please!" Kirti clutched Ruvini's sleeve.

Her mother-in-law shrugged off her hand, and as soon as she heard the honk of Praana's car, left the room slamming the door after her.

Kirti looked after them, shocked, for she had, without a thought for her or her grandchild, driven off into the traffic, leaving her in a shadow land that was between life and death.

Murugan had come into the room silently and looked at her with kindness.

"Don't worry, madam, I am here. Do you think baby is coming?"

"No, no," Kirti whispered. "I think it might have been the stress, but what can we do? How can we save ourselves; the water is everywhere!"

"Madam, our life is in God's hand."

Murugan had not liked the way Kirti was treated and felt sorry for her, but to abandon her in her condition was cruel. He had a daughter and would not have wished in-laws and a husband like Praana for her, he would rather she stay unmarried…

However, they had more urgent things to deal with, so he shut the door, hoping to keep the water out, but knew it was an impossible task and that it would only be a matter of time before the house would be flooded.

"Come with me, Murugan. Hurry up, we will be safer upstairs." Kirti began climbing the stairs.

"No, ma'am, you carry on, I will see that the door is bolted."

"No, Murugan come up, do not worry about that!" Kirti had reached the top of the stairs when she heard a blast and saw that it had caused a piece of ceiling to cave in, and pieces of debris were plummeting down. A steel girder holding the wall had smashed into the wall on one side.

"Murugan, come on!" Kirti said urgently and in alarm from the top of the steps.

Murugan let out a gurgling sound and she saw with horror that not only had the water from the sea seeped into the house, but that a piece of metal from the steel girder was jutting out from his chest.

"Oh, Murugan, don't worry I am coming."

As fast she could, Kirti waddled over to him with difficulty, for he sat against the wall, a piece of metal protruding from his chest. A trickle of blood ran from the corner of his mouth and covered the wall behind him. The blood was oozing from the wound on his chest and she realised that he had already lost a lot of blood.

"Murugan, oh Murugan, why did you stay back? You should have come with me." There were tears in Kirti's eyes as she took his hand and held it to her cheek, her tears soaking it.

"Madam, go, another wave..." But before he could complete the sentence, his body shuddered for a moment then was still.

Kirti wiped the tears from her face as she looked down at Murugan and realised she had to save herself and the baby.

The television was blaring that people should leave low building and try and reach higher buildings and was reminding them there would be another wave on its way.

Kirti knew she could not survive the tsunami, for not only was she fighting the ferocity of the water but was heavily pregnant. But then, she thought of her child who she had to protect, and with that thought, she left her home, hoping she would find help outdoors. And as she turned for a last look at her home, felt that the dreams which she had had when she got married, had vanished, leaving only an echo of them behind.

She waded through the garden that was full of water which had garbage cans, chairs and other bits of scrap floating in it.

By the time she reached the street, she was breathing heavily and there were beads of sweat on her forehead, and a strand of hair had escaped from her bun fell across her clammy temple. She swiped it back with her hand, all the time hoping that either Praana had had a change of heart and would come looking for her, or that she could come across Rasna and her uncle.

But all she could see were a lot of empty cars that had been abandoned everywhere Walking slowly and looking around her, she held on to anything for support, for she was hindered not only by the debris that she came across, but by her weight.

Cars and vehicles had been thrown every which way, and many of them were smashed, and Kirti wondered if Praana was in one of them or if he had managed to escape? She saw one car had been flung so far above the ground, she was sure it must be about twenty feet high.

The streets were littered with pieces of wood, metal, cans, and worst of all, she saw human bodies that lay on the sidewalks.

There were people wandering the streets and she turned to them for help which went unnoticed, and all around her she heard cries, some of rage, other of despair and helplessness, others calling for their missing friends or relatives.

But everyone had two question in common– where were their missing loved ones, and most of all, where was the loving God in all this chaos? It seemed that he had some terrible intention or punishment in mind and was using the Tsunami as His tool to visit the earth to cause chaos and death in the pearl of the south and other parts of the world. Had he asked his angels to call for all the innocent souls?

"Can you please help? I think I am in labour and ohhhh…" Kirti asked breathlessly and clutched her stomach as she felt a searing pain go through it.

Everyone ignored her and hurried away, silently inferring that in the face of calamity, every man looked out for himself. Well, she was familiar with that cruel attitude, for had not her husband left her to fend for herself amidst a tsunami.

The only selfless person was Murugan who had stayed back to help her. There were tears in her eyes as she wondered if she could have somehow saved him?

People were walking and sprinting in all directions whilst small children ran to keep up with their families, and at the same time, tourists, wearing colourful exotic attire, continued to stream out. from nearby hotels.

With the exertion of oncoming labour and trying to find a safe place, Kirti was sweating profusely, so she wiped her arms and brow which were damp with the back of her hand. Just when she thought she was going to collapse, she caught sight of a huge banyan tree and leant on it.

With one hand on the tree trunk, she caught sight of a frothy white mass of water churning and surging towards her, flooding sand destroying everything in its path.

Suddenly a car parked beside her

The driver, a deeply tanned man, pulled down the window of the car, "Hi, you should not be standing there in your condition, here, come get in." Kirti looked at him distrustfully but was reassured when she saw his kind eyes full of compassion." Don't worry, I will see that you are safe, my name is Deva."

Seeing her wavering, he got out, opened the car door, then sat her firmly and gently in the back of the car. "We have to get out of here as soon as possible. See that wave?"

"Oh my god yes! But can we reach any kind shelter before it reaches us? There are roadblocks and I think the baby is coming, Ohhhh. I am so sorry to be a burden, even my husband deserted me because of my condition."

"Don't worry, I see ruins of a building that, hopefully, will protect us." He stopped the car and gently helped Kirti into the remains of the building.

Samudra Devi

26th December 2004

Chapter 55

Urmila, meanwhile, unaware of the impending disaster facing her, got up with a headache which had been brought on by the early morning singing of the birds.

She propped her head on the pillow, listening to the different sounds of the songbirds that were disturbing the peace of the morning. The loudest was called the 'Asian Koel', and Urmila could not help but think that maybe that was the reason everyone got up so early in Sri Lanka?

"Hey, hurry up, Urmila, have you forgotten we are leaving for Matara today?" Puru stretched his arms towards the sky. "Boy, it is good to be home!"

"What, you don't consider London your home?" Urmila teased than yawned. "It is too early…" Urmila answered sleepily

"No, it is not early, the train leaves at 7.55 so we have to reach the rails station at least half an hour before."

"Okay, I thought we had plenty of time, anyway, how could I forget I will at last be meeting Kirti? I still feel we should have gone with Rasna yesterday, anyway; I won't be long."

Urmila hurriedly rose and went into the bathroom. and just as she came out drying her hair, Ramu entered the room with a silver tray with a pot of tea, milk, sugar and two cups of tea on it.

"Whew! I could do with a cuppa!" Puru said as he poured the tea into the cups and handed one to her one. "Mother never forgets her early morning ritual."

"I could do with one too, Puru, and I admire your mother's hospitable nature; she ensures that everyone is made comfortable, down to the last detail." She took the cup from Puru, opened the balcony door. and went out into the balcony. "But Puru, what do we know about this boy, Annama?" Urmila said over her shoulder. "Have you met him?"

Crows were beginning to croak loudly as they hovered and flapped their shiny black wings.

Puru followed her and took a deep breath of the fresh cool air.

"No, I have not, Urmila, he is Praana's cousin, and my mother has met him and guarantees that he is a nice person; and that is enough for me!" Puru replied angrily.

She looked down and saw that a van that had a glass door had stopped outside their house, but instead of passengers, it held a variety of bread.

"Ohhh..Those look so fresh and delicious!" Urmila commented as she looked down at them from the balcony.

She noticed that Ramu had purchased some bread rolls and was hurrying back into the house.

"So, does that mean, that just on the word of your mother, you are willing to make the same mistake as you did with Kirti?"

"Urmila, we both decided that it was the best thing for Kirti."

"You persuaded me into it, Puru, I would have liked her to get married in London. There are nice Tamil boys there too you know. In London, I would have been able to meet her every day and played with my grandchildren! But now I will not only be able to spend a few days with my grandchild, and, back in London, will always be worried as to how she is managing with a new baby, not only that, who will she turn to if she needs advice or is unhappy?!"

"Don't be so dramatic, Urmila, you have been listening to Rasna, your daughter, who, I must say, is like her mother. Dramatic!" he said with a flourish. "Give me an example of one marriage that does not have its ups and down!"

"That is not the point and you know it Puru! Come to think of it, we did not really know anything about Praana, and more importantly whether Kirti would be able to adjust with their family. You know what a gentle Kirti is, not like Rasna, who would not be intimidated by anything or anyone!"

"Exactly my point, Urmila. Kirti is a kind and gentle girl and she is very impressionable. She could have met a wrong boy from London too. And Praana is a good, responsible man, they have tea plantations, and do you want me to go on? What more does a wife want except financial security?"

"What about emotional security, Kirti is unhappy, I can feel it." Urmila insisted stubbornly. "Your mother only visited her once and that too for a very short time, so how can she or you be so certain?"

"I don't want to talk about Kirti, Urmila!"

"Okay, the reason I brought that up was so that we do not make the same mistake again. What do we know really know about Annama or his family and why have you finalised everything without consulting me? Especially when I assured Rasna this was just a holiday with no ulterior motive on our side?" Urmila said angrily and breathlessly as she twisted her hair in a bun.

"Well, he is Praana's cousin and mother said that..." Puru looked uncomfortable.

"Oh no Puru! Not that again! Why does your mother have such a hold on you and your brother?"

"I don't know what you mean, Urmila." He glared at her.

"Well, it is because of your mother that Kadamba, who is such a nice and kind man, is divorced, and she is the reason why Namisha left him. She is also the cause of Lakshmi leaving home and marrying Sarvash!"

"Don't bring Lakshmi into it," Puru growled. "She bought it upon herself! If she had been sensible, she would have seen what kind of man Sarvash really was, and that had she stayed with him, would have ended up being miserable anyway."

"You know that is not what I mean, Puru, just that if Aadi had been a kind person, Lakshmi would have turned to her in her time of need instead of choosing death!"

"Noo…" Puru stuttered. "That is why getting the girls married to suitable men is the only right thing to do."

"You are not thinking in the long term, Puru, what if either Kirti or Rasna find they are unhappy, who are they going to turn to? Your mother? I don't think so, we are in London so what if they too feel the only way out is…"

"Shut up, woman! You think I do not think of our daughter's happiness? Well, the only reason Mother wanted us to stay back was so we could go to Galle from here, because that is where Annama lives. She wanted us to spend time with him and his mother, Mega, Praana's aunt, so you can see their lifestyle for yourself. Now, does that satisfy you, and are we packed?"

"No, it doesn't, and yes we are packed; what time did you say the train departs?" Urmila tactfully changed the subject

"I told you! It leaves at 7.55 a.m. and that we must be there by at least 6.a.m"

"Oh, yes of course you did," Urmila murmured sheepishly then thought she would bring up the Rasna's subject again. "But I still think we should talk to Rasna, for if you are seriously considering Annama for Rasna she should know.

When you mentioned him back in London, I thought you were joking, for you had not told me anything about him…"

"Oh, are you trying to tell me that I don't tell you everything that goes on? Well, I am telling you now that there is no use in talking to Rasna for her marriage will take place on 27th December, that is tomorrow!"

"Oh no, Puru, no!" Urmila cried. "Why the rush? She is not going to agree, but we can get them engaged, return to London, and come back later for the wedding! I want my daughter to have a proper wedding and not hurriedly arranged like Kirti's!"

"Go back, go back to London? Where she will no doubt continue with that boy and… No, I want my daughter to have a wedding that is traditionally arranged, arranged by parents, and if it is done in a hurry, so be it!"

"That boy's name is Mark!" Urmila said indignantly. "And he is a good decent boy. He does not want to elope with Rasna but had only wanted to honourably ask you for her hand with your blessing!"

"Over my dead body," Puru remarked, picking up a suitcase, as Urmila followed him, trying to control her frustration.

Chapter 56

As they went out into the garden, a sweet smell of jasmine and frangipani wafted across the garden where Puru's mother was waiting for them.

"Amma, there was no need for you to get up this early! I would have loved to sleep in bur we have to leave now so we are in time to catch the Samudra Devi."

"Yes, I knew you were leaving, remember we decided on it? Anyway, I always get up early," Aadi replied curtly. "Puru Magan, you must have some breakfast before you leave."

Puru looked at his watch. "We don't have much time, Amma, but something quick and light sounds nice, Urmila, what do you think?"

After Urmila nodded her head Aadi turned to Puru.

"That is a wise decision, come, Ramu has already prepared some light breakfast. In the meantime, I will instruct the driver to put your luggage in the car. He will take you to Fort Station, it is not far from here."

"Thanks, Amma." Urmila said, hoping the light breakfast would include the fresh bread rolls she had had seen Ramu buy from the van.

Ramu had included them the breakfast and were laid out on the table and tasted just as fresh and delicious as Urmila had expected. They finished their breakfast, then went to the car where Aadi was waiting for them.

"Take this with you," she held out a carrier bag "it will get warm later and there are bottles of water and a few snacks in it."

"Thank you, Amma, that is very thoughtful of you."

"Now, Annama will meet you at Galle station." Aadi explained. "They insisted you have lunch at their home before going onto Matara. You can meet him and judge for yourself that, like Praana, he comes from a good stable background. Will that put your mind at rest, Urmila?"

"Yes, it will, although we are sure that you have chosen wisely. Isn't that right, Urmila?"

Urmila glared at him, but nodded whilst Puru touched his mother's feet, embraced her then got into the car followed by Urmila.

Aadi stood waving and Puru turned to wave back.

"Why did you agree to lunch, Puru?" Urmila exclaimed angrily. "You know I want to see Kirti as soon as possible."

In truth, she wanted to warn Rasna, how can one get married within one day nowadays? She was certain Puru must have told Aadi about Mark, hence the rush.

"I know Urmila, and I want to too, but this is the only chance we will get to see how the family's lifestyle, something you insisted on, don't forget."

"Yes, I did, but that was before you told me that Rasna marriage is arranged for tomorrow. Puru please don't let us stay any longer than we have to."

"No, we won't, Urmila, the Samudra Devi only takes about two hours from here and I think Matara is less than an hour from there so we should be there by late afternoon."

"So instead of lunch, I will have tea with my daughters," Urmila sighed.

They drove down Galle road, the famous road which had an entirety of different trades. There were banks, fruit and vegetable stalls, bakeries, restaurants, and cafés and Urmila even saw a dry cleaner, launderette, and supermarket.

"Puru, look!" Urmila cried excitedly. "Look over there, they have food stalls."

"Okay, okay, Urmila, don't get so excited. One would think it is the first time you have been to Colombo! But yes, they are called roadside 'chefs'. There are called roadside 'chefs' because they wave their woks over a flame and greasy hob. The chicken, rice and noodles are tossed into the wok and around it is an odour of spices like cinnamon turmeric and pepper."

"You seem to know a lot about them?"

"That is only because I used to love their food when I was young. In fact, I remember, I used to bunk my college classes just to come here to eat!" He smiled nostalgically. "Those were the days!"

Next to the so called 'chefs' were stalls that sold cold refreshing King coconut, which was called Thambilli, a drink that was unique to Sri Lanka and available in almost all shops and stores. Thambilli was pure coconut milk that was very refreshing and had a slight sweet taste.

"If we had time, I wouldn't have minded one of those, for it is getting warm, as Amma said it would," Urmila said. "I wonder if the coconut milk is better than the one we had at the Galle Hotel?"

All around, Urmila could see stalls stretching across the road, and there were a colourful variety of seasonal fruit and vegetable, fish, pot plants, sweets and household ware, for Galle Road was well known for its vibrancy and productivity - and amongst the crowd of people rushing about, there was the noise of sellers as they tried to attract customers by shouting the prices of their products.

Puru saw the look on Urmila's face and smiled. "No, my dear, no time for stopping here, maybe when we come back next week."

A skilful motor biker swerved around their car with precision and Urmila saw an old man in a sarong waiting to cross the road. But as the cars were just honking and passing by, he got fed up and finally went to a zebra crossing nearby. However, even there, the cars drove past, horns blaring, Urmila held her breath, wishing the best for the old man and as they passed him and Urmila turned her head to look back, he was still waiting at the crossing.

Their car finally stopped outside the station where there were small boutiques and restaurants on the pavement. There were hawkers of all kinds, some selling cheap fake Rolexes, sunglasses, suitcases etc. but it was here it was that the Auto rickshaw drivers reigned, for they made the loudest noises as they blared their horns trying to attract customers.

Their driver got out, took their luggage out of the boot of the car and beckoned to a porter, instructing him to take them to the platform where the Samudra Devi stopped on its way to Galle. The porter nodded his head, arranged their luggage on his head, and whilst clutching on to it with one hand, gestured to Puru and Urmila with the other to follow him.

The station was huge and built at the heart of the city. It had ten platforms and catered to about a thousand commuters a day and was as busy inside as it was outside.

Even though they were early, there was hubbub of commuters inside the station, for people were darting around the platforms, most looking bewildered and confused.

They passed the ticket office where there was a long queue – all pushing and shoving, for, to them, waiting was an unknown concept. They were either using their legs or elbows as weapons and some even resorted to giving deathly stares to help them get to the front.

They overtook a skinny man who was carrying a wicker basket containing slices of pineapple perched on his head.

"Thank god we booked ahead and do not have to stand in that line. Good old Kadamba!" Puru exclaimed. "It was he who thought of booking beforehand."

There were a group of people gathered near a wall, some peering intently at the several framed timetables that were pinned on it, whilst others were making notes. Finally, Urmila and Puru reached their platform, where they had to wait, for the Samudra Devi started from Maradana station.

The porter dropped the luggage near a bench and after Puru had tipped him, sat on an uncomfortable bench beside Urmila.

Puru yawned. "I wonder if we should have gone to Maradana station, it seems to be too crowded here."

"We should be okay, since Kadamba has reserved our seats." Urmila said.

She wiped her forehead then took out a packet of biscuits and a bottle of water that Aadi had thoughtfully provided, but when she saw a young man approaching, quickly put them away.

"Puru, we should have asked the porter to wait, for we won't be able to carry the luggage inside!"

"Don't worry, there are plenty of them around."

In the meantime, the young man had reached their bench.

"Sir, as the train will be full, I can help you get seats," he said.

"No, thank you, we have reservations so should have no problem," Puru told him.

"Ah you are new to this country I see." The stranger eyed them curiously.

"No not at all, we are Tamils and have lived here most of our lives."

"Well, that must be a long time ago, otherwise you would not be travelling by train and would also be aware that there is no such thing as reservations, the train is always too full."

Puru saw that he would not be able to get rid of the young man easily so quickly accepted his help, realising that his assistance would come at a cost.

"All right, but how much do you charge? And can you help us with the luggage too, please?"

"Only… rupees sahib, and don't you worry, I will help with your luggage too and see that you have good seats."

Chapter 57

Finally, the Samudra Devi rolled slowly into the station, and even before it had stopped, Urmila was horrified to see that people were scrambling to get on to it. When it did finally stop, they joined the multitude of other commuters waiting to get on the train.

Urmila looked panic-stricken at the thought of not getting a seat, but the young man had efficiently picked up their luggage and gestured to them to follow him as he jumped on the train nimbly.

"My God, but he does seem strong," Urmila commented, as she struggled to follow him

"He is used to it, for it is his job, come, hurry up."

Once in the carriage, after a lot of pushing and shoving, they finally located the man who was helping them. He placed two fingers in his mouth and let out a shrill whistle as he beckoned them to sit quickly on the two empty seats he had found. They thanked him profusely, and after paying him, seated themselves, but the other commuters had begun to question the man's authority.

"Hey, we were here first, who are you too…?"

"Please do not blame him, he was only trying to help. In any case we have reservations," Puru interrupted quickly.

"As do we," a couple spoke up. "Having reservations makes no difference, the one who comes first gets the seats!"

Puru looked at the angry faces and muttered, "I hope this does not start a riot. I wish Kadamba had told us about this, I would surely have got a taxi, or could have flown to Galle, but I think the reason he wanted us to travel by train was so we get to see the beautiful scenery of this part of Sri Lanka. And had it not been for that boy I don't think we would have found any seats."

"You know, I too had my doubts about him and that he was only out to make money, but you are right. It is thanks to him that we have a place to sit. Anyway, I cannot understand the point in booking tickets if the seats are not reserved?"

Urmila wiped her face then took a plastic bottle of water from her bag and took a gulp. She grimaced for the water was warm and tasted of plastic.

The train waited at the station for ten minutes till all the people who were waiting on the platform were safely inside.

Urmila looked worried.

"Puru, I don't think there should be so many people on the train, it is a health and safety issue, I am sure."

"Ah, I think you have forgotten that in this country there is no such thing as either hygiene or health and safety!"

"Maybe that is because there are too many people who would not abide by the rules and regulations, even if there were?"

The guard, satisfied that the train was full beyond the recommended safety regulations, blew his whistle to alert the driver that all was well to depart.

With the open carriage doors being occupied and commuters hanging on to every available handle, rail or person, the trains engine and gears clinked into place. Finally, the heavily laden Samudra Devi left the station, blaring its horn and slowly gathering speed, sluggishly left Colombo.

"At last, I thought the train would not get going!" Urmila exclaimed as she put the bottle back into her bag.

She turned her head towards the window and watched the view of the city as it slowly moved past.

A cool breeze wafted in through window as the train swung and hooted its way out of the city through several small villages that were surrounded by coconut trees. It rattled on, past the trees that gave of an elusive perfume that filled the compartment with its sweet fragrance.

The people who had been grumbling, soon got bored, and after finding seats, began squeezing in all manner of their luggage in available places.

A middle-aged man unpacked his belongings and spread the food his wife had cooked for him on his lap. Others took out newspapers, and there was a rustle of paper as they fluttered in the soft breeze that was wafting through the open windows.

By now everybody had settled in their seats, and some people had taken out their breakfast and flasks of tea and coffee. So, very soon the smell of curries, Ceylon spices, and in the warmth of the carriage, various body smells, superseded the earlier elusive fragrance of the trees.

The already humid and uncomfortable atmosphere inside the carriage intensified as exhalations and perspirations of dozens of people prevailed in the carriage.

Urmila put the corner of her sari over her nose and mouth and muttered. "Why could not Kadamba have got us first class tickets, or at least second class! This is awful."

"I agree, but I am sure there must be a reason why he didn't. It is not only Boxing Day, but also the day for Buddha and people worship on this day. Added to which you wanted to be with Kirti as soon as possible."

A woman who had objected the loudest had found a seat opposite them. She glared at them as she took a dirty leaf tied up in a parcel which she first placed on her lap, then began to undo. The leaf was full of rice which she began eating hungrily, and she ate in the traditional manner, with her fingers that she licked after each mouthful.

Urmila looked at her with fascination as she finished the food, cleared her throat then belched. She saw Urmila looking at her so licked her lips, wiped her nose with the corner of her sari then pushed the leaf between seats.

A Sinhalese man wearing a smart suit and polished shoes, kept brushing imaginary bits of dust on his suit with his hand. He took out a newspaper and started reading it, occasionally looking over the top. Finally, he put it down and turned to Puru.

"You are not from here, I take it?"

"We are, but we live in London and are here on holiday. I was born and brought up here, as was my wife."

"You must be glad you are going back to England so will not be subject to the terrible things that are happening in our country."

Puru listened politely for he respected people who were opinionated and passionate about their beliefs.

"Yes, it is very disappointing to hear about the riots, demonstrations and kidnappings that are happening here daily. Having said that, I love my country dearly."

"I am glad to hear that, but you know why that is don't you?" the man grumbled. "It is because of the bitterness that has accumulated from century of foreign rule. And what is continuing to disrupt our country today is because certain sects are demanding a separate state." Having made the forceful statement, he folded the paper angrily. "And by their indifferent attitude, our government is not helping either."

"They are not to blame entirely," another man put in. "I am a Tamil, and every day I fear for my life, why only the other day I heard that a small Tamil boy had been taken from his classroom to be recruited as a boy soldier!"

"Ah, I think both sides are responsible for we do not know which side forcibly enlisted the boy."

"You are right, but then who are we to judge? Everybody is on the defensive – it is one of them or one of us – that is the way this county has become."

Urmila was troubled by the conversation, disappointed that despite her organisation's efforts, there were still ongoing struggles and problems that made the political situation in Sri Lanka just as prejudicial and dangerous as when she had left, if not worse.

She shivered with disgust as she saw a dusty cobweb crawl across one of the suitcases.

Opposite her sat a young woman lady with a young child on her lap, who was gazing at everyone with innocent curiosity.

Urmila smiled at the child, thinking how untouched he was by the wars, sins, and materialism of the world. She rubbed her stinging eyes but smiled tenderly when she thought of her grandchild who she would be holding in her arms soon.

"Puru, has your conversation changed your mind?" she asked.

"Changed my mind about what, Urmila?" Puru asked irritably, looking at his watch.

"About getting Rasna married, of course," Urmila replied.

"And what makes you think that? I thought we had decided it was the best thing for her?"

"We had not decided, you had, with your mother! I was talking about the political state of the country, how fragile it is and how people are living in fear. Can you imagine our daughter travelling like this, living in a country under these kinds of conditions? My daughters are not used to this kind of life; I was born and brought up here and love my country but nonetheless, cannot imagine living here now. In your conversation, the man said that Tamil people are struggling against discrimination, and the impression I got was that because of it, they are desperately trying to mask their customs and traditions, instead of being proud of them."

"You are right Urmila, but I don't understand why the Sri Lankan lifestyle and politics should shape your decision; we have examined the families of the boys. They all have cars and are doing well, the girls will travel in cars, not in trains, we didn't have to either, it is only because we have to be in Matara by the 26th and as this is the fastest and only way to be there and meet Annama as well…"

Urmila wished she had not brought up the subject, for nothing and nobody was going to deter Puru when he set his mind on something. She looked around the carriage and saw there were two ladies sitting beside the young woman with the baby. The ladies were Tamil, and she knew this because of the way they were dressed and also because they had red Pottu on their forehead, which signified their marital status. They had draped their saris Tamil style – Palu was wound around the hip then tucked in at the back.

Urmila felt her headache to be looming, the stress of the journey, meeting Annama and then finally the journey to Matara would certainly see the return of her migraine, so she leant her head and closed her eyes, hoping that a short nap would ward it off.

After some time, she opened her eyes sleepily as the train approached a level crossing barrier. She looked out of window and saw a van behind a cycle as the train clanked and creaked to a halt.

Chapter 58

"Have we reached Galle?" she asked.

"We have stopped in Peraliya and as you were sleeping, Urmila, I did not want to wake you, and no, we have not reached Galle, it is only 9.30 a.m.".

"Where is Peraliya?" Urmila asked rubbing her eyes. "I thought this was to be a direct train to Galle?"

"It is, maybe the train is waiting for the signals to change and Peraliya is near the village of Telwatta.."

"Well, I hope we reach Galle soon for I feel another one of my migraines coming on."

"We should be there soon. Peraliya is only about 15 km from Galle."

The train lurched slightly and stopped. Urmila craned her neck out of the window and was surprised when she saw that there was water around the train and that some people were trying to climb on the roof of the train.

"Puru, something strange is going on, there is water everywhere."

Everyone in the carriage groaned and looked at their watches.

"What is going on…" Puru exclaimed as the people in the compartment began to panic.

One man looked out of the window and turned to the others. "I can see that one carriage has been smashed."

At that moment, the driver came to see what damage had been done and informed them that a tsunami was on its way.

"Oh no, Puru what is a tsunami?"

"Well as far as I know, a tsunami is a sea earthquake."

He had barely finished speaking when a wave of water flooded the carriage. Everybody had panicked but calmed down when they saw that the water around the train carriages had suddenly receded.

"Thank God!" Urmila sighed in relief as did the other passengers.

"No, Urmila, we are still in danger for another wave will surely follow, maybe within ten minutes."

The baby on the lady's lap began crying and the mother tried desperately to calm her.

"I think we should shut all the windows," one of the men suggested uneasily.

"I agree," another concurred after looking out of the window. "The other carriages have closed the windows too."

Several of the men began to board the window to keep the second wave out, however, they were stopped by others.

"No, keep them open, we might have to climb out quickly, and some are saying we will be safer on top of the train."

"Urmila, they are right, I think you should leave the train, you will be safer outside." Puru turned to Urmila.

"What do you mean, I will be safer outside? I am not going anywhere without you." Urmila clasped Puru's arm and repeated, "I am not going anywhere without you."

One man exclaimed, "Look, I am not a passenger of this train, but some of us have come from a nearby village, several of whom have climbed the roof of the train thinking it will be safer on the rooftop. The only way to save ourselves is to find shelter on something tall or high till the tsunami subsides, that is the only way we can protect ourselves, and I agree with the man who suggested that we should keep the windows open."

"But did you have to leave your village? You could have gone to a hill or tall building." one of the passengers asked. "Surely that would have been safer?"

"Everybody was frightened, and when one person suggested it, the rest just followed. The Samudra Devi actually does not stop here, maybe it did because of the signal, or maybe because they knew about the tsunami."

"How did the tsunami destroy your village?" was the question on everybody's mind but asked by Puru.

The man who was from Perilya replied, "The tsunami reached our village in the morning about 9.30, and as today is an auspicious day, being the Buddhist full moon and Christmas too most of the fishermen did not go fishing, otherwise they would all have died in the tsunami!"

"That was lucky for them!" Urmila exclaimed

"Don't waste time talking, Urmila, leave!" Puru cried urgently

Suddenly, more water flooded into the carriages and he saw Urmila floundering in it. She was gasping for air and clutching Purus suitcase for support.

"Urmila, are you okay?" Puru cried as he was thrown to the corner of the compartment.

"It is not safe inside, I am going on the roof," one of the men said, trying to prise open the half-boarded window of the train.

"Yes, I agree but we should let the children and window out first." Urmila spluttered.

Puru turned towards Urmila. "Yes Of course the women and children should go first, Urmila you should go as soon as possible with the women."

"Puru, why don't you come as well?" Urmila gasped, drenched in water.

"There are some people here who cannot swim, so I will stay back to help them, please go Urmila, there is no time."

When she saw that Puru was adamant about staying back, she tried to persuade the woman with the baby to come with her but noticed that her arms were empty.

"Where is your baby? Please hurry up and come with me, there is no time to waste." Urmila grabbed her arm.

"No, I won't!" the woman choked, tears in her eyes. "I do not want to save myself for I could not protect my baby, she was swept away by the force of the water, and I don't want to live without her!" There were tears streaming down her eyes as she looked at her arms which, till a few minute ago had held her baby.

Having failed to persuade Puru to come with her, Urmila, with a few others, climbed out of the window and onto the roof of the train, not realising she was still holding on to her husband's suitcase.

Urmila looked at her watch and saw with surprise that they had been on the roof for ten minutes when a huge wave picked the train up and smashed it against the trees and houses which lined the track.

It crashed into the train and scattered the carriages in different directions with such force that heavy concrete forms underneath the tracks were uprooted and turned upside down. Reeling from the wave, the train spun over and over, cartwheeling four times before coming to rest on a house.

Fortunately, the carriage roof that Urmila had been gripping tightly onto was thrown at a house, enabling her and the people who had been on the roof top with her to clamber onto the roof of the house for safety. She looked at what she thought was their carriage and saw Puru floundering in the water than being carried off by a wave as the whole train was finally ripped of the track.

"Puru!" she screamed before she was hit by a rod, and as she fainted, thought she could hear his voice calling her name.

Chapter 59

Urmila had come to after a few minutes and she saw with horror that, after pulling the rail line out of the ground, the powerful wave had thrown the train about twenty-five feet onto the air. The carriages had become a twisted metal wreck, and the force of the waves had torn the wheels of the carriages of them. There were about eight rust-coloured carriages lying entangled in the deep pool of water that surrounded the palm trees that had been ravaged by the tsunami.

From the roof of the house where she had been flung, Urmila saw that the baggage of the passengers had been tossed from the train and was strewn along the tracks. They had been thrown with such force that some of the trunks had opened and pieces of clothing were scattered all over what was left of the track. Urmila thought of the presents she had bought so lovingly for her unborn grandchild and wondered if they too were scattered on the dirty tracks?

Suddenly she trembled in fear. What if the tsunami had struck Matara, which was a coastal town and where both her daughters were at present?

"My god, my whole village has been destroyed," a man clinging on the roof exclaimed.

He pointed to a building that used to be a school, but now just looked like a twisted metal set! The tsunami had crushed every building in the village and even the palm trees had been snapped in half.

"My husband stayed behind, and I think I saw him in the water, maybe he is safe and…" Urmila rubbed her head for it had started throbbing.

"I am sorry, my dear, I don't think so," a middle-aged man who had been in her carriage, then on the train rooftop replied. "I am only grateful that my wife decided to stay back in Colombo."

Urmila gave a cry as she looked at him.

"I am sorry, maybe I should not have been so blunt, maybe he has been thrown free, like we were. There, there, my dear, have hope. Now, I hope somebody can come and rescue us from here?"

"I don't think anyone will be coming soon, for I heard someone who has a radio saying that because of the huge scale of the disaster, the local authorities are unable to cope, as are the emergency services, so immediate rescue is not possible."

They had been on the rooftop for a few hours and just as Urmia lost hope of being evacuated, she saw rescue helicopters flying overhead; and all of them started waving and shouting frantically.

She was to later learn that it was true that the Sri Lankan authorities had no idea where the Samudra Devi was for several hours until it was spotted around 4 p.m., And it was because of this delay that many people, who had only been severely injured in the disaster, had consequently died in the wreckage, whilst there were many bodies that were not retrieved for over a week.

But, when at last they were rescued, she asked about her husband, but was told that most people had either drowned in the train or had perished in the sea.

"Oh no! "Urmila cried then thought of her daughters, "How do I get to Matara, I have to get to Matara, both my daughters are there, and we were on the Samudra Devi to be with them!'"

"I am sorry, madam, Matara too has been badly hit by the tsunami, and there is utter devastation there, even though many people, after the first wave, drove to safety whilst others found high places where they took shelter."

"Oh, I hope my daughters are safe, they must be for my son-in-law has a car, but how can I confirm that they are all right? And if she, they are safe, where would they have been taken to?"

"I sure they would be fine ma'am, there is a shelter nearby where everyone from Matara and around will be taken to,"

Having reassured her, the rescuer moved on, trying to soothe the weeping residents who were crying over the rubble of what had once been their homes.

After a couple of hours Urmila and the others were taken to a Buddhist temple for shelter, and from there to a temporary refugee shelter that had been set up.

"I thought they were here to help us, but I overheard some of the volunteer's talking. They were complaining that the LTTE, who are supposed to be helping us, are actually hijacking food deliveries!" Urmila exclaimed in exasperation for her headache had got worse and she found it difficult to concentrate.

Urmila had begun to feel very tired, and with it came a sense of indifference in everything and everybody around her. However, at times she felt huge waves of emotions, feelings that were exhausting as she could not pinpoint them, however, she knew that they must somehow be connected to the tsunami. She cried in rage and frustration, and after a few days at the refugee shelter she could not even remember her name or how she had got to be there

The strange man with a dark beard and kind eyes, who had been with her throughout, handed her a suitcase hoping it would help her to cope with the trauma.

As Urmila looked at it blankly, he explained, "You have been holding on to it tightly since we were thrown from the train. I presume it holds fond memories of your husband and family?"

Thailand

Phuket
(24ᵗʰ December 2004)

Chapter 60

The plane landed at Phuket international airport on the morning of the 24th, and as soon as Mark had finished the formalities at the airport, he checked his mobile and found that Rasna had been trying to contact him. He frowned when he heard her voicemail informing him that her parents had arranged her wedding, which was to take place on 27th December.

This was followed by another short message informing him that, with the help of her uncle, they planned to leave for Colombo on the 26th, and she again gave her grandmother's address and phone number, which she had also left earlier and which he had memorised in case he lost his mobile; so desperate to meet and save her.

He cursed himself for not catching up with his messages earlier, else he would have taken a flight to Colombo instead of coming to Thailand; so, decided to book his ticket to Colombo immediately before leaving the airport.

He went impatiently to the booking office, but the earliest flight to Colombo was on the 27th which meant he could only reach Colombo by the 28th. He was sure Rasna would wait for him so booked and confirmed his flight to Colombo then left a voicemail on Rasna's mobile to let her know his plans and that he would see her on the 28th.

This unexpected change of plans meant he could only spend two days in Phuket, and as he had no choice but to wait, decided he would explore the city as much as he could in the short time, for he wanted to bring Rasna here for their honeymoon. However, he knew he would not enjoy his short stay for it would be overshadowed by anxiety and worry.

Mark took an auto rickshaw to his hotel, which was about 30 kms from the airport. The drive had taken forty-five minutes through Bangla Road, and as they drove, a slight breeze ruffled his hair.

He had skimmed through a brochure earlier to familiarise himself with Phuket and had learnt that Bangla Road was famous for its night life and entertainments, for as soon as the sun set, it closed all traffic and night action would begin. There were several side roads (called Soi's) leading from Bangla Road, but these were more like entertainment complexes than actual roads and were crammed with beer bars.

Mark was not really looking forward to his short stay in Phuket, also known as 'Pearl of the South', partly because he was worried about Rasna, and partly because he thought this holiday to be jinxed. He had planned the holiday with his close friend, but John had had to cancel due to a family emergency, then his parents had had an accident. Although they had not been seriously hurt, it had been a worrying time and he had thought of cancelling the holiday. But his younger sister, Amelia, Aunt, parents and Rasna had all insisted he go ahead with his plans.

"Don't worry about us now. We are fine, but how can you miss the chance of a lifetime?" his father said disapprovingly. "We went last year, and you just cannot miss the blue lagoons, rainforests, waterfalls hidden deep and waters that shine and glimmer with emerald green tint. I know it will only be for a short while and that you are not going with Rasna, but you must go, son."

"And the pink sunsets, it was just too beautiful," his mother piped up.

"If it is the money you are worried about, son, you know the holiday is on us, so go enjoy yourself!"

Mark had told his parents about Rasna and they had loved her.

His father had clapped him on the back when he had taken him aside "She is a lovely girl, hold on to her!"

"I intend to, Dad. I love her."

He closed his eyes and let his mind wander through the aisle of love and smiled as he thought of Rasna, for theirs was not a romance of grand gestures with dinners, expensive gifts or flowers, but one that was of comfort and affection.

They were simply happy to spend time together be it studying, talking, strolling down the park holding hands or unwinding at a Macdonald's or at a coffee shop. Their love for each other was solid and he missed the intimacy of her company, missed being loved by her, her lovable ways, how she would loop her hair over her ear, the twinkle in her eye, her black hair that framed her beautiful face.

As they arrived at the hotel (which he had booked beforehand as it was peak time), he noticed with delight that it overlooked the whole bay. It was tucked away on a hill that was surrounded by trees, and as there was a slight breeze, he could hear the rustling of their leaves.

As he walked through to the reception desk, he noticed with delight that there was a Chinese restaurant, some coffee shops, and a swimming pool in the hotel itself.

He signed the register and was led to his room where he had a quick shower. He was beginning to feel the jetlag, so thought he would take a quick nap.

He slept for a couple of hours, then went for another bath, but, before he did, ordered tea from room service. He emerged from his bath, rubbing his wet hair with a towel, when there was a knock on the door, and as soon as he opened it, found a waiter with a tray in his hand.

The waiter entered and placed the tray on the table, and after Mark had tipped him, he stirred the teapot and found it was Thai tea, which he quickly drank, then went down the hotel reception.

"I have only two days to see your beautiful country, starting this evening! I would also like to know the names of some restaurants please; I have heard of your delicious food!"

The receptionist smiled as he replied,

"I am glad you like our country, I would suggest you start with a visit to the Hard Rock Café which is located centrally in the Patong Beach area. Most tourists love it because it has a mixture of western and eastern foods and has an original food and drinks menu. It is one of the most popular places, and I consider it to be a must-visit for a meal, a snack, or a drink when in Phuket. It is on Patong beach which is next to the busy Bangla Road in the centre of Phuket.

"The same street that the auto rickshaw brought me from the airport?"

"Yes, the very same. The road is one of the busiest places in Phuket, a street that rises when the sun sets, and is the best place to visit for night life. It is also well known for its music, which you can hear from every pub and bar along the beach. Just walking down the street is an experience in itself, in fact I am sure you will enjoy its atmosphere sir!" The receptionist, Mark sensed, was an ardent enthusiast, for he was flourishing his hands to emphasise his complimentary portrayal of Phuket.

"Yes, my friend came to Phuket for a holiday and told me about it, amongst other nice places he said that I should not miss. Pity it is a short stay and I will only be here for two days."

"What a p for you do need more than two days to see the sights but he was right sir! In your short stay, you should not miss Patong Beach, but although it is popular during the day too, many tourists end up there after sundown, not only to enjoy its nightlife but also its surrounding areas. The lights are bright, as are the go-go dancers, but a word of caution, they will try to persuade you to accompany them to different bars and clubs. It is undoubtedly a wonderful place to just have fun, drink, and just enjoy!"

"Sounds wonderful, can you please give me directions to the place please? Mark asked. "It does sound a good place to chill."

"Any Auto rickshaw driver will know the place, sir, just mention the words Patong Beach and he will take you there!"

"Thanks a lot!" Mark waved to him as he turned and left.

He got into a vacant tuk tuk and the moment he said he wanted to go to Patong Beach the driver replied with a 'no problem, sir'.

Chapter 61

As he sat in the auto rickshaw, Mark admired the beautiful scenery and when he recalled the beautiful snorkelling places he had read about in the brochure, he decided he would find time to snorkel on 26th December, the day after Christmas, provided it was not fully booked!

As soon as he was dropped off, Mark strolled down the beach. Outside, the sky had turned different shades of colour and the roads were busy with three-wheeled-Tuk Tuks, taxis and buses. On the seaside, he saw long tailed boats that transported tourists between the marvellous and splendid islands around Phuket.

After having located Hard Rock Café, he sat for a while, sipping his cold cocktail, and looking out on to the white palm-lined beach. He was feeling peckish so called to the waiter.

"It is my first time here can you suggest what is best?"

"Ah, sir, I recommend you have who Tom Yam Goong."

"Oh dear, I have not heard about it, what exactly are the ingredients?" For unlike Rasna who loved Thai food, Mark was apprehensive in trying new dishes.

"I am sure you will love it, sir, the dish is national to Thailand. The ingredients used in it are fragrant herbs like lemongrass, lime leaves, galangal, and shallots. The dish has flavours of several different spices, with chilis and topped by the fish sauce. The main ingredient is in the form of jumbo shrimp (goong) and mushrooms. The flavour is a combination of spicy hot and sour and makes for an ideal start to a meal, or – with rice – makes for a worthy main dish."

"Does sound nice, and I do want to have something that is cultural and traditional."

"Hi, may I join you?" A young man wearing shorts, a bright shirt and sandals, asked with a smile.

When Mark nodded his head, he pulled up a chair, sat down than added, "I would definitely recommend that dish and this restaurant is the best, in fact, I will have a dish of the same!"

"Tom Yam Goong for me too," he told the waiter then turned his head and introduced himself. "Hi, my name is George." He grinned and his smile reached up to the corner of his twinkling eyes. "I am from England and have been here for a few days."

"Hi, my name is Mark, and I am from England too and, boy, am I glad to meet a fellow Englishman in a strange country!"

"Me too, I have been here for some time and haven't come across many friendly Englishmen!" George said as they waiter brought them their food. "Wow. that looks delicious, first let's eat and later I will advise you about the best places to see here."

They ate in silence and soon as they had finished Mark smiled happily.

"Wow, I enjoyed that!"

"As did I, now as promised, I will recommend a few places that I recommend you should not miss. Phuket is a shopaholic's paradise, that is if you are interested in that sort of thing. It has a variety of shopping super stores, from open-air village food markets, noisy night markets, street stalls to local shops.

They also have western-style department stores and upmarket specialist shops."

",I am not interested in shopping, but I will be coming here for my honeymoon, and my wife would love it. Must be awfully expensive though?"

"Not really, it varies, from bargains to designer labels."

"At the moment. I am only interested in buying souvenirs for my family and fiancée."

"Oh, there are traditional handicrafts, beautifully-designed clothing, jewellery, antiques, housewares and much more to choose from, I tell you the only thing you will regret is that you did not bring a bigger suitcase." George grinned, showing his gleaming white teeth. "Now would you like to try some Thai desert?"

"That was delicious and filling, but what the hell, I am on holiday, even if it is only for two days. What would you recommend?"

"How come you are on holiday for such a short time?" George looked surprised.

"It is a long story, anyway you were going to suggest something for dessert?"

"Of course, sorry, I would recommend Som Chun. It is pieces of traditional fruit in syrup with padan leaves and som sa (rare thai citrus fruit) served in crushed ice made with jasmine water. You can have toppings of either ginger and fried shallots or thin slices of mango, they both give a savoury twist to the refreshing fruity dessert! I love it! The desert is a combination of sweet salty and tangy!"

"You know all the names of the spices, George, but it does sound delicious."

"I liked it so much I made it a point to learn about the ingredients." George replied.

As soon as they had placed their order Mark leant back on his chair and explained.

"The reason I am only here for two days is because my ticket was already paid for and non-refundable, bought by my parents for me, and my girlfriend, who I am going to marry, was going to Sri Lanka."

"So why don't you stay on?" George asked as the waiter brought the dessert.

"I have to meet her in Colombo on the 28th, some personal problem I have to take care of, so have to leave here by the 27th. Gosh, you were right, this is delicious."

George told him he was an army officer and had come for a two-week vacation over the Christmas and new year period.

"Like you, my holiday was set with obstacles, my girlfriend was to join me but was taken ill at the last minute. I wanted to cancel the holiday, for it is no fun alone, but the ticket was non-refundable, same as yours, and she insisted I should go ahead and use it."

"Same situation here, I had originally planned this holiday with John, a good friend of mine, but he had to cancel at the last minute, and my girlfriend had to go to Sri Lanka. But you are spot on, it is not enjoyable alone. In fact, even the two days that I will be here seem too long."

"So, you will have to keep yourself busy, and that should not be a problem since you can cram quite a lot of sightseeing in two days! But is there no chance that your girlfriend's problem will be sorted out before then so you can extend your holiday?"

"No, George, that would not be possible, it is too complicated."

Mark explained Rasna's dilemma, and, in George he found a kind listening ear and thought him to be a cool guy.

"Yes, of course you must support her, but since you are here have you decided on what you will do, which places to see, etc?"

"No, not really, but yes, the hotel did advise me as to which places are worth visiting, so I can take back some memories to convince Rasna, my girlfriend, that this is just the right place for a honeymoon! I have already started out with a taste of nightlife today, and tomorrow, even though it is Christmas, I thought I would do a little bit of sightseeing, then on the 26th go snorkelling then leave for Colombo on the 27th."

"You have planned it well, I see."

"I am sure there is much more to explore than just a little bit of sightseeing. I will miss all the beautiful places, the waterfalls, other islands the caves etc. Oh, well, I will have to do that on our honeymoon, it will be more fun with Rasna anyway. George, if you are free now, I was planning to stroll down the beach. Would you like to join me?"

"I would love that; I could do with some company!" George's eyes crinkled with amusement.

They found it had turned dark outside, its darkness drawing its sea-mist wings over the beach as the waves exploded in clouds of spray. The sea shimmered as the moonlight tumbling its silvery rays over it like a curtain.

Although Mark was expecting something amazing, the breath-taking beauty and splendour took his breath away.

"You know, George, the sea is so beautiful that I am sure there would be years of coral splendour and reef current deep in the sea, and I cannot wait to snorkel to see their beauty! But I do feel uncomfortable about enjoying myself whilst my girlfriend is dealing with her problems alone."

"Don't worry, Mark, I am sure she would want you to experience as much as you can and enjoy yourself."

They strolled down the beach in silence, and night life was just as the receptionist had described, with lights bright and the go-go dancers who tried to lure him and George into bars. After a couple of hours, Mark yawned and turned towards George.

"I am going to call it a night, will I see you again?"

"I doubt it," George shook his head. "I am leaving tomorrow, I think I will celebrate Christmas, or half of it, with my family."

After shaking hands Mark went to back to his hotel.

As soon as the receptionist saw him, smiled. "Did you enjoy yourself, sir?"

"I did indeed, this is a beautiful place, now I need to ask you which beach is best for snorkelling?"

"We have six beaches that are perfect for snorkelling, but I would recommend Phi Phi island. There is a day tour which includes snorkelling and lunch." He handed him a booklet. "In this brochure you will find tours and their times."

Mark went up to his room where he quickly browsed through the brochure. The tour on the 26th appealed to him for the brochure described the palm trees and tropical weather, white beaches with large granite rocks at both ends of the sand. It gave details as to how the tour would explore an island where *'one could swim past fish and several types of coral under the golden sunlight.'*

The sea was emerald green and the snorkeler gave an assurance that they could enjoy Phuket's warm and clean waters to take a closer look at this rarely seen beautiful underwater world. The tour would include a taxi that would take him from his hotel to a ferry that would then take him to Phi Phi island.

He had decided that as he could not see the whole of Phuket in a day, but only visit a few places, Big Buddha being one of them. It seemed interesting for it was 45 metres tall and was situated on a hilltop between Chalong and Kiam.

'What a way to spend Christmas, though. I am alone, no Rasna, no family no John'. He sighed and ran his hair through his hair.

He lay back on the bed, his hands behind his head as he thought of the places, he would take Rasna on their honeymoon. From the brochure he had gathered that there was a romantic side to Phuket that included idyllic strolls to candlelit dinners for two. He would take Rasna to the Andaman Sea on the two-sea boat so they could explore the caves and incredible scenery as they canoed through some of the most beautiful islands around Phuket. And to end a beautiful day, in the evening, they would take part in the hustle and bustle of beach parties.

Just thinking about being in the company of Rasna bought a smile to Mark's lips as he turned on his side and drifted off to sleep.

Chapter 62

When Mark got up the following morning, his anxiety about Rasna dampened the prospect of exploring Phuket, so, before he left the hotel, once again left a message on her mobile that he would be in Colombo on the 28th and would meet her at her grandmother's house.

He went down to the hotel restaurant for breakfast, and as soon as he was seated, a waiter came over with a menu. After he had ordered a traditional Thai breakfast, he sat back and looked around at the people in the restaurant, all of whom he presumed to be tourists, most of whom were with families, however, he saw a single man sitting alone, and as soon as he saw Mark looking at him, came over with a smile.

"Hi, Merry Christmas, may I join you?"

"Hi, Merry Christmas, and please do, I hate dining alone, especially on Christmas Day! My name is Mark." Mark smiled as he introduced himself. "I see you have come prepared for the exotic weather!" he remarked, for the man was wearing a bright floral shirt, shorts, sandals and had a straw hat that dangled from his hand.

"Hi, my name is Simon, and, yes, I have come prepared, suntan cream and all! Oh, and I hate dining alone too." He smiled as he pulled out a chair and put his sunglasses on the table and his straw hat on an empty chair beside him.

They made small talk, and Mark liked him for he seemed a pleasant fellow. Before long the waiter came with his order which consisted of weak Chinese tea and jauk, which was rice porridge made of broken rice that was served with either minced pork cooked in pork stock or chicken meat cooked in chicken stock. The two parts of this dish, the rice porridge and the stock, were served together in a bowl. With it, he had ordered Thai deep-fried donuts or *pa-tong-goh*, hot soy drink or nam tao-hu and Thai mini pancakes or kha-nom krauk.

"Simon, I hope you will share with me. It looks to be too much, and I am not used to eating in the morning, so won't be able to finish it!"

"I have just finished breakfast, but I can assure you, once you have tasted it…!" Simon grinned. "But if you cannot, I will be glad to finish it for you!"

Mark tucked into the food whilst Simon poured himself some Chinese tea.

"So, Mark, how do you propose to spend the day?"

"Well, to start with, I thought of seeing the Big Buddha, but, tell me, how long have you been here and is it worth going to see it?"

"Not long, and I have not seen the Big Buddha, which I believe it is not to be missed."

"You are welcome to join me, I will be glad of the company!"

"I would love to, Mark." Simon replied cheerfully.

So, after breakfast they took an auto rickshaw to the Nakkerd hills, where the statue of the Big Buddha was situated, one of the island's most important and revered landmarks.

"Simon, it is Christmas Day, yet there are so many tourists like us, many of them with children spending Christmas on a holiday! I had always thought Christmas to be a family holiday to be spent at home," Mark looked at them in surprise.

"So did I! But everything is different these days," Simon replied as they joined a group of people, all who were looking in awe at the statue. "I am so glad I decided to come, this is something that should definitely not be missed."

There were yellow Buddhist flags in the compound flapping in the wind, with soft background dharma music.

"You know, I think the atmosphere here is very peaceful, not only because of the music but also because of the tinkling of the small bells!"

"Yes, it is, and again, I am glad I came, I would not have missed it for the world!"

The group of people were joined by a guide who explained that the statue was known among Thais as the Phra Akenakkiri Buddha.

"The whole body of the Buddha is constructed with reinforced concrete that is layered with beautiful Burmese white jade marble," he explained with pride.

"Is there any reason that the Buddha is made in white marble?" one gentleman asked.

"Yes, there is, because it shines in the sun, making it a natural symbol of hope." He pointed to a statue of Buddha which was smaller and positioned nearby. "That statue, although gold in colour, is made of brass. It is not only the statue that is remarkable, if you look around you, there is a 360-degree view of the island, with sweeping vistas of Phuket Town, Kata, Karon beaches, Chalong Bay and I think many more views of the beautiful island."

"It is breath-taking!" Mark said in awe. "Is there anything else to be seen here? I would like to explore the island's natural beauty."

"The best place would be a tour to Phang Nga Bay and its surrounding islands. There are beautiful caves you can explore at Lana Island, and other islands nearby."

"Splendid!" Mark exclaimed. "I think I have time for that, Simon, what about you, would you like to join me for that tour also? I hope so, for I have enjoyed your company."

"I have enjoyed your company too, and yes I will accompany you with pleasure!"

"Good, but before we start, I think lunch is needed! Gosh, I had such a heavy breakfast, yet I am ready for another meal. Is there a restaurant nearby?"

"It is the weather here," Simon remarked. "I feel the same. I suppose being on holiday and relaxed has something to do with it"

The guide had overheard their conversation. "Sorry, I could not help overhearing, there is the Nakkerd Sea View Restaurant that is nearby. And the food there is reasonable in terms of taste and price and the view, of course, is wonderful. A lot of tourists go there after visiting the Buddha."

After thanking him, Mark and Simon walked down the road to Nakkerd Hills towards Nakkerd sea view restaurant.

"You know, Simon, although the road seems to be in good condition, it has too many curves and steep climbs for my liking. Hey, can you spot the restaurant? I cannot, I am too busy trying to avoid the steep curves!"

"No, I cannot, either. Oh yes, I can, at last there it is! Thank God, I was beginning to think we were lost."

"There is no chance of that out here for people are extremely helpful. Whew, I am dying for a cold beer." Mark wiped the sweat off his forehead.

They sat outside the restaurant in the sun drinking chilled beers, and, after a light lunch of mixed vegetable stir fry and spring rolls, again took an auto rickshaw to Phang Nga Bay, which was without a doubt one of Phuket's most fascinating landscape. The scenery was outstanding, and they were told that the best way to explore it was in a kayak that would slowly glide among giant cliffs and its surrounding islands. Although Mark admired the islands, with their beaches of white sand, emerald green sea and the corals, he could but help miss Rasna.

The had just finished the kayak tour and thought they could cram one more excursion.

"Mark, I went to Phuket Fantasea and I thoroughly enjoyed the experience. I do not know whether it is something you would like to visit?"

"It is all so wonderful that it is difficult to decide which one to omit and which one to see. I think, so far, we have varied it a bit by exploring the Phang Nga Bay, natural beauty, and seeing the Statue of the buddha. Before deciding, tell me a bit more about the Fantasea."

"Well, it is kind of an entertainment park that is bright and colourful. There are a lot of shops, and, of course fun fair games, but I found the main attraction to be the stage performances that are given by Thai actors, dancers and acrobats – and to my surprise they were accompanied by their huge elephants. I enjoyed it but I do not know if it is your thing."

"Sounds a bit like Bangla street that is full of entertainment too, I think one needs to spend time to really enjoy Fantasea."

"Maybe you are right, in that case we should go to Rang Hill, it overlooks Phuket town with its lights and there is also a restaurant there that should not be missed, and where we can have dinner. People go up there to admire views of the southern part of the island: Chalong, Panwa and even of the Big Buddha."

"That sounds like a perfect end to a perfect day!"

The took an auto rickshaw again, which was the main mode of transport, that took them to Rang Hill,and as they sat outside the restaurant overlooking the sea, a waiter came up to them for their order.

"What would you recommend, Simon? You have been here before and would know their speciality. I had Tom Yam Goong yesterday and loved it!"

"Then I would recommend Som Tam and please do not ask me the ingredients! I just know that it is delicious and very traditional. Ah maybe you can explain?" He turned to the waiter.

"That is an excellent choice, sir, it is grated green papaya with fish sauce, lime juice, chilies, dry shrimps, green beans and peanuts but there are variations to it."

"Sounds good to me." Mark smiled.

"And I will have that too," Simon added. "And in the meantime, we would like something to drink, it is so hot! I will have iced Thai tea with milk and sugar."

"And I will have the same too." After they had finished dinner Mark turned to Simon.

"I would love to go for a short stroll down the beach, I had a short walk on it yesterday and loved it." Mark said. "I am looking forward to the snorkelling tomorrow, so will need my sleep to be alert to really appreciate its beauty. But thank you for your company today. What a strange way to spend Christmas Day." He added as an afterthought.

"You are right, it is strange, but thank you, the pleasure was all mine," Simon said as they walked into the hotel. "Unfortunately, I am not into water sports so am omitting that part, although I have heard that the underworld is beautiful. Anyway, enjoy yourself, I am sure it is going to be worth it! Goodnight, and I hope to see you before you leave?"

"Yes, I would like that, I will be leaving for Colombo on the 27th so will be in the hotel tomorrow before I go out in the evening. We can have dinner."

"Won't you be tired after your snorkelling?" Simon queried.

"Most probably, but we leave early in the morning so I should be back by late afternoon. Plenty of time to rest and then later come out for dinner."

After having agreed to meet the following evening, Mark closed the door of his room and dialled Rasna's number to confirm that she had received his message. However, there was no reply and he presumed that either there was no signal, the mobile was not charged, or she was just chilling with her sister. He was excited at the prospect of meeting her and planned to marry her in Colombo and bring her back to London as his wife. He was so excited at the thought that he had memorised her address and phone number, hoping he would at least remember one or the other in case he lost his mobile or it got stolen, which was a distinct possibility.

Before going to sleep he requested the hotel lobby to wake him at 6 a.m., then turned on his back and drifted off to sleep, dreaming of Rasna and himself on a Kayak that took them around the Andaman Islands.

December 26th 2004 (Phuket)

Chapter 63

At 6.45 on the morning of the 26th, Mark went downstairs to wait for the taxi that was to take him to the ferry and was pleasantly surprised to find there were a few other people from the hotel who had booked the same tour.

He quickly introduced himself, and in turn Alicia, Jack and Benson did the same. Mark found them all to be pleasant and was talking to them when at 7 a.m. sharp the taxi arrived. A man, who, they assumed to be their guide, smiled amiably as he opened the car door to greet them.

"Hello, my name is Harry and I am here to make your journey and snorkelling as comfortable and enjoyable as possible. The drive to the ferry will take ninety minutes; it leaves at 8 a.m. to take us to Phi Phi islands. Now, as you must have read in the brochure, the island has classic tropical beaches, stunning rock formations and turquoise waters that are so full of colourful marine life that I promise your snorkelling experience will be something to remember!"

"Sounds wonderful, but will the snorkelling gear be provided by you or do we to rent it?"

"Yes, we provide the gear, it is included in the service and includes masks, snorkels and fins for whoever needs it. Many beaches, however, do have stalls that rent out snorkelling gear for the day, but the quality of the gear is better if brought by us, anyway it is included in the price. Snorkelling will be at Maya Bay and I will be your snorkelling guide. You can look forward to an enthralling experience for I know the rock formations, the reef and coral inside out. After snorkelling for a couple of hours, we will then see the monkeys on Monkey Beach, have a light lunch then do some sightseeing around Phi Phi Bay, Pi-Leh Bay, Loh Samah, the Bida's and Viking Cave. After which we head back to Phukhet."

On the drive to the ferry, they passed breath-taking scenery and there were sounds of admiration by everybody in the car.

"Gosh, the scenery is too beautiful, I am so glad I came."

Alicia was a blonde woman wearing a pink dress that set off her complexion and her blonde hair was tied back with a matching pink ribbon.

"Hi, Alicia, will you be snorkelling with us?" he asked curiously.

"Oh no, I am here to support my husband, Jack who is the one who will be snorkelling, in fact he loves it! I am too much of a coward, it looks dangerous to me. I can just about swim, so will relax here on the beach and meet all of you later, when you can tell me about your snorkelling experience."

They had about an hour on the road, so, feeling bored, started chatting. Mark found her to be a nice lady, warm and kind and she exuded such warm motherly love that Mark found he was confiding in her about his dilemma.

"Young man, I am sure you will do the right thing, and I think that young lady of yours is very lucky."

They were interrupted by Harry.

"Folks, the snorkelling will begin at 10 a.m. and we should be in Phi Phi islands by 9.15. Since we left early in the morning, you might not have had any breakfast, so, if you want, you have time to make use of the particularly good restaurants nearby and we will regroup here at 9.45."

As Mark was craving for a hot cup of coffee, and they had time on their hands, Alicia and Jack joined him in finding a restaurant. There were many there, so after they had found one, they took their coffee and sat on sun loungers, admiring the calm, crystal seas, the palm-fringed beaches, and cloudless skies.

Mark finished his coffee then got up in alarm as he looked at his watch.

"Jack, I think we better get going! Alicia, will you be joining us later for the rest of the tour?"

"No, Mark, although I would love to, but you will be going on the tour directly after you finish your snorkelling. Anyway, enjoy your snorkelling!" Alicia smiled warmly, winking at her husband who kissed her on the cheek.

"Yes, Mark, we better be going, I don't want to miss anything." Jack was an athletic man of about thirty years of age.

They went to the meeting place, where they were joined by a young couple, Cynthia, and Tom, who were staying at a different hotel.

They were given the snorkelling gear and taken to a boat, were they quickly changed.

"I am glad we are on time, that will give us more time to spend time underwater," Harry remarked. "Like I said earlier, I know the best places where you will find beautiful reefs and corals, rock formations of the most beautiful kind… the rest you will see for yourself, and for that I will be with you every step of the way."

Mark took a deep breath and dived into what he knew would be a magical kingdom, one that would be as close to aquatic paradise as he would ever get to, and, one by one, he was joined by Jack, Cynthia and Tom.

Mark floated face down in the water, breathing through the snorkel and his mask. He thrust his legs straight up to maintain a streamlined position to glide down into the water and continued to kick with his feet to move down deeper.

He glided around comfortably in his snorkelling fins, keeping his arms at his side and breathing evenly.

The underworld was even more beautiful than he had imagined, for the depths of the sea was bursting with brilliant and colourful marine life. There were corals, reefs and various types of fish and shellfish, some of whom he recognised, others that looked unfamiliar.

They had been floating for about forty-five minutes when the sea suddenly became a bit strange and the visibility changed, as if it were becoming eclipsed. The few fish that he saw, suddenly seemed to be acting strangely, swerving and losing control, Even the look on Harry's face was tense, and all of a sudden, he bumped into a fish that was going around in circles.

Now that is a bit strange for being a guide. I would have thought him to have been more in control, Mark thought. I hope he is feeling alright. By now, the visibility underwater had become very dark, misty and strange.

Suddenly, a strong current sucked them downward into the water. Cynthia and Tom, had been floating nearby when suddenly Cynthia was thrust onto a huge clump of coral whilst Mark and Tom were swept against some rocks; and he could see Jack and the others, including Harry, also floundering in the water.

Chapter 64

Harry looked around him in alarm, then signalled to everyone to surface.

They quickly clamoured on to the boat that was rocking dangerously whilst the sea around them whirled and churned angrily.

"What is happening?" Cynthia asked, looking confused. "The sea suddenly looks strange and dangerous, Harry!"

"I don't know, I have never seen anything like this before! I am going to find out from my boss, but is everybody from our group on the boat?"

"Yes, we are all here." Mark replied looking around at the frightened group huddled together.

"I see a lot of debris floating in the sea, maybe a boat has sunk or something, and that is why there is so much rubbish in the sea?" Cynthia queried. "I wish Harry would tell us what is happening, but he is busy talking on the phone!"

"He is talking to somebody to find out what is happening, obviously there is no signal, so he is using the boat's phone." Mark replied

At that moment Harry walked over, running his hands through his hair in perplexity. "I have just been talking to my boss who has informed me that we have been hit by a tsunami!"

"Why, what is a tsunami?" Cynthia looked at Harry in bewilderment.

"Oh my God! No wonder the sea and the fish have been acting strangely!" Tom exclaimed. "Cynthia, a tsunami is a series of waves that are caused by either earthquakes or undersea volcanic eruptions."

"But we were underwater, apart from the fish acting strangely, the visibility and what I thought to be the force of the water well… I suppose that says it all."

"Actually, we were lucky we were underwater," Harry explained "Apparently the first wave was very destructive, though mild compared to the second one that is coming. My boss said the destruction inland has been massive and that many people on the beach have lost their lives!"

"Oh my God! I hope Alicia is safe, we left her on the beach!" Jack cried. "I told her to stay back at the hotel… I need to find her."

The receding water of the tsunami had hauled not only the debris of the ruins of buildings, trees, tables, and chairs, but also included dead bodies all of which were now floating in the sea.

A body of a woman drifted past their boat, her blonde hair floating in the water, a pink ribbon tied around it, Suddenly Mark saw that it was what Alicia, Jack's wife had been wearing, down to the pink ribbon that held her blonde hair. He looked uneasily at Jack and saw that he too had spotted her.

"Oh, not my Alicia, oh no!" He had tears in his eyes as Mark put his arm around him.

"Oh Jack, I am so sorry! But we must get back quickly, my boss said there is another wave expected shortly!" Harry said urgently.

Somehow, they arrived at the beach and scrambled ashore, frightened, and scared. They looked across at the sea which earlier had been so calm and beautiful, but now looked angry and powerful as a wave emerged, growing higher and higher as it neared the shore. The water rose over 12 feet in seconds,

The roar of the wave, as it neared, became louder and louder and hit them with the strength of a freight train. Its force sent Mark, Cynthia, and the rest flying into the jungle where it pinned them against the trees.

Mark found himself thrust against some trees, fighting to keep his head above water.

"Cynthia are you all right?" he spluttered.

"Yes, I am fine for now, that is, but what is happening? I do not know I can stay afloat for long at this rate! And where are Tom, Jack, and Harry? I cannot see them!"

"Don't worry Cynthia, maybe they swam back," Mark gasped. They saw that their boat had been thrown against some nearby rocks and was continuously being smashed against them. "Cynthia, can you swim on to the boat, I think it best we wait there? Hopefully, we will be rescued soon…"

Cynthia nodded and they started swimming, which they found to be difficult, not only because of the strong current, but because they were being hindered by debris that was floating in the sea.

"This looks impossible, let's try going back to the beach." Mark exclaimed in desperation.

"You are right, Mark," Cynthia choked. "This is too difficult; I don't think I can do this."

"No, Cynthia, don't give up now, we are nearly there."

As they swam, they tried to avoid the debris that was floating in the sea. and finally reached the shore, but the water level and its powerful current had started to pick up again.

"Hey, this does not look like the beach we left from!" Mark shouted, for nothing looked recognizable as almost everything was in ruins. Hundreds of bungalows nearby had been swept away, leaving bare ground whilst many other buildings were smashed to the ground.

There was an eerie feeling of destruction, chaos and death in the atmosphere as some people ran around screaming and yelling in a frenzy whilst others walked around them in a daze, blood dripping from all parts of their bodies.

Mark looked around for a sign of Jack and hoped he was safe.

"Mark, I cannot see Tom, ohhh!" Cynthia around her in desperation, and there was nothing Mark could do to put her mind at ease as they saw the destruction the first wave had caused.

Little kids, parents, and people of all ages were screaming for their missing family members and friends.in despair as they saw the dead bodies that had washed up onto the shore.

Cynthia ran to them and started looking frantically at them, hoping that one of them was not Tom.

"Thank god Tom is not one of them, but I saw the body of Jack. Poor fellow, I liked him." Cynthia said as she came back to where Mark was standing.

Mark had liked him too, but a part of him was glad, for Jack had loved Alicia and would not have been able to live without her, then was mortified at his belief.. Suddenly, it seemed that the sea was receding and there was nothing left but wet sand. They stood gasping and choking water, looking in amazement at the sea that was disappearing into the distance, as if a plug had been pulled out. Ominously, the tide kept going out, further than ever before and the beach, as they knew it, extended as far as they could see.

Chapter 65

"We are safe now," one of the tourists said, clutching her child tightly in her arms.

"I am afraid not," Harry told them, for he had miraculously appeared, soaking wet, but alive. "This is a tsunami, and what you are seeing is a horrible trick that it plays, for it gives false hope that everything is okay. But the first wave is pulled back, only to return bigger, stronger, and deadlier than the one before. And ours is not the only island that has been hit by the tsunami, many others around the world have also been affected."

Mark thought of Rasna, willing her to be safe.

Just as Harry had finished speaking, they saw a wall of foaming water forming out in the bay and heading towards the shore with renewed vigour and venom.

"Look out, it is returning!" yelled frantic voices.

The beauty of Paradise Beach had turned into a death trap and the once beautiful paradise island of Phi Phi turned into a water-logged hell.

Mark and the others saw the height and towering wave heading towards them, and fear replaced wonder as they saw the wave break over a fishing boat and swallow it.

There was mass panic as people began to run into buildings for shelter, but most of them had either drowned, crushed under the wreckage of buildings, or been caught in the stampede. Some people hung on to the remaining walls of hotels, balconies and trees, and screams filled the air as they tried frantically not to let the tsunami break their grip on life.

Mark saw someone entangled in the debris, trying to wriggle out of it, without success, whilst another was decapitated by it. People were trapped in the debris, wrapped around trees, whilst others had drowned in the deluge of water.

He turned towards Cynthia and saw that she had vanished and presumed she had gone looking for her husband.

It seemed the sea had suddenly burst open and smashed everything in its path. It thundered over the beach, saturated the roads along the beach front, and on its route, seized large vehicles or anything else in its path from tree trunks, boats to furniture and any unfortunate person who stood in its way.

He heard a thunderous crash, accompanied by the sound of cracking foundations and falling structures that the force of the wave had demolished., followed by narrow lanes and streets being swamped by water.

A few buildings that had been constructed poorly had capitulated to the force of the wave and were washed away. Most of the shop on the ground floor were wiped out, whilst hotels and guesthouses suffered heavy damages to their ground floors. Hotels and department stores on the sea front suffered heavily too where many dead victims were found. Mark and a few others, who had somehow managed to avoid the wave, were found by rescuers and escorted to the side of a mountain and then to a safe height where there were doctors among the holidaymakers who tended to their injuries.

Mark considered himself lucky to have survived the devastation caused by the tsunami, and looked around, hoping to see Alicia, Cynthia or Tom, and as he recalled that Tom had told him he was an experienced diver, hoped he had been successful in finding shelter and safety. He was glad that George had left the island before the Tsunami and hoped that Simon was safe.

"Are we safe now, is the tsunami over?" Mark asked, still in shock. The doctor who had been tending to the wounds that he had contracted, not only when he was thrust against the trees by the force of the tsunami, but also by being flung against fragments of furniture and other items.

"No, apparently not, but you were very lucky," he replied, "your injuries are not serious, except for a broken arm, but most people have not been that fortunate. Although some survived, they have lost their loved ones, or in some cases more than one. I, myself, was in my hotel when I saw a wall of water sweep ashore onto the island. Just out of nowhere, suddenly the streets were overflowing with water and people were running and screaming."

"I was underwater snorkelling at that time, "Mark explained, "so escaped the destruction the first wave caused. I cannot believe this is happening, I came here only for two days! I have been saying all along that this holiday is jinxed, for everything has been going wrong since the beginning, but, the tsunami just tops it!" Mark winced as the doctor applied some antiseptic cream on his wounds.

"Most of us only came for a holiday to this exotic place!" The doctor finished wrapping bandages and plasters around Mark's minor wounds than cast his arm in a plaster. "Listen, they are organising some rescue methods. I suggest you contact them as soon as possible, and good luck."

As soon as he was finished, Mark contacted some rescue volunteers, and he, together with some other people, were carried off to either hospitals or to Navy ships that had been sent as aid. Mark and the others were eventually rescued by a Thai Cruise Ship called the Ocean Princess.

The next two days were spent with sympathetic Thai cruise workers, and were given hot meals and beds to sleep in.

As soon as he learnt of the magnitude of the tsunami and that it had also hit Sri Lanka, he borrowed a mobile from one of the crew members, frantic with worry and glad that he had memorised Rasna's and her grandmothers' number to mind, for in the chaos he had lost his mobile. As there was no signal from either phone, all sorts of scenarios raged through his mind as he lay in bed,

He relived the scene of the destruction and of the floating bodies in horror; he was distressed, both mentally and physically. He was especially upset as he had not located either Cynthia or Tom, and every time he closed his eyes, he saw Alicia's body in her pink dress floating in the sea followed by the image of Jack's body lying on the shore.

The following day was spent in giving as much information and details to the authorities as they could, not only for identification purposes, but also in trying to locate their lost luggage and money, which according to Mark and most people, would be a waste of time,. Money was the last thing on Mark's mind, except when he thought he would need it to get to Columbo together with his passport, tickets, and other documents.

However, the embassy issued him with a temporary passport and some money, and he left for Colombo, again, grateful that he had memorised the phone number of her grandmother, so keen had he been to meet Rasna.

At the airport, he had phoned her grandmother's house to ask for her address, and he had arrived at her house anxiously. But to his shock, he was told by Rasna's grandmother tersely that neither Rasna, her sister, parents nor her two sons had survived the tsunami.

Mark had looked at her blankly, not believing the sad news, but Rasna's grandmother said repeatedly that Rasna had died with her son. When, finally, the sad news had sunk in, Mark was distraught with grief, and, when he left the house, heartbroken, Ramu, the house servant, had followed him.

"Madam is grief-stricken for she lost both her sons, but I believe that a lot of people are still missing, and Rasna may be one of them"

"Thank you for that ray of hope, my friend," Mark said as he wiped his eyes. "I cannot believe she is dead, but I hope you are right, and if by some miracle she does turn up, this is my mother's phone number where I will be staying."

He patted Ramu on the back then scrawled the phone number on a piece of paper and handed it to him, then with a heavy heart took a flight back to London.

Sri lanka 2004

Chapter 66

Kirti sat looking out at the ocean as the waves heaved and surged, the water a churning mass of silvery black, and Kirti felt that nothing could distinguish it from the dark unending emptiness of the sky that reflected the emptiness Kirti felt at the loss of her family and unborn child.

The physical stitches had healed, but she was still aching, it was a unique kind of pain, an outcome of scars, both emotional mental and physical. But it was when she felt the ghost of her baby lying in her empty arms that she felt the greatest pain.

Kirti did not care much for the new life she had in the shelter, maybe because she had no life left in her to start with? Although her tears had dried, she felt she was not functioning properly.

She ran her hand through her hair as she walked back to the refugee shelter which had been erected for the tsunami victims.

It was made of pieces of metal, bark, palm leaves and although these shelters were supposed to be temporary, there were no signs that the people would be permanently resettled any time soon.

Consequently, this resulted in frustration that was growing amongst the survivors, the angriest were the so-called "100-metre refugees" refugees who had lost their homes close to the sea and who were now forced to live in what they thought to be a halfway house. They did not like the fact that they were barred from rebuilding their homes at the same place where their houses had once been situated but had to depend on the Government to build them a home elsewhere, a place of the Government's choice and a place that would be new and unfamiliar to them.

The only positive aspect in her life, at present, was Deva's friendship. He had rescued her when she had been abandoned by her husband, and singlehandedly and in labour, had been trying to survive a tsunami.

Deva was handsome and distinguished, with a frosting of white on his thick black hair, and not only was he handsome with a tanned complexion, he was also amusing and sensible.

Whenever Kirti felt sad at the loss of her family and child, he would entertain her with stories that would bring a smile to her face. And although he too had lost his family, his wife and daughter in the tsunami, he did not openly demonstrate his grief. He was such a straightforward and honest man that she had regained the self-esteem and confidence that Praana, in his cruel manner, had drained from her.

She had met Deva when she had been at lowest point of her life, but he had switched on a light in her at a time when her life was in darkness.

She smiled as she recalled the time they had met, he had seen her drenched, heavily pregnant, and standing by a banyan tree and had stopped his car. He had not only given her a lift to safety, but stayed by her side all through her delivery, which, sadly had ended in heartbreak for her baby was still born..

All through her labour, Deva had held her hand, and when she had discovered the tragic end of her child, the child she had so wanted to protect against all odds, she had been heartbroken and thought that the demise of her child was her fault.

But Deva had put his arms around her and calmly tried to reassure her, "No Kirti it is not your fault at all, the stress of abandonment by your husband, seeing your servant die in such a horrific manner in front of you, anxiety for your sister's safety, all contributed to the loss of the life of your child."

"And now I remember that before I had met you near the banyan tree, I had tripped and fallen down a couple of times and was trampled on by people who had been trying to run for safety. I could not protect my baby!"

Kirti started crying and through her tears she felt that there were still shadows lying in wait for her and her heart filled with sadness and a premonition of additional heartbreak.

As it turned out her premonition turned out to be accurate, for soon afterwards, she discovered that her parents and sister had died in the tsunami. Deva's heart had gone out to this young, beautiful girl, who, at such an early age had lost so much.

Deva was sitting on a bench when Kirti came up to him.

How long are we going to be here, Deva?" she cried in exasperation.

"I presume by here; you mean at the shelter? If you do, well, you know a lot of people are forced to live in tents, partly due to official incompetence and partly red tape," Deva had replied.

"If that is the case, what do we have to look forward to? We were promised we would be in houses in six months, but we are still living in a tent. We do not even know when, and if, we will ever have a home of our own. And on top of all, I do not like the atmosphere here!"

Kirti could not envisage her life without Deva so always included him in her future, whatever it may hold.

"Why? Has something happened, did someone say something to you?" Deva asked, looking worried, for he was very protective of Kirti.

"There are too many rowdy people here in the shelter that I don't feel safe. Deva, when we initially arrived here, the army had been stationed here and they had imposed order by enforcing a curfew. That curfew had instilled stability and security and the thugs had begun to hold their breath and kept themselves in check. But now that the army has left and the curfew been removed, the thugs have let out their breath in relief by taking control and doing anything they want."

When Kirti had seen the army personnel climb into their trucks and drive away in a line, a convoy of green and brown camouflage, Kirti had foreseen with dismay that things would get worse in the shelter.

"Since the army left the shelter, there has been fighting every day and if things are quiet, the brutes provoke each other till one is started!" Kirti repeated her fears to Deva. "There is also less water available for washing because the so-called non-residents have begun to take water that the army had reserved for people who live in the shelter! Oh, what is the use of complaining, I am going to my room!"

She went to her room and snuggled in her makeshift bed and tried to sleep, and when finally she did, dreamt of her mother.

She got up the next morning with an ache in her heart as she recollected the dream.

Although the dream had been indistinct, in a strange way it was also lucid or she had felt her mother presence, the faint rustling of leaves, and she had even heard, faintly, the snap of a twig, or was it a shot? In her dream, she had parted the branches of a tree so she could see her mother clearly only to find she was merely a shadow.

Chapter 67

'Maybe she wants me to join the Tigers and pick up where she left off? I must talk to Deva about this, for although he is very protective of me at the moment, I cannot depend on him forever, and by joining the LTTE I would learn skills that I will need to not only to safeguard myself but be independent'.

As she went out into the courtyard, she noticed that a brief storm during the night had shaken the mango trees. Their rotten fruit was scattered everywhere whilst ants crawled on the decaying fruit. She wrinkled her nose as a green sickly scent of rotten skin filled the air,

Kirti missed her parents and Rasna and she even thought of Praana. Maybe there was some failing in her that had made him behave so cruelly towards her?

So absorbed was she in her thoughts that it was sometime before she heard Deva.

"Kirti, you have been very quiet this morning, how are you feeling?" Deva looked at her kindly. "I know you are worried about the situation at the shelter, don't worry, I will see to it that you are protected."

Kirti looked young and beautiful, and Deva found her beauty to be subtle yet veiled, a beauty that could endure all trials and tribulations.

"I was thinking of my baby and of my, no, the family that we have both lost. Deva, you never talk about your family, but you must miss them too. If you would like to talk, you know I am always here for you."

As usual, Deva avoided talking about his family. "I have never asked you about this, Kirti, but it has been a year since the tsunami, do you think your husband survived it?"

Kirti hesitated before she replied.

"In the early days when we were bought to this shelter, someone mentioned a place where they had put up photos, ID;s and wallets of victims that had been identified. I went to this place and saw the photos of my husband, his mother, my uncle Kadamba and my parents who had been in the Sumatra Devi. And they are all dead because of me, because they were all coming to visit me!" Kirti wiped her eyes.

"Kirti, please don't say that, it was not your fault! But what about Rasna, I have heard you talk about her many times, did you see her photo also?"

"No, but I rang my grandmother, my father's mother, and she confirmed that not only had my parents died, but so had Rasna, for she had left on the morning the tsunami hit Matara with my uncle, and as his body was identified…!" Kirti wrung her hands. "Deva, I need your guidance on another matter." She related her dream and how she felt she should join the LTTE, not only to follow in her mother's footsteps but so she could gain some independence.

Kirti felt herself to be extremely fortunate to have Deva as a friend, for he was an extremely upstanding and moral man who had eased her pain and shown tenderness and generosity of heart when nobody else had.

Deva on the other hand, felt his friendship with Kirti to be much deeper and could not imagine his life without her. His dream was to buy a plot of land in which he would build a house for her, and where they could plant lemon, mango coconut, jackfruit, and papaya trees.

However, when she told him about her dream and her interpretation of it, he was afraid that he would lose her to the rebels as surely as he had lost his wife and daughter to the tsunami. He felt sad that such a young and beautiful woman would choose death over life.

Moreover, she had such a rosy and glamourous view of the cause, he wondered if he should tell her of the videos that had gone viral of half-naked dead women fighters which he had seen? Of the wounded, mutilated bodies, of the bodies that lay still and that were unidentifiable except for the occasional ornaments like a bracelet or an anklet? He could not get forget the image of a man lying face upward, eyes wide open, of a woman lying unconscious whilst others were covered with sheets. Of people crying as they paid respect to their lost loved ones that were wrapped in orange body bags, and if he did tell her, what would she think of the cause then?

But Deva could not bring himself to shatter her hopes and aspirations, however misplaced; for she would surely discover the truth by herself.

Kirti, on the other hand, when she was younger, had always taken freedom for granted and not understood why her mother, an intelligent, educated woman, had decided to join a terrorist group. However, she recalled that her mother had said that she, and others like her, were not terrorists but freedom fighters.

But when Kirti saw for herself that the suffering in the shelter around her was mostly due to discrimination, she felt she understood her mother's beliefs in a new light.

When she saw Deva looking sceptical, she tried to explain.

"Deva, I am not being naïve, it is not only the dream which made me think about joining The Tigers, but I have also heard their television station broadcast where they show pictures of war, militant training camps, dead bodies and Tamil funerals. I cannot believe this is happening, that too in these days! It worries me and I feel angry that nobody is being held accountable for all the injustices that are happening around us!"

"The television station is one way of marketing their cause, for many people will react the way you have when they see the wrongs being carried out on their people," Deva said mildly. "The other one being that they enlist young children, do you know why? The children are used as protection, in other words, to use them as human shields!"

Kirti knew that Deva was not politically minded so was surprised that he held such strong views.

"However, Kirti, you must do what you think is right, but let me tell you this as a friend, at some point you will feel disillusioned, both physically and emotionally, and I am sure you will, further down the line, and being an intelligent woman, question the purpose of a war that will clearly never be won." However, he looked tense and worried that he had maybe said too much, then ran his fingers through his hair.

With the first brushstrokes of evening, the moon had slipped blood red over the sea and the last of the light seeped across the beach, everywhere around them were silent, coconut palm trees that cast their shadows across rocks as a gentle breeze blew across sky, land and sea.

Epilogue

COVID-19
London 2020

Rasna opened the door of her house awkwardly for she was wearing a mask and gloves whilst carrying bags of groceries.

She had left for the supermarket early in the morning whilst Mark, Sanduni and Mayusha, her young daughter and son, slept soundly. She chose to do so because the stores shelves were usually empty by late morning as the Coronavirus lockdown rules, although eased, were still being applied.

Consequently, queues formed outside the supermarkets as people shopped for essentials whilst trying to observe social distancing; measures that had been set out in the government guidelines. Supermarkets had organised the overwhelming demand of groceries quickly and efficiently by allocating certain times for the NHS staff, vulnerable groups, home deliveries, etc.- and communities too had united in helping isolated and vulnerable individuals.

Rasna was excited at meeting Kirti, her sister, who she had earlier been told by her paternal grandmother, had died in the tsunami.

About two weeks ago, her mother had informed her, in amazement and delight, that Kirti, after 16 years, was discovered to be alive and well. Rasna could not believe the miracle, so Urmila had handed the phone over to Kirti, who she had a brief conversation with, and when Rasna demanded to know why she had vanished all those years, without a word to her, Kirti had told her that she would be coming to London and that all would be explained then!

Although Kirti had arrived with her husband a week ago from Sri Lanka, she had chosen to go into voluntary self-quarantine for a week and was coming to see her today. Not only was Rasna looking forward to meeting her, but she was also anxious to hear about her mother, who she had not been able to contact for some time.

As Rasna placed the shopping on the kitchen surface top, she marvelled at how she had been through two distinct kinds of disasters, one a tsunami, a natural disaster, the other a pandemic, a public health crisis. In one of them, the tsunami, she had lost her family, although miraculously, her mother and Mark had survived and they had been reunited, and now, she had learnt that Kirti, too had unbelievably survived the tsunami!

However, she felt sad that the feeling of joy she felt at being reunited with her sister could not be experienced by Mark, for in the pandemic he had not only lost his sister Amelia, but his Father, Caleb to COVID-19. Amelia had been a kind shy girl, working in the forefront of NHS at the ICU ward of the new Nightingale hospital.

About a month into the lockdown, Amelia had tested positive for COVID-19 so had isolated herself in her room. Mark and Rasna had looked after her, hoping she would recover.

However, when her health had deteriorated, she was taken to a hospital where, after being on a ventilator for a week, and as the virus was contagious and deadly, they had not been able to visit her, however, the nurses had connected her via Zoom, and although Amelia had been sedated, seeing her had somewhat comforted Mark. She had died soon after and Mark had organised her funeral, which only Rasna and himself had attended, and both were grateful that Caleb, at least, would be safe in a care home.

To their astonishment, two days later, the care home called to inform them of Caleb's sudden death, also due to COVID-19. They had found the care home's attitude to be very uncaring, for although Caleb had been ill for a fortnight, they, his family, had not been informed of his ill health.

Rasna had been devasted to hear of his death, for she had come to love Caleb, who had been like a father to her. He had been handsome with white hair and blue eyes and she always used to tease him that she hoped Mark would be as handsome as him at his age! In fact, she could see a lot of Mark in Andrew and vice versa.

Following the death of two family members due to Covid-19, Mark and his family had to go into quarantine for fourteen days- days which were spent grieving for two much loved family members.

Rasna sighed, but before she took the shopping out of the bags, went into the bathroom to wash her hands thoroughly.

When she came out, she saw Mark rummaging through the groceries.

Rasna smiled. "Hey, I have to clean everything first and don't worry, I have got your favourites, barely, for they would have disappeared soon!" Her eyes danced with mischief as she tossed her head back. "Where are Sanduni and Mayusha, and how are they feeling?"

Rasna had had two children, daughter, and son after five years of being happily married to Mark.

Rasna, during the pandemic and also because of what they had endured and lost, was always petrified as to the health of her children and was always looking out for any symptom of COVID-19.

"They are fine, don't worry, Princess! They are watching TV in the other room!"

Mark was coming over to her when Rasna stopped him. "No, Mark, not until I have had a bath and changed my clothes."

"Very wise, I wish more people were like you, anyway, you left quite early, so, whilst you have a bath, I will make you a nice hot cup of tea."

"Thanks Mark, I need that for I did leave the house without one."

Mark filled the kettle and cleaned the kitchen sink as Rasna collected her clothes and went into the bathroom.

After some time, she returned towelling her damp hair.

"Whew! It was horrible out there, the streets are so quiet and eerie, and it breaks my heart to see elderly people quietly standing in the queue yet keeping their distance. I am sure most of them live alone, and for them shopping had been a means of getting out and meeting people."

"I agree, it is very sad, now, for a moment would you stop thinking about others and tell me what you would like for your breakfast?" Mark grinned, his eyes twinkling.

"Mark, you know I do not have breakfast; I am happy with a cup of tea." Rasna spread her towel at the back of chair." You know, the lockdown is only tolerable because I get to spend more time with you and the children? All the same, thank God it is easing.!"

Suddenly she cursed herself for her tactless comment, for Mark was still hurting from the loss of his family. Her heart went out to him for he was mourning for his family, just as she had for hers. She had also grieved for Mark before she found out that he had survived the tsunami.

"No breakfast for me, Mark" she repeated, trying to make light of the situation, "you know I don't have breakfast, but a mug of hot Earl Grey would do nicely, thank you! Oh, and before I went shopping, I made some Sri Lankan breakfast, which I know you love."

"Yes, I noticed that my you have been busy… and one mug of Earl Grey coming up."

After the kettle had boiled, Mark poured it in Rasna's favourite mug, swirled an Earl Grey teabag in it then carried it over to the kitchen table where Rasna was sitting.

After the disaster of the tsunami, the miracle of finding out that Mark was alive, and consequently, their reunion had been surreal and emotional for both.

As Rasna sipped her tea she remarked, "Mark, I hope you have not forgotten hat Kirti will be here today with her husband?"

"How could I forget; you have been talking of nothing else!" Mark grinned "But don't they have to be in quarantine or something?"

"Yes, actually they arrived a week ago and have been in quarantine at the Heathrow Hotel since then. I am dying to meet Kirti, there is so much to be clarified, where has she been all this time, why she has not been in touch till now and how Mum is, for I have not been able to speak to her, there are always internet problem there!"

She had barely finished her sentence when the doorbell rang and Rasna ran to open the door.

Although she was wearing a mask, she recognised Kirti for she had scarcely changed through the years. She was still cool, poised and graceful, and there was maturity and wisdom in her eyes, an understanding and deep found knowledge that had come as a result of the suffering she went through.

Rasna rushed to hug her, disregarding social distancing for once and screaming with excitement.

Kirti stepped back, knowing its importance, only her eyes showing her happiness as she blew her a kiss.

Standing beside her was a distinguished looking man with well-trimmed, salt and pepper hair and dark intelligent kind eyes. He was wearing a white shirt with an open collar that showed his brown throat.

Rasna grabbed Kirti's tightly by the hand and led her into the house.

"Rasna, I can't believe I am meeting you at last after all this time! Anyway, let me introduce you first to Deva, my husband," Kirti said as she introduced Deva.

"And this is Mark, my husband."

"Hi, how are you?" Mark smiled.

"I think we should leave the sisters to catch up, don't you?"

"Yes, but first I think we need to wash our hands, Kirti."

Rasna showed them the bathroom and looked at Mark happily.

As soon as Deva returned, Mark led him to one of the comfortable chairs in the lounge.

"I have not seen Kirti look so happy in a long time." Deva sat on the sofa, stretched his legs, took off his mask and mopped his throat with his handkerchief.

Rasna, meanwhile, called out to Kirti that she was in the kitchen.

"Coming, Rasna!" Kirti entered a kitchen that was bright and airy because of the sunlight streaming in through the high windows that faced the garden.

Playing in the corner of the kitchen were Rasna's children, Sanduni a girl of 10 and Mayusha, her six-year-old son.

"Hey children, I thought you were watching TV in the other room! Look who is here, this is my sister, Kirti, your aunt. She has come all the way from Sri Lanka, where your grandmother lives."

"Hello, how are you? Are you like our aunt Amelia?" Mayusha, Rasna's son, a mischievous six-year-old boy asked.

He was a chubby boy with a smear of jam around his mouth. But Rasna's 10-year-old daughter was a shy girl who looked at Kirti suspiciously. The children had been told to keep their distance from everyone, so after greeting their aunt politely, they turned and resumed their activity.

Kirti looked at them with love and affection, wishing she could give them a hug.

"Kirti, I am so happy to see you that in the excitement, forgot you must be starving!"

"Rasna, don't worry, we had breakfast before we left the hotel" Kirti replied.

Her eyes wandered over to half a loaf of bread that was lying on the bread board with a butter knife next to it and an open marmalade jar that stood nearby.

"Oh no! I forgot to tell you not to, for I have made a Sri Lankan breakfast of egg hopper and some juggery. Oh, and please excuse the mess, "Rasna exclaimed pointing around the kitchen, "I just cleared up an hour ago and it is messy again! I went shopping early in the morning, and even though Mark was home, he keeps getting calls from his office which interrupt his so-called helping me around the house!"

"Don't worry Rasna, it is just lovely being with you." Kirti smiled affectionately when she saw her younger sister's domesticity.

Suddenly the children started to argue and fight.

"Poor things, they get bored indoors!" Rasna explained as she first tried to cajole then, told them to go play in their rooms, and, as a reward, could have ice cream.

"Yehhhhhh!" they screamed at the top of their lungs as they raced upstairs.

"But first, remember to wash your hands and face!" Rasna shouted, tying an apron around her waist.

"Oh, Rasna, they are so cute, I only wish I could hug them. Imagine my little sister, a mother!"

Kirti watched in amusement as Rasna her younger sister, who she remembered as being carefree and mischievous, now twirled around the kitchen efficiently. She put away the cereal bowls of the children in the dishwater, cereal boxes away in the pantry and the marmalade jar in the fridge. She then put the kettle on, polished the kitchen sink with a paper towel as Mark had then, finally took a breath and sat down, resting her elbows on the table, wiping her forehead and waiting for the kettle to boil.

"I meant to have the tea ready, Kirti, sorry, but tell me where you were all this time?" Rasna could not wait any longer. "And where is… you were pregnant in 2004…?"

"Yes, I was," Kirti replied sadly, "but on the day the tsunami hit Matara, Praana drove off with his mother leaving me behind! You know he never did want to have the baby."

"Oh, you poor thing, Kirti. I do not know how many times I have thought that I should not have left you on that day! I am so sorry; it is all my fault. I know Praana was nasty, but to stoop so low! Do you know what happened to him? No, I don't care about him, more importantly, what happened to the baby?" However, judging from the look on Kirti's face, she knew it to be a sensitive subject that maybe she should not have brought up?

Kirti had tears in her eyes as she explained "I think the stress I went through was too much, I had just seen my servant, the only person who cared for me, die in front of me only because he was trying to help me. I left the house and onto the road, trying to save myself and my child from the tsunami thinking that maybe somebody would help me, but instead, I was trampled on by everybody. Because of the stress of abandonment and Murugan's death in front of my eyes, caused me to go into labour and the baby was still born." She wiped the tears in her eyes,

"Kirti, I am sorry to have bought up the subject, please don't talk about it if it is causing so much pain." Rasna looked distressed

"I am only surprised that it is still so painful after all these years, but luckily, I met Deva who took me to a building, no, ruins I should say, but by then it was too late." Kirti's eyes shone with unshed tears. "Deva is a truly kind man who lost his wife and daughter in the tsunami. Soon after, we were placed in temporary shelters, but things were bad there too, in fact many thousands are still living there in unhygienic conditions and now they must contend with the problem of coronavirus too."

Rasna went around the table and put her arms around Rasna. "I am so sorry, Kirti. Everybody faces only one disaster in their lifetime. We have not only survived one natural disaster but are trying to survive the pandemic! But why didn't you contact me earlier? I don't live in London anymore, but I left a forwarding address at our previous house."

"I could have, but you had left with Kadamba Uncle the day the tsunami struck Matara but did not want to believe that you had been affected by the tsunami. But then I saw Chitappa Kadamba's photo, along with those of Mum and Dad, on the wall of the dead people the relief camps had set up, and it was only after that that I assumed you too had died."

"But you do know that Mum is alive, Kirti? Oh of course you must do, for it was she who gave you my phone number and address! I thought she had died in the tsunami for grandmother, father's mum, told me so. And it was only by chance that I came across her in Colombo on the anniversary of the tsunami, where she was with Prathika her mother. Oh my god, what a miracle that was, and not the only one either, I found Mark and now you! How is she, for I have not been able to get through to her! It has been sixteen years since dad drowned and she has been all alone since then, of course with her mother, but grandma must be quite aged now?"

The kettle had boiled, so, before Kirti could reply, Rasna got up to pour the boiling water into the mugs, puzzled by Kirti's reaction, for she had tears in her eyes.

She placed the mugs on a tray, keeping two back for Kirti and herself when Mark entered the kitchen.

"I will take this in, you two have a lot to catch up on." His blue eyes looked at her tenderly, kissed her on the cheek and left.

"You know Kirti, something or the other is always happening in Sri Lanka." Rasna placed the mugs on the table. "There is the political unrest of course, but on top of it there was the tsunami in 2004. And last year I heard 250 people were killed in a bomb explosion during Easter celebrations, and now they are having to deal with the coronavirus, even though that is a global problem. But in Sri Lanka, barely is one disaster over when the next one strikes, and the ongoing political unrest, I think, obstructs, and delays the recovery process. And to successfully combat the coronavirus outbreak demands unity, not communal divisions."

"By political unrest I presume you mean the civil war, Rasna?" Kirti asked.

She wondered what Rasna's opinion of her would be if she knew that she had been part of an organisation that had targeted churches during the Easter period in three cities? That she had played a major part in the bomb that went off in the church in Colombo?

She remembered the day of the bombing vividly and with regret. It had been a bright day in Colombo, and she had been hiding under a bush with four of her comrades with orders to plant the bomb. It had been a chilly morning and dew had dripped from the banana leaves as they waited.

As soon as they had planted the bomb in the church, she had gone home to her mother's, feeling broken, both physically and emotionally.

Even Deva, her kind and gentle husband, did not know how big a role his wife had played in the bombings, and was mortified to think how horrified Deva would be if he ever came to know.

But seeing how happy Rasna was, her lovely children, Sanduni and Mayusha, and Mark's love for her, how could she tell her the truth? How could she tell her that she had taken part in the bombing of a holy temple during one of their holiest festivals?

And Deva had been right, she was now questioning the cause of her organisation and its cruel disregard in the of killing of innocent people just to promote their goal. She was especially remorseful after the catholic church had forgiven the terrorists, though she had not thought of herself as one.

"Kirti, I am dying to know about mother and how she is, I presume you met her before you left?"

"Of course, I did and going back to your question of how I came to know that you were alive and well, do you remember Sudina, Mum's friend? They were together in the rebel army."

"Yes of course I remember her! She was the one who saw Mother at one of the shelters and brought her to Grandma because Amma was suffering from amnesia."

"Yes, she is the one I mean, after some time at the shelter, I joined the Tamil tigers. Oh, I don't know why I did, but after having lived with Praana and his mother and their cruel behaviour I just felt that I had to do something!" The sting of resentment that she felt for Praana and his mother still made her wince. "In addition to which, I missed Mum, and had always admired the loyalty with which she had fought for her county."

"You, a tigress!" Rasna exclaimed in astonishment for she could not imagine her kind gentle sister to be a rebel.

"Surprised, huh? But I had lost everyone, my baby, parents, sister, and was smarting at the way Praana and his mother treated me, so wanted to make a difference, although in his kind way, Deva had tried to discourage me. Anyway, when at the shelter I saw a lot of discrimination, I assumed that is what mother would have wanted and by doing so felt close to her. But even whilst I was away, Deva kept in touch, and over time his letters began hinting at marriage. And he is such a nice man, so honest and considerate, and had helped me through such difficult times and is the exact opposite to Praana, I finally agreed to marry him." She smiled softly; her eyes tender. "And I have not regretted one minute of it. I am incredibly happy, and he treats me with respect, something I had thought no other man would do, for Praana, with his cruelty and ruthlessness, had shaped me into feeling worthless. Anyway, coming back to how I was reunited with Mother... I met Sudina at one of the training sessions. She recognised me immediately and told me Mum was alive and well... the rest you know." Kirti sighed, not knowing how she was going to tell Rasna about their mother, for she had been hedging around at being the bearer of sad news.

"So how was Mother? Is she well?" Rasna asked, her eyes shining. "How come she is not answering her phone, I know that the internet service there is bad there, but it has been quite some time since I spoke to her. Now that you are in London, too, she can come and stay with us. You are not going back, are you? Is that the reason she did not come with you?"

Kirti had decided that the only way to tell her the sad news was to tell her directly.

"Hey, Rasna, slow down with all the questions, I do not know how to say this but to be blunt; Mum will not be coming for she is dead."

"What do you mean Kirti?" Rasna looked confused. "I don't understand."

"The reason you could not get through to her was because she fell victim to COVID-19," Kirti replied sadly, tears in her eyes. "At first, we thought she had mild flu, which turned into pneumonia, and when we took her to hospital she was immediately put on a ventilator, after which she did not regain consciousness…"

"Oh no, Kirti, no, no, no…" Rasna whimpered.

Throughout the disasters, it had seemed to her that nature could not decide whether to cheat her of her loved ones or restore them back to her.

"Amma wanted to come with me, in fact before she fell ill- I spent some time with her, and she apologised that she had not objected strongly to my marriage to Praana. She also told me about Dad's letter and his confession, and that he only married me off in such haste to save himself! I now consider myself lucky, for Praana could have easily killed me at any moment. Anyway, Amma, before she fell ill, had made me promise to come to London, look you up and tell you how much she loves you and to see you are happy and to give her grandchildren her love."

By this time, both the girls were sobbing, and having heard their cries, Mark entered the kitchen, looking alarmed.

Rasna was in no state to speak so Kirti explained the situation

"I am so sorry, Princess." He put his arms around Rasna and gently wiped the tears from her cheeks tenderly with his hands. "Kirti take her into the sitting room, I will join you with a fresh pot of tea. And Rasna, no need to worry about lunch, we will order in."

Rasna sat quietly on the sofa, pained by the fact that the Coronavirus had struck so close to home. First, Amelia, Mark's sister, then his father Caleb and now her mother!

Outside, she could hear the leaves if the trees rustle in the breeze, and she thought she heard them softly whispering the names of the people she had lost, as though the sound of their names just might oust her fear of losing any one of her loved one again? She felt that one minute her arms were bursting with silvery vows that were quickly followed by angry puffs of clouds!

"How is Grandma. Amma's mum?" she asked, for she was very fond of Prathika, her maternal grandmother.

"She is fine, considering her age, but devasted at losing her only child. Luckily, Sudina is living and looking after her, and they have been isolating, as have we, before we left. And then again in London."

They sat silently, each engrossed in their own thoughts; for each person there had been a then, now and an in between – an in-between when there had been a long empty spell of suffering, a period that had led to the present, a time of the lockdown, when there had been happy times and sad, the reuniting of sisters, as well as the loss of loved family members during the pandemic.

Suddenly, an occasion of happiness had turned to one of sadness, and Kirti wished she had not been the one to bring such bad tidings.

She coughed slightly and everybody looked at her in alarm.

"I am fine, everybody, don't worry, must be change of weather, we have been checked, before we left Sri Lanka, at the airport in London and also were quarantined."

Everybody sighed with relief, and she smiled slightly, hoping that her past with the tigers was buried, and that she had a future to look forward to. However, that appeared to be uncertain, for it seemed her future was misty for, whatever it held, it would be under the threat of a deadly virus that nobody could control.

She had survived a tsunami, a natural disaster, which had surfaced in a day, but a disaster that had been so forceful and intense that it had left millions dead and uprooted globally, most of whom were still having to cope with its consequences. On the other hand, COVID-19 was a health and public crisis that was a pandemic, which showed that statistically, there were over 800 deaths occurring daily in most countries.

She was sure the months ahead would be crucial whilst the governments changed rules and regulations that they thought would not only benefit the health and safety of their people, but also secure their failing economy too.

However, her only consolation was that most countries were frantically working towards developing a vaccine by starting drug trials and rapid diagnostic testing. And when they did discover a cure, the other half of the challenge, she speculated, would not only be in manufacturing enough doses, but then being able to distribute them appropriately and justly.

She hoped it would not be too long before an antidote was found, for many innocent lives had and would respond to the call of angels!

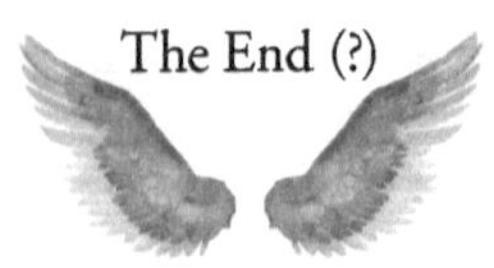

The End (?)